Bloom's Modern Critical Views

Bloom's Modern Critical Views

Bloom's Modern Critical Views

HOMER
Updated Edition

Edited and with an introduction by
Harold Bloom
Sterling Professor of the Humanities
Yale University

CHELSEA HOUSE
PUBLISHERS
An imprint of Infobase Publishing

Bloom's Modern Critical Views: Homer—Updated Edition

©2007 Infobase Publishing

Introduction ©2007 by Harold Bloom

Chelsea House
An imprint of Infobase Publishing
132 West 31st Street
New York NY 10001

Library of Congress Cataloging-in-Publication Data
Homer / Harold Bloom, editor. — Updated ed.
      p. cm. — (Bloom's modern critical views)
   Includes bibliographical references and index.
   ISBN 0-7910-9313-1 (hardcover)
 1. Homer—Criticism and interpretation. 2. Epic poetry, Greek
—History and criticism. 3. Mythology, Greek, in literature. I. Bloom, Harold.
   PA4037.H774 2006
   883'.01—dc22   2006025325

Chelsea House books are available at special discounts when purchased in bulk quantities for businesses, associations, institutions, or sales promotions. Please call our Special Sales Department in New York at (212) 967-8800 or (800) 322-8755.

You can find Chelsea House on the World Wide Web at http://www.chelseahouse.com

Contributing Editor: Pamela Loos
Cover designed by Takeshi Takahashi
Cover photo © Peter Will/SuperStock

Printed in the United States of America
Bang EJB 10 9 8 7 6 5 4 3 2 1

This book is printed on acid-free paper.

All links and web addresses were checked and verified to be correct at the time of publication. Because of the dynamic nature of the web, some addresses and links may have changed since publication and may no longer be valid.

Contents

Editor's Note

My introduction contrasts the *Iliad* with the Hebrew Bible, and in particular with the archaic War Song of Deborah and Barak in Judges 5.

Scott Richardson examines the Homeric narrator's powers, which are godlike but, like the gods', are bound by fate, while Louise H. Pratt mediates upon the relation between poetry and truth both in the *Iliad* and the *Odyssey*.

The paradox of vocal authority and written text, as exemplified by the Homeric hero, is set forth by Ahuvia Kahane.

Andrew Ford greatly illuminates Homer's freedom in manipulating the conventions he had inherited from archaic song so as to create the epic genre, as we have come to know it from him, while Richard Gotshalk addresses the same process of transformation.

A feminist perspective is introduced in Nancy Worman's consideration of Helen's speech patterns as the representative of Nemesis, after which Margalit Finkelberg argues that the Homeric poems were deliberate revisions of the heroic tradition, and thus intended to usurp earlier epics.

In this volume's final essay, D. N. Maronitis explains the Homeric theme of *homilia*—which can be marital, extra-marital, or friendship—and which is counterpointed with war in both the *Iliad* and the *Odyssey*.

HAROLD BLOOM

Introduction

Hektor in his ecstasy of power / is mad for battle, confident in Zeus, / deferring to neither men nor gods. Pure frenzy / fills him, and he prays for the bright dawn / when he will shear our stern-post beaks away / and fire all our ships, while in the shipways / amid that holocaust he carries death / among our men, driven out by smoke. All this / I gravely fear; I fear the gods will make / good his threatenings, and our fate will be / to die here, far from the pastureland of Argos. / Rouse yourself, if even at this hour / you'll pitch in for the Akhaians and deliver them / from Trojan havoc. In the years to come / this day will be remembered pain for you / if you do not.

    (*Iliad*, Fitzgerald translation, bk. 9, II. 237–50)

For the divisions of Reuben there were great thoughts of heart.

    Why abidest thou among the sheepfolds, to hear the bleatings of the flocks? For the divisions of Reuben there were great searchings of heart.

    Gilead abode beyond Jordan: and why did Dan remain in ships? Asher continued on the sea shore, and abode in his breaches.

    Zebulun and Naphtali were a people that jeoparded their lives unto the death in the high places of the field.

    (Judges 5:15–18, King James version)

1

I

Simone Weil loved both the *Iliad* and the Gospels, and rather oddly associated them, as though Jesus had been a Greek and not a Jew:

> The Gospels are the last marvelous expression of the Greek genius, as the *Iliad* is the first ... with the Hebrews, misfortune was a sure indication of sin and hence a legitimate object of contempt; to them a vanquished enemy was abhorrent to God himself and condemned to expiate all sorts of crimes—this is a view that makes cruelty permissible and indeed indispensable. And no text of the *Old Testament* strikes a note comparable to the note heard in the Greek epic, unless it be certain parts of the book of Job. Throughout twenty centuries of Christianity, the Romans and the Hebrews have been admired, read, imitated, both in deed and word; their masterpieces have yielded an appropriate quotation every time anybody had a crime he wanted to justify.

Though vicious in regard to the Hebrew Bible, this is also merely banal, being another in that weary procession of instances of Jewish self-hatred, and even of Christian anti-Semitism. What is interesting in it however is Weil's strong misreading of the *Iliad* as "the poem of force," as when she said: "Its bitterness is the only justifiable bitterness, for it springs from the subjections of the human spirit to force, that is, in the last analysis, to matter." Of what "human spirit" did Weil speak? That sense of the spirit is of course Hebraic, and not at all Greek, and is totally alien to the text of the *Iliad*. Cast in Homer's terms, her sentence should have ascribed justifiable bitterness, the bitterness of Achilles and Hector, to "the subjections of the human force to the gods' force and to fate's force." For that is how Homer sees men; they are not spirits imprisoned in matter but forces or drives that live, perceive, and feel. I adopt here Bruno Snell's famous account of "Homer's view of man," in which Achilles, Hector and all the other heroes, even Odysseus, "consider themselves a battleground of arbitrary forces and uncanny powers." Abraham, Jacob, Joseph and Moses clearly do not view themselves as a site where arbitrary forces clash in battle, and neither of course does David or his possible descendant, Jesus. The *Iliad* is as certainly the poem of force as *Genesis, Exodus, Numbers* is the poem of the will of Yahweh, who has his arbitrary and uncanny aspects but whose force is justice and whose power is also canny.

II

The poet of the *Iliad* seems to me to have only one ancient rival, the prime and original author of much of *Genesis, Exodus, Numbers*, known as the Yahwist or J writer to scholars. Homer and J have absolutely nothing in common except their uncanny sublimity, and they are sublime in very different modes. In a profound sense, they are agonists, though neither ever heard of the other, or listened to the other's texts. They compete for the consciousness of Western nations, and their belated strife may be the largest single factor that makes for a divided sensibility in the literature and life of the West. For what marks the West is its troubled sense that its cognition goes one way, and its spiritual life goes in quite another. We have no ways of thinking that are not Greek, and yet our morality and religion—outer and inner—find their ultimate source in the Hebrew Bible.

The burden of the word of the Lord, as delivered by Zechariah (9:12–13) has been prophetic of the cultural civil war that, for us, can never end:

> Turn you to the stronghold, ye prisoners of hope: even today do
> I declare that I will render double unto thee;
>   When I have bent Judah for me, filled the bow of Ephraim,
> and raised up thy sons, O Zion, against thy sons, O Greece, and
> made thee as the sword of a mighty man.

Like the Hebrew Bible, Homer is both scripture and book of general knowledge, and these are necessarily still the prime educational texts, with only Shakespeare making a third, a third who evidences most deeply the split between Greek cognition and Hebraic spirituality. To read the *Iliad* in particular without distorting it is now perhaps impossible, and for reasons that transcend the differences between Homer's language and implicit socioeconomic structure, and our own. The true difference, whether we are Gentile or Jew, believer or skeptic, Hegelian or Freudian, is between Yahweh, and the tangled company of Zeus and the Olympians, fate and the daemonic world. Christian, Moslem, Jew or their mixed descendants, we are children of Abraham and not of Achilles. Homer is perhaps most powerful when he represents the strife of men and gods. The Yahwist or J is as powerful when she shows us Jacob wrestling a nameless one among the Elohim to a standstill, but the instance is unique, and Jacob struggles, not to overcome the nameless one, but to delay him. And Jacob is no Heracles; he wrestles out of character, as it were, so as to give us a giant trope for Israel's persistence in its endless quest for a time without boundaries.

The *Iliad*, except for the Yahwist, Dante, and Shakespeare, is the most extraordinary writing yet to come out of the West, but how much of it is spiritually acceptable to us, or would be, if we pondered it closely? Achilles and Hector are hardly the same figure, since we cannot visualize Achilles living a day-to-day life in a city, but they are equally glorifiers of battle. Defensive warfare is no more an ideal (for most of us) than is aggression, but in the *Iliad* both are very near to the highest good, which is victory. What other ultimate value is imaginable in a world where the ordinary reality is battle? It is true that the narrator, and his personages, are haunted by similes of peace, but, as James M. Redfield observes, the rhetorical purpose of these similes "is not to describe the world of peace but to make vivid the world of war." Indeed, the world of peace, in the *Iliad*, is essentially a war between humans and nature, in which farmers rip out the grain and fruit as so many spoils of battle. This helps explain why the *Iliad* need not bother to praise war, since reality is a constant contest anyway, in which nothing of value can be attained without despoiling or ruining someone or something else.

To compete for the foremost place was the Homeric ideal, which is not exactly the biblical ideal of honoring your father and your mother. I find it difficult to read the *Iliad* as "the tragedy of Hector," as Redfield and others do. Hector is stripped of tragic dignity, indeed very nearly of all dignity, before he dies. The epic is the tragedy of Achilles, ironically enough, because he retains the foremost place, yet cannot overcome the bitterness of his sense of his own mortality. To be only half a god appears to be Homer's implicit definition of what makes a hero tragic. But this is not tragedy in the biblical sense, where the dilemma of Abraham arguing with Yahweh on the road to Sodom, or of Jacob wrestling with the angel of death, is the need to act as if one were everything in oneself while knowing also that, compared to Yahweh, one is nothing in oneself. Achilles can neither act as if he were everything in himself, nor can he believe that, compared even to Zeus, he is nothing in himself. Abraham and Jacob therefore, and not Achilles, are the cultural ancestors of Hamlet and the other Shakespearean heroes.

What after all is it to be the "best of the Achaeans," Achilles, as contrasted to the comparable figure, David (who in Yahweh's eyes is clearly the best among the children of Abraham)? It is certainly not to be the most complete man among them. That, as James Joyce rightly concluded, is certainly Odysseus. The best of the Achaeans is the one who can kill Hector, which is to say that Achilles, in an American heroic context, would have been the fastest gun in the West. Perhaps David would have been that also, and certainly David mourns Jonathan as Achilles mourns Patroklos, which reminds us that David and Achilles both are poets. But Achilles, sulking in his tent, is palpably a child, with a wavering vision of himself, inevitable since his vitality, his perception, and his affective life are all divided from one another, as Bruno Snell demonstrated. David, even as a child, is a mature and autonomous ego, with his sense of life, his vision of other selves, and his emotional nature all integrated into a new kind of man, the hero whom Yahweh had decided not only to love, but to make immortal through his descendants, who would never lose Yahweh's favor. Jesus, *contra* Simone Weil, can only be the descendant of David, and not of Achilles. Or to put it most simply, Achilles is the son of a goddess, but David is a Son of God.

III

The single "modern" author who compels comparison with the poet of the *Iliad* and the writer of the J text is Tolstoy, whether in *War and Peace* or in the short novel which is the masterpiece of his old age, *Hadji Murad*. Rachel Bespaloff, in her essay *On the Iliad* (rightly commended by the superb Homeric translator, Robert Fitzgerald, as conveying how distant, how refined the art of Homer was) seems to have fallen into the error of believing that the Bible and Homer, since both resemble Tolstoy, must also resemble one another. Homer and Tolstoy share the extraordinary balance between the individual in action and groups in action that alone permits the epic accurately to represent battle. The Yahwist and Tolstoy share an uncanny mode of irony that turns upon the incongruities of incommensurable entities, Yahweh or universal history, and man, meeting in violent confrontation or juxtaposition. But the Yahwist has little interest in groups; he turns away in some disdain when the blessing, on Sinai, is transferred from an elite to the mass of the people. And the clash of gods and men, or of fate and the hero, remains in Homer a conflict between forces not wholly incommensurable, though the hero must die, whether in or beyond the poem.

The crucial difference between the Yahwist and Homer, aside from their representations of the self, necessarily is the indescribable difference between Yahweh and Zeus. Both are personalities, but such an assertion becomes an absurdity directly they are juxtaposed. Erich Auerbach, comparing the poet of the *Odyssey* and the Elohist, the Yahwist's revisionist, traced the mimetic difference between the *Odyssey*'s emphasis upon "foregrounding" and the Bible's reliance upon the authority of an implied "backgrounding." There is something to that distinction, but it tends to fade out when we move from the *Odyssey* to the *Iliad* and from the Elohist to the Yahwist. The *Iliad* may not demand interpretation as much as the Yahwist does, but it hardly can be apprehended without any reader's considerable labor of aesthetic contextualization. Its man, unlike the Yahwist's, has little in common with the "psychological man" of Freud.

Joseph, who may have been the Yahwist's portrait of King David, provides a fascinating post-Oedipal contrast to his father Jacob, but Achilles seems never to have approached any relation whatever to his father Peleus, who is simply a type of ignoble old age wasting towards the wrong kind of death. Surely the most striking contrast between the *Iliad* and the J text is that between the mourning of Priam and the grief of Jacob when he believes Joseph to be dead. Old men in Homer are good mostly for grieving, but in the Yahwist they represent the wisdom and the virtue of the fathers. Yahweh is the God of Abraham, the God of Isaac, the God of Jacob, even as He will be the God of Moses, the God of David, the God of Jesus. But Zeus is nobody's god, as it were, and Achilles might as well not have had a father at all.

Priam's dignity is partly redeemed when his mourning for Hector is joined to that of Achilles for Patroklos, but the aged Jacob is dignity itself, as his grandfather Abraham was before him. Nietzsche's characterization is just. A people whose ideal is the agon for the foremost place must fall behind in honoring their parents, while a people who exalt fatherhood and motherhood will transfer the agon to the temporal realm, to struggle there not for being the best at one time, but rather for inheriting the blessing, which promises more life in a time without boundaries.

Yahweh is the source of the blessing, and Yahweh, though frequently enigmatic in J, is never an indifferent onlooker. No Hebrew writer could conceive of a Yahweh who is essentially an audience, whether indifferent or engrossed. Homer's gods are human—all-too-human—particularly in their abominable capacity to observe suffering almost as a kind of sport. The Yahweh of Amos and the prophets after him could not be further from Homer's Olympian Zeus.

It can be argued that the spectatorship of the gods gives Homer an immense aesthetic advantage over the writers of the Hebrew Bible. The sense of a divine audience constantly in attendance both provides a fascinating interplay with Homer's human auditors, and guarantees that Achilles and Hector will perform in front of a sublimity greater even than their own. To have the gods as one's audience enhances and honors the heroes who are Homer's prime actors. Yahweh frequently hides Himself, and will not be there when you cry out for Him, or He may call out your name unexpectedly, to which you can only respond: "Here I am." Zeus is capricious and is finally limited by fate. Yahweh surprises you, and has no limitation. He will not lend you dignity by serving as your audience, and yet He is anything but indifferent to you. He fashioned you out of the moistened red clay, and then blew his own breath into your nostrils, so as to make you a living being. You grieve Him or you please Him, but fundamentally He is your longing for the father, as Freud insisted. Zeus is not your longing for anyone, and he will not save you even if you are Heracles, his own son.

IV

In Homer, you fight to be the best, to take away the women of the enemy, and to survive as long as possible, short of aging into ignoble decrepitude. That is not why you fight in the Hebrew Bible. There you fight the wars of Yahweh, which so appalled that harsh saint, Simone Weil. I want to close this introduction by comparing two great battle odes, the war song of Deborah and Barak, in Judges 5, and the astonishing passage in book 18 of the *Iliad* when Achilles reenters the scene of battle, in order to recover his arms, his armor, and the body of Patroklos:

> At this,
> Iris left him, running downwind. Akhilleus,
> whom Zeus loved, now rose. Around his shoulders
> Athena hung her shield, like a thunderhead
> with trailing fringe. Goddess of goddesses,
> she bound his head with golden cloud, and made
> his very body blaze with fiery light.
> Imagine how the pyre of a burning town
> will tower to heaven and be seen for miles
> from the island under attack, while all day long
> outside their town, in brutal combat, pikemen
> suffer the wargod's winnowing; at sundown
> flare on flare is lit, the signal fires
> shoot up for other islanders to see,
> that some relieving force in ships may come:
> just so the baleful radiance from Akhilleus
> lit the sky. Moving from parapet
> to moat, without a nod for the Akhaians,
> keeping clear, in deference to his mother,
> he halted and gave tongue. Not far from him
> Athena shrieked. The great sound shocked the Trojans
> into tumult, as a trumpet blown
> by a savage foe shocks an encircled town,
> so harsh and clarion was Akhilleus' cry.
> The hearts of men quailed, hearing that brazen voice.

Teams, foreknowing danger, turned their cars
and charioteers blanched, seeing unearthly fire,
kindled by the grey-eyed goddess Athena,
brilliant over Akhilleus. Three great cries
he gave above the moat. Three times they shuddered,
whirling backward, Trojans and allies,
and twelve good men took mortal hurt
from cars and weapons in the rank behind.
Now the Akhaians leapt at the chance
to bear Patroklos' body out of range.
They placed it on his bed,
and old companions there with brimming eyes
surrounded him. Into their midst Akhilleus
came then, and he wept hot tears to see
his faithful friend, torn by the sharp spearhead,
lying cold upon his cot. Alas,
the man he sent to war with team and chariot
he could not welcome back alive.

Exalted and burning with Athena's divine fire, the unarmed Achilles is
more terrible even than the armed hero would be. It is his angry shouts that
panic the Trojans, yet the answering shout of the goddess adds to their panic,
since they realize that they face preternatural powers. When Yahweh roars,
in the prophets Isaiah and Joel, the effect is very different, though He too
cries out "like a man of war." The difference is in Homer's magnificent
antiphony between man and goddess, Achilles and Athena. Isaiah would not
have had the king and Yahweh exchanging battle shouts in mutual support,
because of the shocking incommensurateness which does not apply to
Achilles and Athena.

I began this introduction by juxtaposing two epigraphs, Odysseus
shrewdly warning Achilles that "this day," on which Hector may burn the
Achaean ships, "will be remembered pain for you," if Achilles does not return
to the battle, and a superb passage from Deborah's war song in Judges 5.
Hector's "ecstasy of power" would produce "remembered pain" for Achilles,
as power must come at the expense of someone else's pain, and ecstasy results
from the victory of inflicting *memorable* suffering. Memory depends upon
pain, which was Nietzsche's fiercely Homeric analysis of all significant
memory. But that is not the memory exalted in the Hebrew Bible. Deborah,
with a bitter irony, laughs triumphantly at the tribes of Israel that did not
assemble for the battle against Sisera, and most of all at Reuben, with its
scruples, doubts, hesitations: "great searchings of heart." She scorns those

who kept to business as usual, Dan who remained in ships, and Asher who continued on the sea shore. Then suddenly, with piercing intensity and moral force, she utters a great paean of praise and triumph, for the tribes that risked everything on behalf of their covenant with Yahweh, for those who transcended "great thoughts" and "great searchings of heart":

> Zebulun and Naphtali were a people that jeoparded their lives
> unto the death in the high places of the field.

The high places are both descriptive and honorific; they are where the terms of the covenant were kept. Zebulun and Naphtali fight, not to be the foremost among the tribes of Israel, and not to possess Sisera's women, but to fulfill the terms of the covenant, to demonstrate *emunah*, which is trust in Yahweh. Everyone in Homer knows better than to trust in Zeus. The aesthetic supremacy of the *Iliad* again must be granted. Homer is the best of the poets, and always will keep the foremost place. What he lacks, even aesthetically, is a quality of trust in the transcendent memory of a covenant fulfilled, a lack of the sublime hope that moves the Hebrew poet Deborah:

> They fought from heaven; the stars in their courses fought
> against Sisera.
>   The river of Kishon swept them away, that ancient river, the
> river Kishon. O my soul, thou hast trodden down strength.

SCOTT RICHARDSON

Special Abilities

W_e have seen how the narrator makes his presence in the text felt by leaving signs of his manipulation in telling the story. By speeding the story up, by bringing it to a halt, by making a character's words his own, and by rearranging the sequence of events, a narrator shows his hand in presenting the story to which only he has direct access. We must see the story through his eyes, but his activity involves much more than merely recording, in his own way and in more or less detail, what he sees in his vision of the story. His role as storyteller can be a powerful one, and in the following three chapters I shall examine the manifestations of that power, the ways in which the narrator shapes our perception of the story while we watch it. I shall begin with his special abilities in viewing and understanding the events of the story and then move on to his overt commentary on the story and on his discourse.

The narrator's advantages over us extend beyond his exclusive vision of the story. He has extraordinary abilities empowering him to do what no others can do, neither the readers nor the characters. But just as Faust avails himself of Mephistopheles' magic to defy the laws of nature and time, we too are taken in hand by the narrator and benefit from his superhuman capabilities.

Physically, the narrator has the ability to move at will and instantaneously to any location. The two manifestations of this power pertinent to the Homeric poems are the abrupt change of scene and the

From *The Homeric Narrator*. © 1990 by Scott Richardson.

perspective on the scene from on high. More impressive is his knowledge: he knows what none of the mortal characters can know, especially about the activity of the gods; he can see into the characters' minds; and he knows beforehand what is going to happen.

<h2 style="text-align:center">CHANGE OF SCENE</h2>

The narratee is the narrator's constant companion on his visits to the various locales of the story, and it is this relationship that the narrator of *Tom Jones* pretends to take literally: "Reader, take care. I have unadvisedly led thee to the top of as high a hill as Mr. Allworthy's, and how to get thee down without breaking thy neck I do not well know."[1] Fielding in fact knows full well how to get the reader down safely—he only has to change the scene, and with a word we are having breakfast with Mr. Allworthy and Miss Bridget. While the reader relies on the narrator for conveyance through the world of the story, the narrator depends on nothing but his own volition.

The novelist thinks nothing of abrupt changes of scene, but the Homeric narrator, though he recognizes his privilege of unfettered movement, usually declines it and lets himself be led from scene to scene by one of his characters.[2] Even when the distance is as great as from Olympos to an earthly setting, his habit is not to switch one camera on and the other off simultaneously, but to attach himself to a god who is making the journey. In *Odyssey* 5, for example, the scene switches from a council on Olympos to Kalypso's cave, and the change is made by following Hermes, whose course is described in detail—he leaves Pieria, flies across the sea, approaches the island, steps out of the water, walks on land, arrives at Kalypso's cave, and finds her inside (49–58). This change of scene is unusual in its elaboration but typical in its method. Normally we get to the next scene almost immediately and without a word about the journey itself, but we still follow a character in getting there, as in this walk to Diomedes' tent:

> and many-wiled Odysseus, going into his hut,
>   put the variegated shield on his shoulders and went
>   after them.
> They walked to Tydeus's son, Diomedes, and found him
>   outside of his hut with his armor.
> (Il. 10.148–51)

Homer retains the advantage of swift movement between scenes, but he lends the narrative a continuity that would be lost by an instantaneous change of scene.

Although the majority of the hundreds of scene changes in the two poems are effected in the way described, many are not connected by the physical movement of a character whom we accompany. When a character leads us to the next scene, we lose sight of the true guide. The Homeric narrator is usually a silent companion, hiding behind the movement of his characters. But when the change is abrupt, the narrator's hand in conveying us to each location is more apparent, even if he is not self-referential in the manner of the narrator of *Tom Jones*. The instances of these abrupt scene switches in Homer fall into a few distinct categories, and I begin with by far the largest class, which is in fact but a variant of the customary method of getting from one scene to another.

In the early part of Diomedes' *aristeia*,[3] we switch from the scene of his slaughter of Trojans to the part of the battlefield where Pandaros is stretching his bow. The distance separating them is bridged not by a character but by a line of vision:

Thus the thick ranks of the Trojans were routed by
Tydeus's son, and they did not withstand him, though
    they were many.
Then as the brilliant son of Lykaon watched him
rushing along the plain routing the ranks before him,
he quickly stretched his curved bow at the son of
    Tydeus....

                    (*Il.* 5.93–97)

Instead of following a character from Diomedes to Pandaros, we move from an action to a character watching that action.

In a sense, such changes of scene[4] are even less noticeable than the usual mode. When we speak of accompanying the narrator or a character to a new location, it is sometimes the case that we view the scene as though physically present at a character's side,[5] but normally we are no more than witnesses of the action on the outside looking in—we watch the action from an external point of view, usually unspecified. Scene changes such as the one above can be considered no changes at all but a revelation that we are sharing our viewpoint with one of the characters. We are watching Diomedes rout the Trojans and so is Pandaros, and it turns out, as we find in line 95, that we are looking on the slaughter from the same vantage point. Our movement is nil; we simply shift our attention from the view to the place of viewing.

The span is wider and the implications greater when the character who is looking on the scene with us is a god.[6] When Achilleus is chasing Hektor around the citadel before the inevitable duel, we are joined as spectators not only by the Greek army and the Trojan populace, but also by the gods:

> Thus three times the two whirled around the city of Priam
> with swift feet; and all the gods were looking on.
> And among them the father of men and gods began to speak:
> "Oh woe, beloved is the man being chased around the wall
> whom I see with my eyes; my heart grieves
> for Hektor...."
>
> (*Il.* 22.165–70)

We suddenly find ourselves on Olympos, though after a fashion we have been viewing the chase from there as long as the gods have.

The gods' realm is the most appropriate place for us to follow the action below, because our relationship to the mortal characters, and the narrator's, is in significant respects no different from theirs.[7] Zeus's heart goes out to Hektor, to be sure, and Athena champions more than one Greek hero. At times it appears that the outcome of the activity on earth really matters to the gods, but ultimately the conflicts and sufferings are a game to them and the fates of the mortals affect them only a little more than they do us. We, like the gods, are fascinated and absorbed by the characters and their actions, but in the end we emerge unscathed, though not untouched; to the gods they are not far different from the fictional characters they are to us. When a god's line of vision, then, takes us from the scene of the action to Olympos or Ida, the change of scene is not as great as it at first appears.

The switching of scenes along a line of vision has a variant that occurs several times.[8] In *Odyssey* 1 we leave the hall and enter Penelope's chamber upstairs by following the sound of Phemios's voice:

> The very famous singer sang to them, and they in silence
> sat listening; he sang of the Achaians' mournful
> return, which Pallas Athena had laid upon them from Troy.
> And in the upper chamber she heard in her mind his
>   inspired song,
> the daughter of Ikarios, circumspect Penelope.
>
> (325–29)

A change of scene based on hearing is somewhat more noticeable as a narrator's contrivance than those above because the image that the text evokes is more visual than auditory.[9] But in both cases the perception by someone at one place of what is happening at another is a sufficiently natural connection between scenes that the narrator's involvement in the transference is concealed.

Sometimes we follow the line of vision in the opposite direction, from the spectator to the action,[10] as when Zeus watches the *Theomachia*:

> And Zeus heard,
> sitting on Olympos, and his heart laughed
> with joy when he saw the gods joining in strife.
> (*Il.* 21.388–90)

Line 391 takes us to the gods' battlefield that Zeus has been viewing. On a few occasions[11] Homer plays on this type of connection between scenes by basing the change on a character's ignorance of what is happening elsewhere:

> Zeus stretched out such an evil toil for men and horses
> over Patroklos that day; but not yet did
> divine Achilleus know that Patroklos was dead.
> (*Il.* 17.400–402)

Because so often it is an onlooker we turn to, someone who has been sharing our experience in following the course of the action, it is all the more pathetic (or, in the case of the suitors, comically ironic) when we find that our knowledge of the situation has not reached the new location.

Before we proceed to scene changes that point up the narrator's special powers of movement, let us have a brief look at those that in effect involve no movement for the reader. Most of them[12] conform to the pattern of the following example. When Telemachos returns to the shores of Pylos, he asks Peisistratos to go back to the city without him in order to prevent any delay in his journey. Nestor's son bids him farewell and leaves:

> Speaking thus he drove away the beautifully maned horses
> back to the Pylians' city, and quickly he arrived home.
> And Telemachos urged on his companions and commanded
> them.
> (*Od.* 15.215–17)

Though Peisistratos arrives at his home in line 216, we never really leave Telemachos's side, so 217 is not so much a return to where we left off as it is a continuation after a parenthetical interruption.

The remaining changes of scene are effected in ways that break the chain and thereby call attention to our dependence on the narrator and his ability to travel from one location to another in an instant. But whereas modern narrative is accustomed to switching the scene with the same disregard for continuity as the theater's curtains and blackouts, Homer usually manages to keep some logical connection between the scenes even when he makes a clean break from one to the other.

Frequently the logical connection is parallelism, or at least correspondence, of actions, usually with the implication of simultaneity.[13] The parallelism is often emphasized by particles, especially , "on the one hand/on the other," or by, "on the other side." We frequently move from the Greek camp or segment of the battlefield to the Trojan side (or vice versa) where the enemy is engaged in the same activity—

> Thus on the one hand beside the hollow ships the Achaians
> armed themselves around you, son of Peleus, insatiate
>   of battle,
> and on the other side the Trojans by the rise of the plain—
>   (*Il.* 20.1–3)

or the opposite activity—the Trojans rejoice over their victory and the killing of Patroklos, while the Greeks lament:

> For on the one hand they gave their approval to Hektor
>   who plotted evil,
> but do one to Poulydamas, who had offered good advice.
> Then they took their supper along the camp; the Achaians,
>   on the other hand,
> groaned and lamented all night long over Patroklos.
>   (*Il.* 18.312–15)

The physical distance between the two points may be far, but the effect is not of a disruptive change, because the actions on each side are responding to the same stimulus—a renewal of the fighting, a slaughter.

A similar continuity of thought obtains in another set of scene switches in which the action in one scene has a great bearing on the other or is the topic of conversation of the other.[14] At the end of *Iliad* 3, the initial cause of the war is reenacted when Paris is whisked away by Aphrodite to his bedroom and is joined by Helen.

> He spoke and led her to bed, and his wife followed with
>   him.
> Then, on the one hand, the two slept in the inlaid bed,

but the son of Atreus, on the other hand, was wandering
   through the crowd like a beast
to see if he could somewhere catch sight of godlike
   Alexandros.

(447–50)

The immediate switch from the lovers in bed to the wronged husband
searching for his rival is a masterful comic finale to this lighthearted book,
and though a character or a line of vision does not provide the continuity
between the two, there is no question of a break in the chain—one scene
follows naturally upon the other and the narrator's part in whisking us back
to the battlefield goes largely unnoticed.

Sometimes a change of scene occurs when a character leaves or arrives,
even though he does not act as our guide to the new location. In some cases we
are told his destination, and we get there before him or by a different route by
following someone else.[15] Patroklos is sent to reconnoiter in *Iliad* 11.617; he
does not arrive at Nestor's hut until 644, but since we are taken there
immediately (618), we are on hand to greet him when he does. Just as often, we
are suddenly conveyed to a new scene at the time when a character arrives at the
new location.[16] Sometimes his departure from the previous location has also
occasioned a switch of scene, so that the pair of scene changes is linked by the
implied movement of the character from one place to the other. At *Iliad* 6.119
Hektor leaves the battlefield for the city, but we do not accompany him there nor
do we go there immediately in anticipation of his arrival. Instead we turn to the
site where Glaukos encounters Diomedes, and at the end of their conversation
we switch immediately to the Skaian gates just as Hektor approaches. Each of
these is but a deviation from the usual method of changing scenes—by following
a character from point A to point B—but the instantaneous change of location
accentuates our reliance on the narrator's extraordinary mobility.

We now move to those scene changes that, by their absence of physical
or logical continuity, most noticeably involve the narrator's maneuvering. Of
the six cases in the *Iliad* of a clean break between scenes,[17] all but two seem
to involve a continuation of the action from one scene to another but with a
change of characters. Consider, for example, the change of scene at 3.121:

Then lord Agamemnon sent forth Talthybios
to go to the hollow ships and bade him bring
two jambs; and he did not disobey divine Agamemnon.
And then Iris came as a messenger to white-armed
   Helen....

(118–21)

The messenger Talthybios is sent to the ships, but suddenly the messenger Iris steps in with her own message for Helen. The scene change comes upon us unawares—we are not prepared for it by any of the means discussed so far—but the same type of action is being undertaken by both, so the break from the first scene is not as harsh as it might have been.[18]

There is more skipping back and forth in the *Odyssey* than in the *Iliad*.[19] Because the geographical compass is much wider and the plot has several strands unwinding at the same time, there is not always a handy way to go from one land to another except by the narrator's stepping in and taking us there in an instant. Still, it is remarkable that even with these difficulties, the clean breaks from one scene to another are quite few and far rarer than in a novel of a similar size and of a much narrower geographical range.[20]

The classic novelist works with detached units, scenes in the theatrical sense, that he joins one to another to form a whole. The Homeric narrator, on the other hand, sees the plot as a continuous succession of events. Just as he does his best to avoid ellipses to prevent the story from being divided up into temporal segments;[21] and just as he manages to avoid an interlacing chronological structure even when it means falsifying the temporal relations of events in the story;[22] so he goes to great lengths to construct his plot not by connecting together a series of discrete episodes at the various locations, but by unfolding a chain of actions in which each link, with only a few serious exceptions, leads naturally to the next. One of Hitchcock's films, *Rope*, is noteworthy for being the only feature-length film with no breaks in the filming: the camera is never switched off and then switched on with a different focus or at a different scene, but follows the action with no clean break in the filming, as though it were the eyes of an onlooker. Homer is singular among narrators, especially in the *Iliad*, in much the same way that *Rope* is unique among films. Equipped with immortal characters who fly, he is capable of following the story with very few breaks in the filming. Homer's distinctiveness in his practice of changing scenes typifies his attitude toward the telling of the story—he wants us to watch the story as though it were presented to us with no mediation. He fosters the illusion that his vision of the events and characters of the story is our vision.

BIRD'S-EYE VIEW

Beyond his ability to move within the world of the story in literally no time with no physical restrictions, the narrator also has the superhuman power to soar above the earth for an expansive view of the scene. The Homeric narrator takes advantage of his privilege of a bird's-eye view, but the use of this technique in the Homeric poems is different from that in most other narratives—in these poems the narrator is not the only one who can fly.

Uspensky (1973, 64) explains the most common use and function of the bird's-eye view in narrative:

> Frequently, the bird's-eye view is used at the beginning or the end of a particular scene.... For example, scenes which have a large number of characters are often treated in the following way: a general summary view of the entire scene is given first, from a bird's-eye viewpoint; then the author turns to descriptions of the characters, so that the view is broken down into smaller visual fields; at the end of the scene, the bird's-eye view is often used again. This elevated viewpoint, then, used at the beginning and the end of the narration, serves as a kind of "frame" for the scene.

Homer's use of the bird's-eye view is consistent with what Uspensky describes as usual. He rises from the ground to view the whole panorama in only a few situations and almost solely in the *Iliad*: when the characters gather together in preparation for battle,[23] when they scatter to their ships or homes[24] and, by far most frequently, when they fight.[25] Similes are a common expedient in describing mass movement as seen from above. Prior to the final battle marking the return of Achilleus to the fighting, the Greeks rush from the ships to gather for the attack:

> ... and they poured themselves away from the swift
>   ships.
> As when thickly packed snowflakes of Zeus flutter down,
> cold, under the sweep of sky-born Boreas,
> thus then thickly packed helmets, shining brightly,
> were carried from the ships, and also studded shields
> and strong-plated cuirasses and ashen spears.
> The radiance reached heaven, and the entire land
>   laughed around them
> under the gleam of bronze; and under their feet stirred
>   the rumble
> of men.
>
> (Il. 19.356–64)

From this comprehensive view of the army's movements we descend for a closer look at the leader:

> And in the middle divine Achilleus armed himself.
> And there was a gnashing of his teeth, and his eyes
> glowed as if a flame of fire....
>
> (364–66)

Likewise the end of an assembly scene is often seen from afar while all the men (or gods) scatter to their various dwellings, before the camera zooms in on one of the characters:

> Then after the bright light of the sun dipped down,
> they each went homeward to sleep
> where the famed Hephaistos, strong in both arms, for each
> had built a house with his knowing skill;
> and Olympian Zeus of the lightning-bolt went to his
>   bed....
>
> (*Il.* 1.605–9)

The bird's-eye view frames a scene of mass movement, usually only at the beginning or at the end, and serves as a transition between episodes.

In a general description of a battle, the fighting is seen from a point of view distant enough to take in the whole spectacle but with a consequent lack of detail. The bird's-eye view of a battle often introduces a battle scene or "serves as the bridge between two sections of single combats" (Fenik 1968, 19)—again it is a framing and transitional device.[26] For example, after the fall of Sarpedon, Poulydamas stirs the Trojans to retaliate, and Patroklos encourages the Aiantes to stand firm. The armies clash, but before we look at individual combats, we get an overview of the fighting:

> When they had strengthened their ranks on both sides,
> Trojans and Lykians, Myrmidons and Achaians,
> they threw themselves together in battle over the dead
>   body,
> yelling terribly; and the men's armor clashed loudly.
> Zeus stretched deadly night over the fierce conflict
> so that there would be deadly toil of battle over his
>   dear son.
> And the Trojans first pushed back the quick-eyed Achaians.
>
> (*Il.* 16.563–69)

With line 570 we are back on ground level watching one of the Myrmidons die at the hands of Hektor, the first in a series of duels that leads to another summary description of the fighting from a distant perspective beginning in line 633.

In these passages we view the scene from on high where none of the mortal characters can go, nor could we but for the narrator's taking us there.[27] But as the mention of Zeus in the example above reminds us, we are not alone. In the previous section I noted that one of the ways Homer switches scenes is to rise from the earthly action to Olympos or Ida, where one or more gods are viewing the whole panorama, just as we do during the moments when we soar to the upper regions and look down over the scene we have just been watching at close range. Because we are accustomed in Homer to supernatural flight and to the gods' distant perspective, the sudden ascent to a bird's-eye view does not so much highlight the narrator's manipulation of our perception of the story as it establishes a strong relationship between the narrator and the gods, a bond we will explore later with regard to the development of the plot.[28] Like the gods, the narrator (and his companion, the reader) can rise high above the scene and return to earth at will. The ability to get a bird's-eye view of the world of the story is not only one of the narrator's special powers in perceiving the story—it is also a sign of his godlike status with relation to the story.

PRIVILEGED KNOWLEDGE OF EVENTS

The transition from physical abilities to mental is no abrupt one. What a narrator knows is in part a function of what he can see,[29] and if he is not tied down to one spatial point of view and is capable of watching more than any one character can, he is "privileged to know what could not be learned by strictly natural means" (Booth 1961, 160). We must distinguish between the privilege of mobility and that of knowledge, as Chatman (1978, 212) points out:

> This capacity to skip from locale A to locale B without the authorization of an on-the-scene central intelligence should be called "omnipresence" rather than "omniscience." Logically there is no necessary connection between the two. Narratives may allow the narrator to be omnipresent but not omniscient, and vice versa.

We have seen that Homer is omnipresent and will now examine his omniscience. Even the issue of the narrator's omniscience involves different kinds of knowledge that should be considered separately, for he may have access to one kind of information but not to another.

The implied author knows all, but he may deny any part of his knowledge to the narrator. A homodiegetic narrator, one who is a character in the story he is telling, knows how the story will turn out but is incapable of knowing everything that is happening at locations where he is absent (although he might subsequently learn some of what he has missed),[30] and he certainly cannot delve into other characters' minds—Marlow is as ignorant as we are about the workings of Kurtz's mind or Lord Jim's.[31] Even an extradiegetic narrator who tells the story from one character's point of view, Henry James's "central intelligence," is granted the knowledge of other characters' thoughts and feelings only by their outward manifestations. Genette (1980, 189) sees three general possibilities: in the first, "the narrator knows more than the character, or more exactly says more than any of the characters knows"; in the second, "the narrator says only what a given character knows"; and in the third, "the narrator says less than the character knows."[32] Homer is clearly one of the first class, an "omniscient" narrator, but since the extent of a narrator's omniscience and the forms it takes are variable, a more specific analysis of the Homeric narrator's knowledge is needed to determine the nature of his omniscience.

The privileged knowledge that the Homeric narrator exhibits is of three kinds. The first will be discussed in this section: the knowledge of events or facts about which the (mortal) characters could not possibly know; the second is the ability to see into characters' minds; the third is the knowledge of the future. In the first category, two sorts of information held by the Homeric narrator are unavailable to the characters. One is common in narrative, while the other is peculiar to the few narratives in which the machinations of supernatural characters are hidden from the humans.

An ordinary onlooker will be able to make certain observations about a scene, but there are details and pieces of information that even the most acute observer cannot divine. When these details are supplied, we recognize that they come from the narrator, who is privy to what lies concealed from the characters. For example, in chapter 4 of Thomas Pynchon's *V.*, Esther walks into a plastic surgeon's waiting room and surveys the deformed patients:

> And off in a corner, looking at nothing, was a sexless being with hereditary syphilis, whose bones had acquired lesions and had partially collapsed so that the gray face's profile was nearly a straight line, the nose hanging down like a loose flap of skin, nearly covering the mouth; the chin depressed at the side by a large sunken crater containing radial skin-wrinkles; the eyes

squeezed shut by the same unnatural gravity that flattened the rest of the profile.[33]

Some of these observations could be Esther's—the gray face, the collapsed profile, the loose nose, the sunken chin, the closed eyes—but who is telling us that the cause of the deformities is hereditary syphilis, and who peers under the surface to see lesions on the bones? Only the narrator knows these facts. He is not only giving us a visual picture of what we could see if we were in Esther's place, a description unnecessary in cinema or on the stage. He is supplementing the visual description with detail unavailable to anyone but him. The Homeric narrator often demonstrates a privileged knowledge comparable to the knowledge of the bone lesions and the disease that produces the outer symptoms, facts requiring superhuman powers of vision.

When a warrior is killed or wounded in the *Iliad*, it often happens that every detail of the injury is given, including the exact course of the missile through the body (and sometimes the shield):[34]

> Him Meriones, when he overtook him in the chase,
> wounded in the right buttock; and clean through
> went the spear's point all the way under the bone into
>   the bladder;
> he fell to his knees groaning, and death enveloped him.
> (5.65–68)

An observer might be able to tell just when death envelops the fallen soldier, but the passage of the spear could not be told in such detail except by a narrator with more than ordinary vision. A Hemingway narrator, who is regularly denied such knowledge, would have described the wound as seen from the outside, unable to see the spear pass under the bone and into the bladder. The Homeric narrator has access to all that transpires in the world of the story.

The knowledge of all the details of an injury is not greatly significant in itself but only as an indication of the narrator's powers. Of great importance, on the other hand, is his ability to see into the world of the gods. The roles played by the gods in the *Iliad* and the *Odyssey* are so fundamental to the plot and thematic structure and their appearances are so numerous that a catalogue is neither necessary nor practical. What is noteworthy is that the gods' activity is almost entirely concealed from the mortal characters. At most one character at a given time will be aware briefly of a single god's presence and influence on the action—when Athena takes Achilleus by the hair (*Il.* 1.197ff.), for example—but the gods operate for the most part on a separate plane, the vision of which must be granted as a special power, as it is to Diomedes briefly during his *aristeia* (*Il.* 5.127ff.).[35] When men and gods do speak face-to-face, the latter are usually disguised as mortals. Generally, when the gods marshal the warriors and rouse them to battle, when they take part in the fighting, when they put ideas into the characters' heads, when they preserve the bodies of the dead, when they deflect missiles from a potential victim, and when they plan the course of the plot, the gods' industry in shaping the lives and fates of the mortal characters goes virtually unnoticed except in the effects of the immortals' activity. The men know who control their universe, but they are incapable of seeing into the gods' world. Only the gods and the narrator see the entire picture, and we profit from the narrator's clear vision.

INNER VISION

In his epic drama, *The Dynasts*, Thomas Hardy portrays a Napoleon who believes, falsely, that his campaigns against England are determined solely by his decisions and ambitions, much like the Napoleon of *War and Peace*. While Tolstoy undermines the general's self-importance with philosophical and literary arguments against any individual's control over the course of history, Hardy illustrates the same point on a cosmic level by turning at crucial points to the "Phantom Intelligences," who can see the workings of the universe and are conscious of the inscrutable design of the "Immanent Will." Periodically the opacity of human vision is replaced by a celestial clarity, and we are given a glimpse of the complexity of human activity, as in this "stage direction":

> At once, as earlier, a preternatural clearness possesses the atmosphere of the battle-field, in which the scene becomes anatomized and the living masses of humanity transparent. The controlling Immanent Will appears therein, as a brain-like network of currents and ejections, twitching, interpenetrating, entangling, and thrusting hither and thither the human forms.[36]

Napoleon and his fellow characters are not attuned to the powers that control and shape their lives. To the Intelligences of the story alone belongs the true and complete vision of human affairs.

In the *Iliad* and the *Odyssey*, the narrator is one of the Intelligences. He sees the world with the same eyes as the gods and in fact has a more comprehensive view of the gods' activities than they do—even Zeus sleeps. The Homeric narrator's omniscience concerning the workings of the world might lead us to infer that there is nothing beyond his ken, that he indeed knows all, but this conclusion does not necessarily follow. The Phantom Intelligences of *The Dynasts* can see the "brain-like network" of the Immanent Will, but they do not, as far as we can tell, see into the characters' minds, nor do we. In drama, what we know of the characters' minds and thoughts comes to us only from their own words, not from any privileged direct knowledge of their psyches. Just as omnipresence does not always entail omniscience, so does omniscience of external matters not necessarily imply omniscience of internal processes. We must examine the latter separately.

Booth (1961) claims that "the most important single privilege is that of obtaining an inside view of another character, because of the rhetorical power that such a privilege conveys upon a narrator" (160–61), but he reminds us that

> narrators who provide inside views differ in the depth and the axis of their plunge. Boccaccio can give inside views, but they are extremely shallow. Jane Austen goes relatively deep morally, but scarcely skims the surface psychologically. All authors of stream-of-consciousness narration presumably attempt to go deep psychologically, but some of them deliberately remain shallow in the moral dimension. (163–64)

Homer does have access to his characters' minds, and he plunges to some extent along more than one axis, but his method of presenting the inner processes of his characters involves a singular combination of techniques. Before launching into the peculiarities of Homeric psychology, let us first look at the straightforward types of mind reading.[37] Most of the passages involving mental activity are brief statements of an emotion or attitude: a character is pleased, troubled, afraid, courageous, reluctant, angry, kind, sorrowful, impassioned, disappointed, sympathetic, amazed, and so on. Such observations are the shallowest form of inner vision, not only because the expression of the emotion is unembellished, but also because the emotion is usually manifested by the character's words or action:

> Thus he spoke, and ox-eyed queen Hera was afraid,
> and she sat quietly, bending down her heart.
> (*Il.* 1.568–69)

It does not take any powers of divination to see Hera's fear. Nevertheless, to speak with absolute certainty about someone's mental state is not a privilege granted in real life. No one is completely aware of another person's feelings, and any authoritative statement by an outside party does imply special ability.[38] Occasionally the character's action conceals what he really feels, but the narrator sees through to the truth of the matter:

> And though they were in distress, they laughed gaily at him.
> (*Il.* 2.270)

Such statements asserting positive knowledge of an emotion demonstrate that the narrator does indeed have access to the characters' minds,[39] but they do not attest to his ability to penetrate any further than the narrators of the tales in *The Decameron*.

Slightly greater powers are required to tell what someone knows, as when a character recognizes a god in disguise—

> Thus she spoke, and he recognized the voice of the
>   goddess who had spoken—
> (*Il.* 2.182)

but even these cases are usually accompanied by a verbal declaration of recognition, such as Helen's outburst upon seeing through Aphrodite's impersonation:

> And then as she recognized the goddess's beautiful neck
> and her desirable breasts and her flashing eyes,
> then she was astonished and spoke a word and addressed her:
> "Goddess, why do you desire to deceive me in this? ... "
> (*Il.* 3.396–99)

Frequently a statement of a character's knowledge simply introduces a speech based on that knowledge: Zeus's rebuke of Athena and Hera is introduced by the assurance that he knows what is bothering them—

> But he knew in his mind and spoke.
> (*Il.* 8.446)

So far the evidence of the narrator's ability to delve into the minds of the characters has been limited to authoritative statements of what could easily be conjectured by those standing by. But when the narrator explains the reason for an action or verbalizes the intention, he demonstrates a somewhat deeper knowledge of the character's private thoughts.[40] Only he, for example, shares Diomedes' knowledge that the spear he hurls at Dolon misses him deliberately (*Il.* 10.372), and only he knows that the reason Aineias wanders through the battlefield is to find Pandaros (*Il.* 5.166–68). But even in the cases of the character's purpose the narrator lets us barely pierce under the surface of the mind. We do not see the workings of the mind, even if the narrator does; we hear only the narrator's summary.

When someone is planning a course of action, we may, again, be given only a summary account of the character's thoughts:

> ... and Athena and Hera muttered;
> they were sitting close together, plotting evil for the
>   Trojans.
>
> (*Il.* 4:20–21)

But the narrator may also tell us in so many words the plan that has taken shape within a character's mind:

> This seemed to his mind to be the best plan,
> to go first among men to Nestor, Neleus's son,
> to see if he could devise some faultless scheme with him
> which would be a defense against evils for all the
>   Danaans.
>
> (*Il.* 10.17–20)

Other kinds of decisions reached but not expressed openly can be laid bare by the narrator:

> At once war became sweeter to them than to return
> in the hollow ships to their dear fatherland.
>
> (*Il.* 2.453–54)

The narrator has gone further than to say, "They returned to battle formation joyously." He has expressed the thought in a full sentence, resembling, as it were, a collective indirect speech by the warriors.[41]

Chatman (1978, 181) explains that "one can separate two kinds of mental activity: that which entails 'verbalization,' and that which does not." Some of the thoughts discussed above are most likely not verbalized (presumably Hera does not say to herself, "I'm afraid of my husband"), while some perhaps are, though we are not told so (Aineias might well be thinking, "I have got to find Pandaros"). But when some of the verbalization is expressed either directly or indirectly, we carry internal vision a step further. The extreme is stream-of-consciousness narration, a purported transcription of "the random ordering of thoughts and impressions" (Chatman 1978, 188), the greatest sustained example of which is Molly Bloom's "monologue" closing *Ulysses*. Homer, of course, never tries to imitate verbally the thought processes in the manner of Joyce or Woolf, yet he does quite frequently disclose mental operations in his own way.

His own way is to portray the workings of the mind in the form of an address to oneself or of a dialogue, usually with a god. Russo and Simon (1968, 487) have demonstrated that the following two characteristics arise from the very nature of the tradition of oral poetry, which culminated in the *Iliad* and the *Odyssey*:

> 1) The Homeric representation of mental life shows a strong tendency for depicting that which is common and publicly observable, as contrasted with that which is idiosyncratic and private.
>
> 2) This tendency is manifested by representing inner and (to us) internalized mental processes as "personified interchanges." The interchange may be between a hero and a god, or between a hero and some other external agent (e.g., a horse, a river), or between a hero and one of his "organs," such as his *thymos* or *kradie*.

They claim that any in-depth probing of a character's private thoughts is alien to Homer's practice, not because he does not have the ability to do so, but because the oral poet tends "to favor external over internal determinants of mental activity" (494).[42]

Homer sees into the workings of his characters' mental life with no less clarity than a modern narrator who makes frequent use of the interior monologue or stream of consciousness; his knowledge is simply presented in a different form. For fairly brief and shallow incursions into the mind, Homer proceeds straightforwardly by stating the emotion, intent, thought, or plan he has the ability to see. But to present an extensive picture of what is going on in a character's mind, he externalizes the thought processes in ways alien to most other narrative—the thinking is cast as a conversation with an extension of the self (the nearest modern equivalent is the dramatic soliloquy). His most profound demonstration of omniscience, complete access to private thoughts, is thereby disguised and made to seem no privilege at all.

FOREKNOWLEDGE

While some narrators, like Homer, are granted all the special abilities discussed so far, many, intradiegetic narrators in particular, are denied some or all of them. Foreknowledge, however, is the possession of virtually everyone who tells a story—the narrator can see into the future and knows how the story will end. There are exceptions—epistolary or diary novels or an occasional community endeavor, such as the mystery, *The Floating Admiral*, whose chapters were written successively each by a different author—and there are disclaimers of foreknowledge, especially by narrators who claim a certain amount of autonomy for their characters,[43] but these are rare. Because narrative is almost always retrospective, the story's future is the narrator's past.

Genette (1980, 40) borrows the term *prolepsis* to refer to "any narrative maneuver that consists of narrating or evoking in advance an event that will take place later."[44] Even though all narrators are capable of prolepses, not all of them avail themselves of the privilege of anticipating future events. Prolepses are in fact rather scarce in the classic novel, as Genette explains:

> The concern with narrative suspense that is characteristic of the "classical" conception of the novel ("classical" in the broad sense, and whose center of gravity is, rather, in the nineteenth century) does not easily come to terms with such a practice. Neither, moreover, does the traditional fiction of a narrator who must appear more or less to discover the story at the same time that he tells it. (67)

But as we see from works that at the beginning tell or hint at the ending— *Lolita*, *The Death of Ivan Ilych*, *The Immoralist*, *Frankenstein*, *The Catcher in the Rye*, to name a few—a prolepsis does not necessarily lessen the interest in the episodes leading up to the disclosed event, but might rather whet it like a good appetizer.[45]

Mystery and secrecy play little part in the telling of the *Iliad* and the *Odyssey*. A modern reader completely unfamiliar with the traditional stories is at little disadvantage beside one better informed, for an outline of the plot introduces each poem and allusions to the future are scattered liberally throughout in several different ways. Todorov (1977, 64–65) remarks that the plot of the *Odyssey* is a "plot of predestination," and his assessment holds for the *Iliad* as well:

This certitude as to the fulfillment of foretold events profoundly
affects the notion of plot. The *Odyssey* contains no surprises;
everything is recounted in advance, and everything which is
recounted occurs. This puts the poem, once again, in radical
opposition to our subsequent narratives in which plot plays a much
more important role, in which we do not know what will happen.[46]

Duckworth (1933, 1) sees this penchant for telling plot elements in advance
as typical of classical literature in general:

The epics and dramas of Greece and Rome do not, in general,
strive to keep the reader in the dark concerning the subject-
matter, but tend to give him a foreknowledge of the events to
come; modern literature, on the contrary, places a greater
emphasis upon the elements of unexpectedness and surprise.
Especially prominent in the field of ancient epic is this tendency
to prepare the reader for the incidents that he is to expect during
the course of the poem.

The epics are distinct from most classic novels in more than their frequent
announcements of what is yet to occur; they stand out also in the variety of
means available to make the announcements and in the variety of the
prolepses' purposes and effects.[47]

The proems are wide-ranging versions of the prolepses that will recur
throughout both poems. As proleptic prefaces, they resemble the unusual,
synoptic opening paragraph of Nabokov's *Laughter in the Dark*[48] rather than
Marlow's quite normal preface to the tale of his journey into the heart of
darkness:

I don't want to bother you much with what happened to me
personally, ... yet to understand the effect of it on me you ought
to know how I got out there, what I saw, how I went up that river
to the place where I first met the poor chap. It was the farthest
point of navigation and the culminating point of my
experience.[49]

Some of the events are revealed in advance—that he does make it up the
Congo as far as anyone could, that he does meet Kurtz—but since we do not
at this point know what river or what poor chap, our attention is directed not
toward the fulfillment of what we find out later to be his intentions, but
toward the profundity of the journey's effect on him.

Homer's preludes are certainly more than mere plot synopses, but unlike this example from Conrad, each of them is a genuine, though elliptical, summary of the story we are about to hear. The proems do not summarize the plots of either poem to the end—that of the *Iliad* does not go beyond the fulfillment of Zeus's decision to honor Achilleus, and that of the *Odyssey* mentions his homecoming but only hints at troubles awaiting him there without a word about the conclusion.[50] They do, however, give away some of the crucial facts that most novelists would be careful to conceal: the Apologue, of Odysseus is "spoiled" in the proem by disclosing the fact, the nature, and the cause of the crewmembers' destruction; the main narrative of the *Odyssey* by revealing that Odysseus does make it home; and the *Iliad* by announcing that Zeus will accomplish his decision to slaughter a great number of Greeks on account of Achilleus's wrath.

Homer was clearly no more interested in surprising his audience with plot twists or unexpected events than the tragedians of Athens, especially Euripides, whose prologues are often plot synopses.[51] The story exists quite apart from any telling of it. The Homeric narrator sees it entire and he sees no reason to pretend otherwise, to act as though he is discovering it along with us, nor does he see a problem in advance notices to the audience—if they serve a purpose. We saw earlier that the narrator interrupts the flow of the story with a descriptive pause or an analepsis only if it enhances the immediate surroundings. The same is not true of prolepses. We shall see presently that the immediate scene is indeed enriched by a prolepsis, and there are a number of cases in which that is its only function, but more often the glimpse into the future is part of a larger framework affecting our perception of the whole work.

Several of the prolepses in the *Iliad* refer to events in the very near future and do not go beyond the context in significance,[52] but they do show something of how Homeric prolepses work. Duckworth (1933) demonstrates that, whereas characters are party to predictions of events beyond the scope of the *Iliad* or the *Odyssey*, "the events which occur within the poem are forecast to the reader, but the characters themselves are kept in the greatest possible ignorance of their fate" (116). The narrator uses their ignorance to make our awareness something more than mere foreknowledge. For example, when Dolon is given his commission, he readies himself and heads for the Greek ships;

But he was not going to
come back from the ships to bring his tale to Hektor.
(10.336–37)

With these words we know the outcome of the episode: Dolon will encounter the Greek spies and die. But the narrator has done more than give us advance information. His tone has changed to one of warning, steering our sympathy toward the unwary victim. Our knowledge of the ending, far from spoiling the tale, only increases the tension throughout the scene between the prediction and the fulfillment. When Dolon begs for his life and many-wiled Odysseus reassures the captive,

> "Be brave, and let not death be any concern at all to your heart,"
> (383)

our feelings of sympathy and tension gain strength from our certain knowledge that his death is inevitable. As Alfred Hitchcock has often ably demonstrated, suspense is heightened by full disclosure of the facts—the uncertainty is not of what but of how and when. When the predestined finally occurs, when Diomedes finally slashes Dolon's throat, the impact is more powerful and profound than the jolt of horror a surprise murder would have produced.

If a proleptic announcement is effective within the compass of a short scene, so much greater will be the effect if the anticipated event is delayed. The eventual death of Asios, for example, at the hands of Idomeneus is told when he disobeys Poulydamas's order to leave his horses by the ditch (*Il.* 12.113–17), and we fully expect him to meet his end during his charge. Yet after his angry speech about the impossibility of breaking through the wall (164–72), Asios drops out of the picture. It is not for several hundred lines, when Asios steps forward to challenge Idomeneus (13.384), that the foretold is finally fulfilled.

The *Iliad* is not centered on the deaths of Asios or Dolon; the interest, pathos, and tension produced by the foretelling of relatively unimportant incidents, though forceful while they last, are evanescent. The prolepses with the greatest effect are those that foresee the events forming the core of the plot—the deaths of Patroklos and Hektor and the fulfillment of "the plan of Zeus."

Patroklos is mentioned occasionally beforehand, but it is not until Book 11 that he becomes important in the plot, and his emergence into the foreground is marked by an intimation of his death. Achilleus has been watching the battle and decides to send Patroklos to find out who has been taken wounded to Nestor's tent:

> At once he spoke to his companion, Patroklos,
> calling from his ship; and he heard from his hut

and came out, equal to Ares, and this was the beginning
 of his evil.

(11.602–4)

The tremendous pathos and sympathy that the death of Patroklos produces
is attributable in large part to the frequent direct addresses by the
narrator,[53] but even these would not be nearly as effective if they were not
accompanied by the numerous allusions to his impending fall—indirectly
in Book 8, at the outset in Book 11, at the time of his request to lead the
Myrmidons to the Greeks' defense, and with increasing concentration
throughout his *aristeia*.[54] Our prior knowledge of the denouement casts the
events leading up to it in a more serious light than the events themselves
would warrant.

The three prolepses relating to Hektor shift the stress successively
from his glory to his death. At 12.173–74 the narrator announces Zeus's
intention of reserving the honor of breaking through the Greek wall for
Hektor. At 15.612–14 Zeus is enhancing his glory because he will have only
a short while to live. After the killing of Patroklos, the act that will mean
Hektor's death, Zeus grants him one last honor, to wear Achilleus's helmet:

Then Zeus gave it to Hektor
 to wear on his head, and his destruction was close at hand.
(16.799–800)

The two crucial deaths come as no surprise to the audience. We are warned
well in advance, and our certainty of their deaths is the cause of great tension
and sympathy as we watch them pave their own ways toward the fates of
which they are ignorant.[55]

Tension and sympathy, however, have less to do with the prolepses
concerning Zeus's plan to honor Achilleus by giving the victory temporarily
to the Trojans.[56] With these the emphasis is not on the feelings evoked by
the knowledge of what is to come but on the inevitability itself. Zeus's nod to
Thetis in Book 1 is irrevocable, and the frequent references to his plan
prepare us for the success or failure of the particular action at hand, and more
important, they drive home the fact that the conclusion is foregone. When
the narrator makes this statement after the oath sealing the terms of the
truce,

Thus they spoke, but the son of Kronos would not bring it to pass
 for them,

(3.302)

at the same time that he is letting us know that the intentions of the truce will riot be carried out, he is reminding us that the intentions of the mortal characters have no bearing on what will happen—the decision has already been made by Zeus.

The narrator's allusions to the "the plan of Zeus" lead us to the prolepses, which the narrator does not make in his own voice but puts in the mouths of his characters.[57] In the Homeric poems the narrator is not the only one with foreknowledge, for he shares this power with the gods and the prophets. Many of the conversations on Olympos concern the course of the plot, and though there is at times a dispute over what should be done at a given point in the story,[58] all agree about what is fated and all challenges to fate are in the end rebuffed. Both poems are filled with characters' predictions of the future, and many turn out to be accurate. When gods and prophets speak of the future, there is no question but that their predictions will be fulfilled. They, like the narrator, know what is fated—that is, they know how the story goes.

Of the several passages in which the future course of the plot is revealed by a god or a prophet,[59] the most far-reaching is at *Iliad* 15.56–77, in which Zeus, *volvens fatorum arcana*, picks up where the proem leaves off and gives an outline of the rest of the *Iliad* and beyond[60]—Hektor will drive the Greeks back to their ships; Hektor's rout will bring Patroklos to battle, and he will kill Sarpedon only to be killed by Hektor; Achilleus will kill Hektor in revenge and turn the war around until Troy is captured. The only important event not disclosed here is the death of Achilleus, the prophecy of which is made many times elsewhere throughout the poem. The actions on the earthly stage may seem to the human actors to be at least partly in their control and the possible outcomes limitless, but to those of us with foreknowledge—the gods, the prophets, the narrator, and also the narratee, who is privy to their knowledge—the die is cast and the course of the action already determined.

The Homeric narrator has all of the special powers a narrator may have in perceiving and understanding the world of the story. His exploitation of those powers is idiosyncratic, but his possession of them is perfectly normal. What is unusual is that his abilities are in every instance mirrored by the supernatural characters within the text. The gods take on the attributes of the narrator and the narrator those of the gods. Like the gods, the Homeric narrator uses his special powers without being seen. And just as the gods are bound by the dictates of fate, Homer's omniscience does not entail omnipotence—he knows how the story goes, but he is powerless to change it.

NOTES

1. Henry Fielding, *The History of Tom Jones* (New York: Modern Library, 1943), 10.
2. See Bassett (1938, 47–56) and Hellwig (1964, 89–107).
3. An *aristeia* is a sequence of battle scenes highlighting one hero.
4. Il. 5.95, 5.166, 8.76, 10.339, 11.581, 11.599, 15.484, 16.278, 16.419, 17.1, 17.483, 17.626, 21.526, 22.25, 23.448. In the following, the watching is implied by the context, though not stated: Il. 16.124, 17.237, 17.498, 22.405; Od. 13.165. Line numbers refer to the first line of the new scene. De Jong (1987c, 102–7) discusses perception as embedded focalization.
5. See especially the discussion of tableaux of arrival in chapter 2, 52–57.
6. Il. 5.711, 7.17, 7.443, 8.397, 10.515, 13.1, 13.10, 14.153, 15.4, 16.431, 17.198, 17.441, 19.340, 22.166, 24.23, 24.331; Od. 5.282, 5.333, 5.375, 5.382. That the gods have been watching is implied at Il. 4.1, 5.29, 8.69, 11.75, 11.182, 16.666, 17.582, 18.356, 21.435; Od. 5.1, 13.125, 24.572.
7. See "Plot Decisions" in chapter 7, 187–96.
8. Il. 1.43, 8.198, 10.532, 11.463, 14.1, 15.377, 15.379, 16.527, 17.456, 18.35, 21.388, 24.314; Od. 1.328, 4.767, 6.117, 6.328, 17.492, 20.92.
9. An oral performance makes the auditory aspect of the action more vivid than a silent reading does only when what is heard has been cited in direct speech.
10. Il. 5.37, 16.257, 21.391.
11. Il. 11.497, 13.521, 13.674, 17.377, 17.401, 22.437; Od. 4.768.
12. Il. 1.308, 1.313, 1.457, 1.474, 1.479, 2.419, 6.287, 8.170, 10.295, 11.3–4, 11.52, 15.377, 16.249, 16.684, 17.268, 17.648, 22.209, 23.771; Od. 1.26, 1.365, 2.146, 3.4, 3.10, 4767, 4.795, 5.81, 5.85, 5.462, 6.224, 6.328, 6.330, 7.81, 15.217, 17.541, 19.53, 20.102, 20.159, 20.373, 21.359, 22.381, 23.297. Note that a god hearing a prayer is a common instance of this change of scene that turns out not to be a change. At Il. 24.677 it is unclear whether Hermes is in fact in a different location. The three times when a second messenger is delayed in his mission in the text until the first is carried out (Il. 15.220ff., Il. 24.143ff., and Od. 5.1ff., discussed in chapter 4, 91–94) are extended and modified examples of the same situation—in a sense we have not really left Zeus and what intervenes is a sort of digression from the dispatching scene.
13. Il. 5.668, 7.311, 7.419, 7.430, 8.55, 8.384, 10.25, 10.299, 11.56, 11.597, 12.196, 13.83, 13.351, 13.489, 13.835, 14.388, 15.390, 15.501, 15.515, 15.516, 15.518, 15.560, 16.553, 18.243, 18.314, 20.3, 20.4, 20.364, 22.3, 23.1; Od. 2.382, 3.431, 3.432, 3.435, 17.506, 17.507, 19.51, 20.57, 23.289. On simultaneity, see chapter 4, 90–95.
14. Il. 3.449, 8.213, 8.489, 16.102, 17.210, 17.412, 23.110; Od. 4.787, 4.842, 16.342, 16.409, 17.166, 17.182, 18.158, 20.1, 20.241.
15. Il. 6.503, 8.438, 11.618, 22.188, 24.349; Od. 16.1, 16.322, 24.489.
16. Il. 6.119/237, 9.669, 13.43, 16.2, 18.2, 18.148/369; Od. 15.1, 15.301/495, 16.452.
17. 1.430, 1.488, 3.121, 20.42, 21.520, 22.7. In Od.: 3.464, 4.625, 6.2, 7.2, 7.14, 13.187, 20.124, 24.1, 24.205, 24.413. These are the only ones I could detect, though I do not doubt that a case could be made for others, or even that some of these might show a continuity I do not see.
18. It is interesting that this is the only time we are not told who sends Iris. I see a similar correlation at these three points in the *Iliad*: 1.430—both Thetis and Odysseus are going out to sea; 1.488—Odysseus and his men go to their huts, but it is to Achilleus's hut

we turn; 20.42—the gods array themselves for battle, but Achilleus is the one who now fights. This type of switch occurs at least once in the *Odyssey* (24.1)—at the end of the previous book, Athena guides Odysseus and company out of town in darkness; the next book begins with Hermes leading the suitors' souls down to Hades.

19. Hölscher (1939) discusses scene changes in the *Odyssey* (22–36) and compares the techniques with those in the *Iliad* (37–50).

20. Hellwig (1964, 97–107) overstates the difference between the two poems in the number of abrupt scene changes.

21. See chapter 1, 20–21.

22. See chapter 4, 91–95.

23. *Il.* 2.86–94, 2.455–73, 2.808–10, 19.356–64, 20.153–58, 24.707–9 (gathering not for battle but for mourning).

24. *Il.* 1.487, 1.605–8, 19.277, 23.1–3, 24.1–3; **Od.** 2.257–59, 13.17–19.

25. *Il.* 3.1–14, 4.422–56, 8.53–67, 11.47–91, 11.148–53, 11.214–17, 12.2–3, 12.35–39, 13.126–36, 13.169, 13.330–44, 13.540, 13.789–801, 13.833–37, 14.153–58, 14.388–401, 15.1–8, 15.301–28, 15.353–69, 15.379–89, 15.405–14, 15.636–38, 15.653–58, 15.696–703, 16.211–17,16.364–98, 16.562–.69, 16.633–46, 17.262–78, 17.342–43, 17.366–77, 17.543–44, 17.736–61, 21.606–22.4.

26. See also my chapter 1, 14–17, and Fenik (1968, 79–80). Uspensky (1973, 64) refers to the overview of the troops before the Battle of Austerlitz in *War and Peace* 3.14, which is functionally similar to the general descriptions in the *Iliad*.

27. We must be careful not to assume that every description of this sort presupposes a viewpoint from one hovering above the scene. Nestor at one point stands outside his hut to see what the clamor signifies:

> ... at once he looked on a disgraceful action,
>   some being routed, others rushing behind them,
>   mighty-hearted Trojans, and the wall of the Achaians
>   was thrown down.
>
> (**Il.** 14.13–15)

The account of the chariot race in **Il.** 23.362–81 also gives a broad and comprehensive picture, but we are clearly watching the race from the point of view of the spectators. These episodes do emphasize the theme of viewing in the *Iliad*, seen most prominently when gods are the spectators.

28. Chapter 7, 187–96.

29. οἶδα, "to know," is in effect the perfect tense of a verb "to see."

30. When Odysseus, for example, tells of Helios's threat and Zeus's conciliation after the eating of the oxen, a scene at which he could not have been present, he quickly explains how he arrived at this information—Hermes had told it to Kalypso, who then had told it to Odysseus (**Od.** 12.389–90). We had not heard Hermes mention this during their conversation in Book 5. As usual, Homer withheld a piece of information that was irrelevant at the time, only to bring it up when it matters—a paralipsis (see chapter 4, 99–100) with a twist, since it owes its place in the discourse to an intradiegetic narrator. Odysseus does not explain how he could narrate the portion of the Laistrygonian episode occurring inland (10.103–17). We are to presume, not unreasonably, that he learns the details from the men he had sent to reconnoiter, just as he hears what happens to his men at Kirke's hands from Eurylochos (10.244–60). Even in the latter case, Odysseus tells the story in much more detail than Eurylochos does in direct speech, and we must presume

that the outline was filled in subsequently or that his direct quotation of Eurylochos's account has been abbreviated for the sake of his own story. More mysterious is Odysseus's detailed knowledge of the unusual astronomy and consequent customs in the Laistrygonians' land (10.81–86); here is an instance of unwarranted knowledge on the part of a secondary, homodiegetic narrator, as in the case of Achilleus discussed in note 31 below. On limitations on Odysseus's knowledge, see Suerbaum (1968, 153–64) and Effe (1975, 142–44).

31. De Jong (1985c, 17) points out the interesting assumption of authorial omniscience on the part of Achilleus, when he tells Thetis about the quarrel (Il. 1.366–92): "Achilles knows the inner thoughts of Chryses and Agamemnon and reconstructs the scene between the priest and Apollo, without having been present."

32. For fuller discussions of the narrator's knowledge, see Booth (1961, 160–64), Genette (1980, 185–211), Chatman (1978, 211–19), and Füger (1978).

33. Thomas Pynchon, V. (New York: Bantam, 1964), 90.

34. 3.318–49, 3.357–60, 4.132–39, 4.459–61, 4.480–82, 4.502–3, 4.521–22, 5.66–67, 5.73–74, 5.106, 5.281–82, 5.290–93, 5.305–8, 5.538–39, 5.661–62, 5.694–98, 6.9–11, 7.245–48, 7.251–54, 8.325–28, 11.266–68, 11.351–53, 14.404–6, 16.504–5. Occasionally in Od.: 18.96–97, 19.449–51, 22.15–16, 22.82–83, 22.294–95.

35. In Virgil's Aeneid, Aeneas is likewise favored with such a vision during the fall of Troy (2.604ff.).

36. Thomas Hardy, The Dynasts (New York: St. Martin's Press, 1965), 118. Since The Dynasts was clearly not written to be produced, the stage directions function in the play as descriptive pauses between direct speeches.

37. Because the instances of inside views of all types are so prevalent throughout bath poems, on almost every page, I see no need to document each one but only to suggest the general categories that include the hundreds of individual cases. See de Jong (1987c, 110–14) on characters' thoughts.

38. See Füger (1978, 208–9).

39. Felson-Rubin (1987, 70) cites Od. 18.281–83, where the narrator asserts that Penelope had other things on her mind while flattering the suitors, and asks, "How accurate an assessment [of her motivation] is it? Is the narrator totally cognizant of his own character's intentions?" The narrator of The French Lieutenant's Woman denies such powers ([New York: New American Library, 1969], 80–82). Homer, on the other hand, has nothing of this assumed ignorance; his words about a character's mind are authoritative.

40. See also chapter 6, in the section "Interpretation," 148–53.

41. See the section "Pseudo-Direct Speech" in chapter 3, 79–82.

42. The page numbers for these passages in Wright's collection (1978) are 45 and 52, respectively. See this article for a good bibliography on Homeric psychology.

43. See, for example, John Fowles's excursus on the creator's role in the story in The French Lieutenant's Woman, 80–82.

44. See his discussion of prolepsis on 67–79. Prolepsis is an overt reference to an event of the future and is therefore not the same as foreshadowing.

45. One of Duckworth's principal intentions in his systematic study of foreshadowing in classical epic (1933) is to refute the commonly held view that the announcement of future events "lessens the interest and weakens the effectiveness of the poems" (3–4).

46. It is not, by the way, entirely true that "everything which is recounted occurs" in the Odyssey, since Teiresias's prophecy extends beyond the scope of the poem to the time of Odysseus's death. This exception reinforces Todorov's point about no surprises—not even the events after the narrative ends are left open for speculation.

47. Bergren (1983) shows that Odysseus skillfully uses prolepses in the Apologue in the same manner as the main narrator in the *Odyssey*.

48. See chapter 1, 34.

49. Joseph Conrad, *Heart of Darkness* (New York: Washington Square Press, 1972), 8.

50. For an ingenious explanation of the curtailment of the summary, see Minton (1960, 306–8). That the outline is given backward in the *Iliad* and forward in the *Odyssey* is a function of their respective structures. The former has a geometrical design in which the events of the first half of the poem and of each section are mirrored by those of the second half; the proem, then, is a reflection in miniature of what follows. The *Odyssey*, on the other hand, proceeds linearly, just like its proem. See Whitman (1958, 249–309).

51. Euripides, of course, is noted for surprise twists on the myths, as in the *Helen*, but the surprise is not within the play.

52. 5.674–76, 6.393, 10.332, 10.336–37, 12.3–4, 12.113–17, 13.602–3, 13.644–45, 16.460–61, 17.277–78, 17.497–98, 18.311–13, 20.466, 21.47–48.

53. See chapter 7, 170–74.

54. 8.476, 11.602–4, 16.46–47, 16.249–52, 16.644–55, 16.685–87, 16.692–93, 16.707–9 (his failure to take Troy is foretold by Apollo), 16.787.

55. The prolepses in the *Odyssey* in the narrator's voice tell us of the suitors' impending doom and likewise heighten the suspense, though not the pathos—17.364, 18.155–56, 18.345, 20.392–94, 21.418, 22.32–33; the death of Antinoos's father is also told in advance—24.470–71.

56. 2.36–40, 2.419–20, 2.694, 3.302, 8.69–74, 11.54–55, 11.79, 16.249–52.

57. It is noteworthy that, after the proem, there are no prolepses in the *Odyssey* in the narrator's own words, only in the speeches of gods and prophets.

58. See "Plot Decisions" in chapter 7, 187–96.

59. Some of the more notable are these (some in the Apologue): Il. 13.663–70, 15.56–77, 16.707–9, 18.59–60, 20.337–39; Od. 4.561–69, 11.101–37, 12.39–141, 13.339–40, 15.31–37., 15.172–78, 20.45–53, 20.351–57, 20.364–70.

60. On four other occasions the narrator in his own voice refers ahead to events that occur outside the scope of the *Iliad*: 2.724–25, 12.8–35, 17.197, 24.85–86.

LOUISE H. PRATT

Aletheia *and Poetry:*
Iliad *2.484–87 and* Odyssey *8.487–91*
as Models of Archaic Narrative

Do you think that such an intense power of memory as yours has
inhibited your desire to invent in your books?
No, I don't think so.
    —From an interview with Vladimir Nabokov*

Before we can begin to discuss the issue of lying and deception in archaic
poetry, it is necessary to look at the archaic evidence for a connection
between poetry and truth. Modern scholarship's persistent emphasis on this
material has created the impression that archaic poetry is fundamentally
committed to truth (aletheia), and this has become an underlying assumption
in much recent work on archaic poetics. This assumption has led many
scholars to believe that the archaic poets and their audiences could see no
natural affinity between poetry and lying or falsehood, such as that created
by modern reflection on fiction and invention, and it has led some to doubt
that the archaic Greeks even recognized poetic fiction as a legitimate
category of discourse.

But the evidence for a general poetic commitment to truth, to aletheia
in particular, is not nearly as certain as it has come to seem. It does not
suggest a shared notion of poetic truth that can be universally applied to all
archaic poetry, so as to exclude an appreciation of the false and deceptive
aspects of fiction and invention. Claims to truth in archaic poetry are better

From *Lying and Poetry from Homer to Pindar: Falsehood and Deception in Archaic Greek Poetics.* ©
1993 by the University of Michigan.

treated as individual claims applicable only to specific circumstances within particular poems, rather than as evidence for a widespread belief that all poetry was, or ought to be, in all senses true. Such claims are by no means uniform in their language, nor in the variety of truth they embrace. We therefore need to carefully examine both the language and the implications of the essential passages before we can draw final conclusions.

TWO MODEL PASSAGES: *ILIAD* 2.484–87; *ODYSSEY* 8.487–91

In the second book of the *Iliad*, before launching into the lengthy catalog naming the Greek contingents at Troy and their leaders, Homer calls on the Muses:

> Tell me now, Muses, who have Olympian houses—
> for you are goddesses, and are present,[1] and know everything,
> and we hear only report [*kleos*] and know nothing—
> who were the leaders and chieftains of the Danaans.
>   (*Il.* 2.484–87)

This famous invocation has typically served as the starting point for modern work on truth in early Greek poetics. According to the conception suggested here, the divine Muses dispense not beauty or poetic inspiration but a knowledge of people and events that would otherwise be inaccessible to a mere mortal. In shorter apostrophes elsewhere in the *Iliad*, the poet likewise asks the Muse for specific bits of information (e.g., *Il.* 11.219, 14.509). The Muses are summoned at the beginning of all four of the earliest surviving Greek poems and frequently in other archaic poetry. If the primary function of the patron goddesses of poetry is indeed to provide accurate information, as these passages suggest, it can be inferred that the archaic poets must have seen the preservation of a true (accurate) account as the primary aim of successful poetry. This passage and others with similar implications have given archaic poetry, particularly Homeric hexameter, its close identification with truth (aletheia) in modern scholarship.

An often cited passage from the *Odyssey* confirms this interest in truth and extends it beyond the bounds of the *Iliad*. In the eighth book of the *Odyssey*, Odysseus praises the singer Demodocus, apparently for the accuracy of his account:

> Demodocus, I praise you beyond all mortals.
> Either the Muse, the child of Zeus, or Apollo taught you.
> For exceedingly rightly[2] you sing the fate of the Achaeans,

all the things they did and suffered and all their toils,
as though somehow you yourself were present or heard from
another.

(*Od.* 8.487–91)

Since Odysseus was present as a witness to the events described by
Demodocus, and Demodocus presumably was not, it can be inferred that
Odysseus is impressed by how accurately Demodocus has managed to record
the events of the war without being present himself ("as though you yourself
were present"). If the passage is interpreted this way, it suggests the poet's
almost miraculous ability to recreate accurately events that he himself has
not witnessed, an ability that may be credited, as we know from the *Iliad* 2
passage, to the aid of the all-knowing Muses (or possibly, as the passage here
may imply, to Apollo).

In both passages, the poets recount past events. Scholars working in
this area have therefore identified the truth about the past to be the archaic
poets' predominant concern. As the daughters of Memory, the Muses enable
the poets to negate memory's opposite, forgetfulness, and so to preserve the
truth about past events. The Greek word for truth, *aletheia*, can be analyzed
etymologically to be the alpha-privative plus *lethe* (forgetfulness), so it might
be rendered "unforgetfulness."[3] Thus, the archaic poets may be considered
the historians of their culture, their function primarily conservative, and
their aim to preserve the traditional lore of their society. This interpretation
of the archaic poets' role fits well with the now widespread belief that among
these early poets, at least Homer is an oral poet, and with work that stresses
the essentially conservative and traditional nature of oral poetry.

The importance of the commemorative function of archaic poetry is
unmistakable. Poets from Homer to Pindar frequently boast of the power of
poetry to confer lasting memory on worthy individuals and deeds. Achilles
balances a long life against the immortality he can win through song, and
apparently chooses the latter. Pindar's victory odes represent a thriving
genre, epinician, that had as its primary aim the commemoration of victories
in the great athletic contests of Greece. Moreover, narrative poems like the
Iliad and the *Odyssey* were not wholesale fictions to their Greek audiences.
The Trojan War was considered a historical event by even the relatively
skeptical Thucydides, and the gods and the heroes we enjoy as literary
figures were worshiped in Greek religion and cult. Thus, the picture of the
archaic bard as a "master of truth" (to use Detienne's term) is immediately
compelling.

All archaic poetry is not, of course, primarily commemorative or
exclusively narrative. Archaic poetry contains numerous statements that are
explicitly didactic, offering advice and precepts for behavior (see especially

Hesiod's *Works and Days* and the lyrics of Callinus, Tyrtaeus, and Solon). Much of early lyric directly asserts an opinion or a value held by the poet. Although such statements fundamentally differ from the commemorative type described above, their presence in archaic poetry tends to reinforce our conception of the archaic poet as sage and truth-teller. Indeed, early criticism of the archaic poets makes clear that they had a reputation for authoritative wisdom that had to be challenged by any other claimant to knowledge, and this supports our overall conception of the poets as possessing the highest truth.[4]

We must, however, be most careful at precisely this point, because the belief that a poet is a purveyor of wisdom, of what we might call gnomic or general truths, is distinct from the belief that a poet truthfully preserves the past. That some archaic poets may offer prescriptions and opinions that were apparently received as sage truths tells us nothing about whether they and their audiences regarded poetic narrative as an accurate account of the past, and therefore nothing about archaic awareness of fiction.[5] Certainly many modern poets and writers of fiction offer general pronouncements that we are asked to admire as sage truths without our thereby supposing that their narrative is a truthful account of real events. I think, for example, of Trollope or Fielding, who often make such general observations. Their fictional narratives may even be said to convey accurate perceptions about human nature or apt observations about their society, but that does not mean that we believe they accurately commemorate past events. This strange property of fiction, its ability to make falsehood credible so that it may induce belief in its underlying precepts, confounds the categories true and false, belief and disbelief, so that they can not be seen as mutually exclusive.

I do not dispute that the archaic poets were supposed to possess a general sort of wisdom (*sophia*), and that their audiences and critics treated their advice and opinions as authoritative. But this position is different from their supposing that all archaic narrative was intended to be an accurate account of the past, different from their failing to appreciate that narrative may be fictional. We must strongly resist the temptation to use passages that suggest an interest in other varieties of truths as evidence for a commitment to a nonfictional variety of truth in poetic narrative, and vice versa. For the moment, I am interested only in archaic awareness of fiction in narrative, particularly in the kind of narrative represented by Homeric poetry (the *Iliad*, the *Odyssey*, and the Hymns), that is, narrative about events far removed in time. I therefore set aside discussion of poetic statements that make claims to validity that are not immediately relevant to archaic awareness of narrative fiction (e.g., victor praise in epinician and advice on how to live one's life in

Hesiodic poetry). Since such claims have sometimes shaped scholarship's interpretation of Hesiodic and Pindaric attitudes toward narrative fiction, I discuss the issue of narrative fiction in Hesiod and Pindar separately in later chapters.

If we use the *Iliad* 2 and *Odyssey* 8 passages alone to establish the poetics of archaic narrative, we are forced to concede that the archaic poets had no awareness of fiction or poetic invention. Poetic narrative is divine revelation, and the ancient poet and his audience had the faith of fundamentalists. If the *Iliad* 2 and *Odyssey* 8 passages represent archaic notions of poetic narrative, all narrative becomes an account given to the poet by all-knowing and entirely reliable eyewitnesses of past events, that is, an account of "what really happened."

It might be argued that this interpretation of the *Iliad* 2 passage is too strict, that the poet is only asking for the full account according to the traditional story, which suggests no commitment to the factuality of the events reported, no suggestion that they actually happened this way (as if, for example, the poet had said, "Tell me the names of the three bears who scared Goldilocks"). The poet is interested exclusively in what is preserved in the tradition and has no interest in the reality of the past. We might then posit that the passage implies an interest in an entirely nonreferential poetic truth. The truth (aletheia) that has always been associated with this passage becomes "that which is remembered in the tradition," an "unforgetfulness" that is a remembering only of traditional words, not of real deeds. Such a definition of poetic truth would not necessarily exclude that many of the events narrated might be believed to have some relationship to real past events. Both factual and nonfactual information could be preserved in the tradition, but the poet and his audience would never be interested in sorting out the one from the other, nor capable of it. Truth (aletheia) would be defined simply as "all that which is preserved in the tradition," without discrimination of fact or fiction. All innovations, all departures from the tradition, would be lies.

If we were to say that the Homeric poet values this brand of truth as his primary aim, we might speak of a fictional variety of narration, because the narrative has no primary connection to real past events in the minds of either poet or audience. An interest in fact, in what actually happened, is subordinated to an interest in how the traditional story goes. (Anyone who has ever told a familiar story to a critical child will recognize the attitude of this particular type of audience.) Nonetheless, this kind of fictional narrative presumably could never be distinguished from a nonfictional one as lies from truth, because traditional fiction would be as "true" (*alethes*), as unforgotten, as traditional nonfiction. Moreover, we certainly could not have any positive notion of poetic invention, because the poet's primary responsibility would be to preserve the tradition, not to innovate or invent.

This interpretation, however attractive it may be to those of certain philosophical persuasions, does not fit well with our two model Homeric passages. The contrast of the Muses' knowledge with the *kleos* (report) available aurally to mortals in the Catalog-invocation makes it unlikely that Homer appeals here to the tradition alone and not to a past that is felt to be entirely real. In the oral culture that we presume to have been Homer's, it would be virtually impossible to contrast knowledge of a traditional story with the hearing of mere *kleos*. The word *kleos* designates information that is obtained by word of mouth.[6] In an oral culture, all traditional stories would be transmitted by word of mouth. They would all therefore technically be *klea*. In fact, one of the Homeric designations of traditional narratives is the phrase *klea andrôn* (see below for further discussion of the phrase). Moreover, the Greek word used of the Muses' knowledge (*iste*, "you know") is closely associated with visual observation. The contrast here therefore seems to depend on a distinction between the certain and reliable information obtained firsthand from a trustworthy eyewitness, and the fallible reports that circulate anonymously and orally. Such a contrast seems to presuppose a distinction between what really happened and what is said to have happened. Indeed, Homer seems to claim here, rather strikingly, that he can actually bypass the mortal limitations of the tradition itself, by going directly to a knowledgeable, divine source. The *Odyssey* 8 passage seems to be even less ambiguous on this point. Odysseus, whom the passage assumes was present at the Trojan War, is praising Demodocus not for telling a traditional story correctly but for presenting the events as they really were, "as though you yourself were there, or heard from another."

ALETHEIA: AN EXCURSUS

At this point, it is useful to consider the Greek word for truth, *aletheia*, which has been given extraordinary prominence in scholarship on archaic poetics.[7] Interest in the apparent etymology of this word (alpha-privative + *lethe* = unforgetfulness) can lead to some flawed conclusions if we do not carefully consider all usages of both *aletheia* and *lethe*.

The etymology is misleading if it leads us to conclude that aletheia in archaic poetry ever denotes only a nonreferential "unforgetfulness" or "that which is remembered," making the word *aletheia* a virtual synonym of the English word *memory*. Nor should we think that the opposition between aletheia and lethe (forgetfulness) ever makes irrelevant other significant oppositions that are far more explicitly expressed, such as the opposition between aletheia and *pseudos* (truth and falsehood) or that between aletheia and *apate* (truth and deception).[8] Aletheia always excludes falsehood and deception, and in some instances the presence of memory may be entirely irrelevant to the speaking of aletheia.

For example, at *Odyssey* 17.10–15, Telemachus gives the following advice to the swineherd regarding his beggarly guest (also present and listening):

> Send the wretched stranger to the city, so that there
> he can beg for his dinner. Whoever wishes to will give him
> wheatcake and drink. But it is not possible for me to
> receive all men, since I have sorrows on my mind.
> But the stranger, if he is very angry, it will be more sorrowful for him.
> For it is dear to me to speak forth true things [*alethea*].[9]

In saying that it is dear to him to speak forth true things, Telemachus seems to mean that it is dear to him to speak without hiding what he thinks, even though in this case his frankness may give some pain to his guest. In this passage, the importance of memory is negligible. But it is critical that Telemachus does not hide what he thinks, either by not speaking out or by expressing an insincere sentiment. The former would be a kind of deception; the latter would entail not only deception but a falsehood.

Even in the one Homeric passage cited by Heitsch in support of an association of aletheia with memory, the opposition between truth and its absence or substitution remains implicit. The poet describes Achilles' preparations for the chariot race:

> And he sent forth as an eyewitness
> the godlike Phoenix, the companion of his father,
> that he might remember the chariots and speak forth the truth.
>   (*Il.* 23.359–61)

Memory is mentioned in the passage as a necessary condition of Phoenix's speaking *aletheia*. But this does not mean that memory alone guarantees *aletheia*. Achilles wishes Phoenix not only to retain in his mind what he sees (to remember it) but also to report what he sees without hiding or distorting it. The request is more than a request for memory; it is a request for a frank and reliable report of what is remembered. It excludes deliberate falsification or suppression of information as much as it excludes forgetfulness.

The etymology of *aletheia* creates confusion if we dwell too much on a simple meaning of the noun *lethe*, "forgetfulness."[10] If we look at the verb *letho* (= *lanthano*), used much more frequently in Homer than the related noun *lethe* (used only once in Homer), it becomes clear that the lethe excluded from *aletheia* can not be associated exclusively, or even primarily, with the semantic field of memory and forgetting.[11]

The verb *letho* occurs in a wide range of contexts, all of which share a common feature; all entail an absence of awareness. Forgetfulness is one example of such an absence, but it is by no means the only type of lapse created by the action of the verb *letho*. For example, when Helen goes through the city of Troy unperceived by the Trojan women, wrapped in her shining cloak and her silence, Homer comments that she escapes their notice (*lathe*) (*Il.* 3.420). The point is not that Helen has induced the Trojan women to forget her, but that by her silence and her cloak she has managed to go unperceived by them. Likewise, when Hera questions Zeus closely and all too perspicuously about his meeting with Thetis, Zeus responds in some frustration, "Always you know, and not at all can I escape your observation [*letho*]." (*Il.* 1.561). Again, it is not that Hera is able to remember everything Zeus does, but that he is unable to conceal anything from her. Thus, unlike *forgetting*, which tends to imply one's losing what was formerly in one's consciousness, *letho* has no special connection with a loss of a hold on the past.[12] Most occurrences of *letho* have nothing to do with a loss of memory, but rather with an absence of perception, recognition, or awareness that may be caused by a whole range of things, including secrecy, deception, or invisibility on the part of the unperceived, or ignorance, inattention, or forgetfulness on the part of the one unaware. The absence of lethe implied in the etymology of *aletheia* is thus better identified as an absence of hiddenness that might give rise to a failure of perception or awareness, rather than as the absence of forgetfulness and the presence of memory exclusively.

Moreover, if *aletheia* describes an absence of lethe from the entire process of communication rather than from the speaker or from the matter communicated alone, as Thomas Cole persuasively argues it does,[13] these verbal expressions have particular significance (as descriptions of processes). An absence of lethe from this process implies not only the speaker's not forgetting, or not permitting the audience to forget, but the speaker's not hiding anything from the audience's attention in communicating, either deliberately—out of tact or the desire to deceive—or through neglect, ignorance, or forgetfulness. The speaker of aletheia does not hide but reveals. This interpretation of the etymology of *aletheia* suits the usage of *aletheia* and the adjective *alethes* (true) in Homer, where the speaker's remembering, though sometimes a necessary condition for the speaker's communication of aletheia, is never sufficient and in many cases seems entirely irrelevant.

Thus, aletheia always excludes, at least implicitly, anything false or invented (any pseudos) that might hide or disguise the real nature of the subject under discussion, so as to cause a failure of perception. As physical manifestations of lethe may involve not only hiding (physical absence) but also disguising, verbal manifestations of lethe may involve not the mere absence of expression (silence) but the creation of a lie (pseudos). The movement from hiding what you think or know to speaking something false is very swift, as Achilles' famous declaration makes clear:

As hateful to me as the gates of Hades is that man
who hides one thing in his heart and speaks forth another.
(*Il.* 9.312–13)

The absence of truth and the speaking of a substitute are thus seen as two sides of the same coin. Cole characterizes aletheia nicely: "What is involved is strict (or strict and scrupulous) rendering or reporting—something as exclusive of bluster, invention or irrelevance as it is of omission or understatement" (1983, 12). Aletheia thus excludes not only forgetfulness but also invention, falsehood, fiction, intentional omission, insincerity, equivocation—anything that might prevent the hearer's perceiving accurately the subject matter under discussion, anything that might interfere with the process of communication. Aletheia tends therefore to characterize speech that is simple and direct, unduplicitous and straightforward, clear and nonenigmatic. It is seemingly not an appropriate designation for speech that refers only indirectly—that makes use of ambiguous or metaphorical language or of fiction—and we have no early instance of its being used this way.

The archaic notion of aletheia comes close to a notion of truth still present in modern literate society, namely, the kind of truth requested in an American court of law under the name "the truth, the whole truth, and nothing but the truth." This notion of truth is not dependent on our literacy but is fundamentally associated with the oral testimony of an eyewitness.[14] Aletheia too seems to have quite close associations with eyewitness accounts. When applied to narrative accounts in Homer, it is virtually always applied to eyewitness accounts.[15] Moreover, like the legal phrase, *aletheia* has overtones of honesty and fullness. The speaker's sincerity and the desire to communicate fully what is known (or in the case of Telemachus quoted on page 18, what is merely thought) seem both to be essential conditions of aletheia.

Homeric attitudes toward aletheia seem to presume, as do modern American legal practices, that as long as the speaker does not deliberately obscure a set of events in reporting them, the listeners can know what happened, at least well enough to act on it. There seems to be no evidence in Homeric poetry for the widespread modern perception that the witness, no matter how honest in intention, is incapable of giving the hearer an undistorted account of what was seen. Falsehoods are attributed either to ignorance (the person did not actually see what happened), to forgetting, or to deliberate; falsification, not to an inherent inability of language or subject to express what took place.[16] Aletheia in Homeric diction does not resemble another prominent modern conception of truth: it is not a hidden or esoteric property of things (e.g., "the truth about the universe"), attainable only by the initiate or the specialist, or held secretly by the gods, but a kind of straightforward and sincere speech, produced by the average, honest speaker.[17]

Because it excludes any kind of invention or distortion, any kind of ambiguity that might conceal, distort, or mislead, aletheia is not appropriately used to describe speech that contains fiction or invention of any kind. Therefore, if we are to agree with many scholars that archaic poetics is committed to aletheia, we must accept the conclusions of some of those scholars that the archaic poets and their audiences could not regard anything reported in archaic poetry as the product of human invention and had no appreciation of poetic fiction. This would be consistent with a notion of the poet as the mere mouthpiece of the divine Muses, who faithfully report all that they have witnessed (i.e., everything).

ILIAD 2.484–87 AND *ODYSSEY* 8.487–91 AS MODELS OF HOMERIC NARRATIVE

With the exception of the opening invocations to the *Iliad* and the *Odyssey*, which name a general theme for the Muse to sing (or speak of), the other invocations of the Muses in Homeric poetry constitute requests for specific information: Who was the first of the Achaeans to carry off the bloody spoils? (*Il.* 14.509) Who was the first to advance against Agamemnon? (*Il.* 11.219). Which of them was the very best and which of their horses? (*Il.* 2.761). By analogy with the *Iliad* 2 passage, the poet would seem, in these passages too, to be requesting from the Muses the nonfictional truth about the past. Because the Muses are also invoked at the very beginning of both the *Iliad* and the *Odyssey*, and thus are seemingly made responsible for the entire poems, must we conclude that the model of narrative created in our two model passages was assumed by both audience and poet to apply to the *Iliad* and the *Odyssey* in their entireties? That the poet and audience accepted these poems as eyewitness reports conveyed verbally through the poet by the consistently reliable Muses? That the function of the Homeric poems was therefore primarily the accurate preservation of the past (aletheia), a function that excludes the poet's invention and an appreciation of poetic fictionality?

So scholars have frequently concluded, compelled by the force of these few passages. Thus, the archaic narrator was no more supposed to invent than is an eyewitness in a court of law. In fact, the poet must be considered a much more reliable reporter than your standard eyewitness, because the poet has the Muses to help should any gaps in his memory arise. This turns the archaic poets and their audiences into fundamentalist interpreters of Homer and other early poets, intolerant of any kind of falsity, convinced that Homeric and other early narrative accurately represented the past. Homeric narrative is equivalent to nonfiction, to history, insofar as it is taken to represent accurately the events of the past.

Such a view of poetry seems hard to reconcile with the archaic narrative that survives. To our literate minds, the *Iliad* and the *Odyssey* are full of patent inventions, the products of a great imagination (or imaginations). We may believe that these stories originated in real events, but the representation of these events has been so transformed by the artists' imaginations as to become fictional. The works are no longer reliable accounts of the past but seem to have an entirely different function, a distinct one that we recognize as artistic. How can we explain archaic culture's failure to recognize the imaginative and fictional qualities of the accounts? How could the poets who were engaged in this inventive enterprise, an enterprise that so clearly seems to involve making things up, have been so entirely self-conscious?

For the scholars working in this area, the answer lies in the fundamentally oral nature of archaic culture. Even though oral poets may invent, they have no awareness of their invention; their dependence on the formulae and traditional themes of oral narrative give them the impression that they are reciting the traditional tales as they have always been told.[18] The audience, in turn, had no fixed text that it can use as a standard of comparison for the oral poet's new version, so it too is unaware of the subtle shifting and changing that occurs in the course of poetic composition. In the absence of evidence to the contrary, the audience can accept all poetic narrative as (nonfictionally) true. The Muses offer a religious, representation of these phenomena.

INNOVATION AND VARIATION

Though it has an internal logic and consistency that is hard to resist, this picture is difficult to reconcile with certain features of archaic narrative. Given what we know of archaic poetry, it seems unlikely that even in this very early period the audience and the poet were aware of only one essentially unchanging version of a story, one single tradition, that they might uncritically accept as the true version transmitted accurately through the divine Muses who had witnessed the events. Mark Griffith has argued that the competitive context of Greek poetic performance virtually demands multiple accounts, requires improvement on one's predecessors and explicit comparison with one's rivals. He has documented the self-conscious contradicting of other poets that pervades Greek poetry, both archaic and later.[19]

Thus, poetic statements sometimes call attention to alternate versions of the story they recount, as does the poet of the *Homeric Hymn to Dionysus*:

Some say that you were born in Drakane, others in windy Ikaros,
Others in Naxos, O divinely-born one, Eiraphiota.
Others say that at the deep-whirling Alpheios river
Semele, having conceived, bore you to Zeus who delights in thunder.
And others say that you were born lord in Thebes.
All of them lie.[20] he father of men and gods bore you
Far from men, hiding from white-shouldered Hera.
There is a certain Nysa, a very high mountain ...
                                                (*H.Dion.* 1–8)

Such self-conscious comments as these will not long permit the audience to accept that all poetic narrative derives from the Muses' eyewitness accounts and is consequently nonfictionally true. Moreover, given that the audience can not know which of these competing versions is in fact true,[21] it has a fairly complex critical task to perform: How should it respond to a particular claim made by a given poet when it contradicts other poetic accounts? What standards should it adopt in judging these accounts? Why should the audience accept the *Hymn to Dionysus*' account as superior to that of the other accounts so helpfully listed by the poet? Explicit contradictions in archaic poetry demand greater sophistication on the part of the audience and ultimately, due to the absence of secure knowledge, a greater appreciation of certain qualities of narrative apart from its truth-value.

In the notion of truth it embraces, the *Hymn to Dionysus* passage quoted above seems to assert precisely what the *Iliad* 2 and *Odyssey* 8 passages do. By criticizing alternate versions as false, the poet of the *Hymn to Dionysus* would seem to imply that the account he himself retails is the true one, the real one, an actual, nonfictional account of Dionysus' birth (though the poet does not actually say so). But, unlike in the *Iliad* 2 passage, the author of the *Hymn* makes no attempt to explain the mechanism by which the poet, a mere mortal, has been given the knowledge of the true account of the god Dionysus' birth; there is no appeal to the Muses. Moreover, by criticizing other traditional accounts, the poet of the *Hymn to Dionysus* raises disturbing questions about the validity of traditional narrative. The audience is forced to acknowledge the existence of competing, false traditions, a recognition that undermines any assumption that poetry, because it is traditional, is true, and that even casts some doubt on the whole possibility of certain knowledge about events so remote.

Because the passage undermines any assumption that all poetry is true and does not provide any account of this poet's special access to the truth, the only reason for the audience to choose this author's version as superior is because it likes it better. The notion that Zeus was hiding from Hera perhaps makes this author's version more credible, because it suits the character of the two gods in their persistent marital jousting. Might the audience then conclude that this credibility translates into an eyewitness-like truth, into aletheia? Or does the poet's knowledge of a plethora of alternate accounts perhaps seem to guarantee also his knowledge of the only true one? Or maybe the implied etymology of the name Dionysus (= Son of Zeus, born on Nysa) ratifies the poet's new version so as to confirm its (nonfictional) truth.[22] Though these features may contribute to the effectiveness of the passage, it seems unlikely that an ancient audience to this claim, faced with a proliferation of various possible accounts, would be so convinced of this particular claim's truth that it would replace the traditional version of Dionysus' birth at Thebes (now exposed as a falsehood) with this new version (the truth, at last revealed), or that the poet of the passage could really have expected them to.

The structure of the claim seems to be more appropriately explained by the notion of the poetic agon (contest); the poet advances his version in open competition with alternate versions. This suggests a rhetorical function distinct from its apparent purpose. The condemnation of other poets as liars dramatically clears the ground for the poet's version. It does not necessarily translate into the poet's sincere claim for the nonfictionality of his account. The audience may understand it as a conventional device within a poetic competition, as part of a narrative game, at which the poet strives to better his rivals. The apparent criticism may even be taken playfully and ironically: the poet announces the poetic tendency to falsify just as he embarks on his own fiction, a fiction that he asks the audience to admire, but not necessarily to adopt as fact, that is, as an account of what actually happened.[23]

The reception of the poet's implicit claim to know the true version may in this sense be comparable to our reception of similar claims in modern fiction. Though obviously not comparable in all respects, the following passage from *The Pickwick Papers* provides a particularly elaborate and entertaining example:

> We are merely endeavouring to discharge in an upright manner, the responsible duties of our editorial functions; and whatever ambition we might have felt under other circumstances, to lay claim to the authorship of these adventures, a regard for truth forbids us to do more, than claim the merit of their judicious arrangement, and impartial narration. The Pickwick papers are our New River Head; and we may be compared to the New River Company. The labours of others, have raised for us an immense reservoir of important facts. We merely lay them on, and communicate them, in a clear and gentle stream, through the medium of these numbers, to a world thirsting for Pickwickian knowledge. (Charles Dickens, *The Pickwick Papers* [Oxford, Clarendon Press; 1986], chap. 4; 53)

Because we are familiar with the conventions of fiction, we are unlikely to apply such a claim outside the fiction, to misread it as a claim that the events depicted within the fiction actually occurred in the world of our own experience. The claim is itself part of the fiction. The notion of truth represented by such passages is not different from the notion we use in everyday language. Dickens speaks of "facts" and "impartiality," denies authorship of the adventures, just as a historian might. His claim is not to a separate and distinct fictional "truth" but is itself what Austin has called "parasitic" on serious (nonfictional) discourse.[24] Though it resembles in its external features a sincere claim to nonfictional truth, it is intended only in play, is part of a shared game of make-believe, and is not taken outside the fiction as an assertion about the world external to the fiction, the world in which the audience lives and acts.

This calls our attention to a more basic problem in the interpretation of truth claims in archaic narrative. Without an understanding of the conventions that govern the reception of the claims, they can tell us little about the audience's reception of the narrative as fictional or nonfictional. Depending on how we construe the understanding that exists between poet and audience during the poetic performance, we can take such claims as themselves fictional or nonfictional.

The most receptive audience for the sort of claim made in the *Hymn to Dionysus* would be one both skeptical and tolerant, willing to contemplate a range of possible accounts with positive pleasure, to smile at the poet's amusing account of Dionysus' birth, rhetorically set off against other, more partisan versions familiar to their archaic audience. An audience looking for certain knowledge of the past, for the absolute truth, could hardly feel comforted by the poet's initial list of possibilities, particularly because the canonical account of Dionysus' birth at Thebes is boldly rejected. Instead, the structure of the poem (the *priamel* form), common in archaic poetry, asks the audience to admire the poet's ability to present a variety of accounts and then to cap these with his or her own account better than all the others.[25] Two abilities would therefore be paramount: knowledge of a variety of different possible accounts and the ability to present a new and striking best account. Neither skill would have to do exclusively with the preservation of tradition or with an attempt to present a nonfictional account of the past (aletheia). They are rather the sort of skills appropriate to a fictionalizing poet within a tradition. Such a poet would need both the knowledge of many different ways of telling the traditional stories and the ability to innovate in a way that would be acceptable to those familiar with previous versions, a way that improves strikingly on the poet's predecessors.[26]

This openness to variation and innovation suggests an audience that is far from fundamentalist in its approach to narrative. Even in the context of a hymn to a god, a context within which we might expect a more rigid adherence to tradition, the poet may openly confront traditional versions and assert a clever alternative for the admiration of his audience, both human and divine.[27] Apparently, Dionysus will not take offense at the poet's' invention, but will appreciate the poet's offering, his cleverness and even his originality, but this should not surprise us unduly, since it seems a fundamental assumption of Greek religious practices that the gods like to be entertained by humans engaged in contests, both athletic and poetic.[28]

The *Hymn to Dionysus* passage may suggest an important distinction between the poet's function as a "bringer to mind" of and as a teller of nonfictional truths. The poet here certainly makes his audience think of Dionysus, bringing the god to mind in a vivid way. In this sense, he may be said to commemorate the god. Yet it is very difficult to suppose that the audience to the *Hymn* somehow left the performance believing that they had just been given access to the true account of Dionysus' birth, to a knowledge of what really happened, and that all the other stories that had been told had been revealed to be false.

Open rejection of established traditions is already visible in Stesichorus' *Palinode* in the late seventh or early sixth century B.C. Griffith argues that many Hesiodic passages should be similarly construed (e.g., Hesiod's account of Eris at *Works and Days* 11–12, which seems to correct the genealogy of Eris advanced in the *Theogony*; and his account of the number and names of the Muses, which differs from the Homeric account; Griffith

1990, 193). Though the narrators of the *Iliad* and the *Odyssey* never explicitly condemn a previous tradition for lying, characters in the poem do sometimes raise questions about the validity of traditional *klea*.[29] Moreover, readers have noted that the poet does seem aware of alternate versions of certain events that he recounts.[30] Indeed, in the *Iliad* 2 passage, the poet seems to acknowledge quite openly the possibility that the traditional versions may be flawed, when he calls our attention to the inferiority of mortal *kleos*; for if mortal *kleos* were reliable, the poet would not need to invoke the Muses. Thus, it seems unlikely that, even in the very earliest period represented by surviving poetry, we can have an audience or poet so uncritical as to imagine that poetry consistently offers access to an eyewitness-like truth about the past. Any such illusion would have to be shattered as soon as any two poets who invoked the Muses of differing accounts, which is bound to happen in the agonistic context of archaic poetry. The audience must consequently value other qualities of narrative, must appreciate, for example, the poet's ability to create a pleasing and appropriate story, to create a credible and engaging semblance of truth in the absence of certainty, to amuse and to entertain.

The author of the *Homeric Hymn to Apollo* recommends that the audience evaluate the poet in terms of the sweetness of the song and the pleasure it gives them:

> Girls, what man has traveled here as the sweetest of singers,
>   and by whom have you been most pleased?
>   (*H.Apollo* 169–70)

In characterizing song, archaic poetry repeatedly singles out for mention the beauty of the song and the emotions it arouses, rather than its truthfulness.[31] The giving of pleasure (*terpsis*), in particular, is frequently named as the proper function of the poet.[32] Thus, for example, Alcinous describes the poet Demodocus' function: "to give pleasure, in whatever way his impulse (*thumos*) urges him to sing" (*Od.* 8.45). In contrast, truth (aletheia) is never actually named in connection with poetry in Homeric poetry, not in the *Iliad*, the *Odyssey*, nor in any of the Homeric Hymns. The association of poetry with truth in Homeric poetry is almost entirely dependent on our interpretations of certain claims, in which notions that we identify as truth lurk unnamed by any specific Greek term.[33]

Even the Muses, who are the guarantors of a truthful account in the *Iliad* 2 passage, have different associations and functions elsewhere. For example, the names Hesiod gives to his nine Muses in the *Theogony* (77–79) more closely call to mind the realm of beauty and pleasure than truth and accuracy: Melpomene (Singing/dancing one), Kalliope (Beautiful voice), Erato (Desire), Euterpe (Well-pleasing), Terpsichore (Dance-delighting), Thaleia (Festivity), Polyhymnia (Many-hymns), Kleio (Glory), and Ourania (Heavenly one). Moreover, because Hesiod locates the houses of the Muses near those of Himeros (Desire) and the Graces, we may feel that Hesiod does not have truth (aletheia) predominantly in mind when he considers the Muses.

Though poetry's giving pleasure and being beautiful or sweet obviously does not prohibit it from being (nonfictionally) true, the general tendency to characterize poetry in these terms creates a hierarchy of values that leaves room for fictional representation. With pleasure and beauty as preeminent goals, the poets need not promise that all their stories are (nonfictionally) true.[34] This is clearly the view of the fourth-century sophist who wrote the *Dissoi logoi*: "Poets create with pleasure, not truth, as their goal" (*Dissoi logoi* 2.28 Diels-Kranz). Many scholars have considered this an entirely new, hedonistic theory of art, but it seems consistent both with the emphasis of the archaic poets on pleasure and with certain later critiques of poetry (see chapter 5). It is not that narrative can not be both true and pleasurable. But in making pleasure the object of poetry, its preeminent function, truth (aletheia) becomes nonessential, so that neither poet nor audience need be unduly concerned about the truth-value of narrative as long as the narrative gives pleasure. Poetic narrative may be nonfictionally true, but it is not necessarily bad poetry if it is not.

Once we have acknowledged the possibility of a more critical audience, an audience that might look to poetry for pleasure and not necessarily for truth, we need to reconsider our model passages. Perhaps the *Iliad* 2 passage is not a real claim to truth at all but a device of the kind used by writers of modern fiction in play or to lend psychological credibility to the narrative. If the *Iliad* 2 invocation is comparable to modern fictional practices, we could interpret around the poet's request for information a fictional frame representing the poet and audience's implicit agreement to pretend that the poet gets information from the Muses about a past he then pretends to represent accurately.

Odysseus' comment to Demodocus can equally be treated as entirely fictional if we can see the *Odyssey* as creating a fiction in which all the events depicted, including Odysseus' fantastic adventures, are treated as real, but only as long as we are within the frame of that fiction. Because the events that Demodocus sings about are supposed to be real within the fiction created by the *Odyssey*, Odysseus' comment on the accuracy of Demodocus' representation is appropriate, but only within the *Odyssey*'s fictional world. It can not be taken outside this frame as a general reflection on the way poetry works in a real world, where (1) all the events depicted in the *Odyssey* may not be assumed to be real and (2) the audience does not stand in the same relationship to the events described in the *Odyssey* as Odysseus does to the Trojan War. By such interpretations, we would no longer have to take either the *Iliad* 2 or *Odyssey* 8 passage as representing a notion of the way the archaic poet and audience conceived poetry to work, but only as part of the game of the fiction, a game whose rules were entirely familiar to the archaic audience (i.e., "let's pretend these events really happened precisely as I recount them and that the Muses enable poets to know exactly what went on"). This is similar to the game played by all authors and audiences—to fiction when the fiction has an omniscient narrator.

COMMEMORATION AND TRADITIONAL NARRATIVE

This does not seem to be an entirely satisfactory solution to the problems posed by these passages. Early Greek response to poetry has also led scholars to think that the culture regarded poetry nonfictionally. Response to the Catalog of Ships, in particular, suggests that it was taken entirely seriously as an important document, a list of names of heroes and city-states really present at the Trojan War. The story that the Athenians had themselves spuriously inserted into the catalog suggests both the importance of being included on the list and also the concern that the catalog be authentic. Thucydides, though skeptical about Homer's accuracy in enumerating the ships, nonetheless treats it as reflecting, however imperfectly, the truth about the past (1.10.3). Moreover, modern scholarship on the catalog has pointed out that the catalog includes some city-states that were inhabited in the Mycenean period, but not subsequently.[35] This suggests that the catalog is not simply a list composed on the spot of the first names that would have been likely to occur to the poet, not only a way of flattering his audience and giving them pleasure, but may really be an attempt to preserve the past. And the catalog is not the only part of the *Iliad* and the *Odyssey* that is treated as a source of factual information about the past or that preserves detail drawn from a period preceding our estimated date for the poems. Any attempt to account for the *Iliad* and the *Odyssey* as fiction must take this commemorative function into consideration, its function as a preserver of klea.

We must bear in mind, however, that the ancient perception that these poems preserve information about the past they represent does not necessarily translate into an interpretation of the entire narrative as a nonfictional representation of that past. Modern scholars have also used the poems as a source of information about the past without thereby imagining that these narratives are true in their entireties. (I am doing something of the kind right now.) Indeed, Herodotus and Thucydides, though they behave as though Homeric poetry can provide clues to an accurate reconstruction of the past, clearly perceive that poets are prone to certain kinds of misrepresentation, to exaggeration, for example, or even to outright invention.[36] Both historians attempt therefore, much as do modern historians (though modern historians may use different techniques and types of evidence), to sort out fact from poetic invention through rational argument. In so doing, they treat Homeric poetry as a fictionalized representation of real events, neither entirely true (*alethes*) nor entirely false, but rather an imaginative representation of these distant events, one that may offer clues to the past, but not one that can be regarded as consistently reliable, because poets are clearly recognized to exaggerate and to make things up.

Even as the early Greek historians were attempting to distinguish true from false in these accounts, we have evidence that audiences were continuing to enjoy them as performances; the poems were not losing their hold on the popular imagination. Such audiences seem to be evaluating the Homeric epics almost purely in terms of the emotional effect that performance of the poems creates. The rhapsode Ion in Plato's *Ion* makes his professional success dependent entirely on the extent to which he is able to move his audience in retelling the familiar stories,[37] to involve them emotionally so that the pathos does not become laughable. After discussing his own emotional involvement as he performs particularly moving sections of the poems, Ion describes audience reaction to his performance:

> Ion: If I make them weep, I myself will laugh, as I take their money, but if I make them laugh, I myself will weep, because I'll lose my fee. (*Ion* 535e)

Though the interests of the rhapsode's audience are entirely different from those of the two historians, both types of audience response are compatible as responses to an account of the past that was widely accepted as a fictional representation of real events. The historians seek to sort out the facts from an amalgam of fact and fiction. The rhapsode's audience enjoys its emotional involvement in the world of the past without attempting to define the borders between real and unreal, true and false, actual and fictive. Such distinctions are not relevant to their experience of the performance. The latter attitude of mind seems to be characteristic of audiences to fiction when immersed in the fiction, for we can not follow the logic of the narrative if we attempt to make distinctions in the status of the various statements we are asked to entertain.[38] This does not mean that such an audience can not step back from the fiction and analyze it more critically in the same sorts of terms advanced by the historians, at least to the extent that they may recognize it as a mixture of true and false. But an audience out to enjoy a performance is unlikely to attempt to segregate elements of the narrative into distinct categories of real and unreal, true and false, actual and fictive, though upon reflection members of the audience may have certain opinions about which elements are more plausible or more likely to be true (obviously, they can not know which is which).[39]

Since most of our evidence for response to Homeric poetry is later than the estimated date of the poems' composition, we can only ask whether such a response is also a possible construction of the response to Homeric narrative in an earlier period as well. It would seem to fit well with three things that are testified to in an earlier period: (1) the emphasis within the texts themselves on pleasure and other psychological effects in connection with poetic narrative, an emphasis that suggests a type of narrative functionally similar to fiction, insofar as fiction works primarily by engaging the imagination and emotions of its audience, rather than by promising it consistently factual information;[40] (2) the apparent tolerance for certain kinds of (sometimes explicit) change to traditional narrative, a tolerance that suits an audience interested more in novelty and effect than in obtaining information about "what really happened" (the latter goal, I assume, perhaps erroneously, to be the primary goal of the audience to nonfictional narrative); and (3) the affinity between the poet and the liar to be discussed in the next chapter. These features of early response to Homeric narrative suggest a genre that has an uncertain truth-value and is valued more for its effects than because its information is felt to be consistently reliable. This does not mean that the audience felt there was nothing true or real or factual in Homeric narrative. But it suggests that the audience accepted that it was not all true or real or factual and that the poet might invent or alter to give pleasure or to create certain other effects.

Theorists of fiction have pointed out that audiences to fiction do not regard fiction as composed exclusively of the false, the invented, and the unreal as opposed to the true, the actual, and the real. We may, for example, believe that London is real, but that Sherlock Holmes is not. Once we appreciate the complexity of fiction's relationship to truth and falsity, its marriage of the real and the imaginary, we may be more willing to tolerate the suggestion that Homeric narrative is essentially a fictional variety of discourse.

Folklorists have called into question the usefulness of the opposed categories "true" and "fictional" as ways of categorizing folklore genres.[41] This is perhaps because fiction does not exclude truth or fact or reference to reality. Consequently, fictional and truthful speech overlap and intersect. Nonfiction is the more exclusive category. Like Homeric aletheia, nonfiction has a privative prefix and requires absence, particularly the absence of deliberate invention. Fiction necessitates the presence of invention, but does not exclude mention of real people, events, and places. It does not demand an absence of all kinds of truth.

COMMEMORATIVE FICTION

When I speak of fiction in connection with Homeric poetry, I am not talking about a modern novel, in which most of the characters and events are presumed to be the author's invention (and in which any similarity between anyone living or dead is purely coincidental, an obvious legal fiction). The Greeks seem to believe that Homeric poetry represents real events and people, and the poet certainly relies heavily on traditional material in composing his narrative. But fiction does not exclude the representation of the real. It merely alters the nature of the representation, so that we permit the author to make things up, if such inventions can be somehow revealing. For example, we permit Garry Trudeau in the cartoon strip Doonesbury to create a fictional representation of President George Bush and to give him an invisible twin named Skippy. Though we are unlikely to believe that the real George Bush has an invisible twin named Skippy, the cartoon strip's depiction of this twin and his relations with a fictional George Bush may influence the way we feel and think about the real George Bush. This is one way in which fiction and the real may interact. This type of fictional representation is recognizable in ancient comedy, where the audience probably does not confuse the fictional Socrates of Aristophanes' *Clouds* with the real Socrates to the extent that it comes to believe that the real Socrates floats in a basket and measures the leaps of fleas. Nonetheless, Aristophanes' representation may encourage the Athenian audience to think of the real Socrates in ways that may not be entirely flattering (as Plato's Socrates suggests in the *Apology*). In such ways as these, fiction may evaluate and comment on the real.

For Homeric poetry, a fictional status means that, although the poet was telling a traditional story with some tie to what was felt to have really happened, he could at any time alter the tale or invent a new detail if he felt that these changes would permit the audience better to imagine the events he narrated. The story is felt to have a connection to the past, but instead of trying to recreate the past accurately, the poet tries to recreate it imaginatively.[42] The poems merge the commemorative function of history with the imaginative function of fiction. The story commemorates real deeds but in an imaginative way that does not require that the poet consistently vouch for the truth (aletheia) of his story. The goals of the narrative leave room for deliberate poetic invention and self-acknowledged artfulness.

The notion of "commemorative fiction" that I am advancing here is akin to our own notion of historical fiction,[43] though the material out of which the narrative is constructed is not "history," which does not yet exist, but the "memories" preserved in the tradition. The poet will have a certain stock of such "memories," of traditional characters, events, ways of saying things, and ways of doing things, but he may combine and recombine these variously to create new versions of the stories, even to contradict openly versions that are part of the traditional repertoire, if this may create a desirable effect. Thus, an entirely new version of Dionysus' birth, for example, or Odysseus' parentage, or Helen's defection may be added to the repertoire to give pleasure or because such an account is more "beautiful" (*kalos*).[44] (What this might entail, I will discuss further in chapters to come.) Such inventions unquestionably interfere with both poets' and audiences' ability to reconstruct "what really happened," but if reconstruction is not the primary goal of the narrative, invention does not have to invalidate the narrative for its audience.

The difference between this sort of fiction and history is that the former asks us to entertain a possible construction of these events, a hypothetical construction, and the latter asks us to believe such a construction. Commemorative fiction says "imagine that it happened this way." History argues that it did happen this way.[45] The author of commemorative fiction consequently need not attempt to prove the truth-value of the individual statements he or she makes, and the audience need not weigh the individual claims of each of the author's statements. Both accept that the author may invent if that will help the imaginative process. In contrast, however much able writers of nonfiction may appeal to the imagination, they are supposed to keep that appeal subordinated to their own commitment to their facts. That their facts may be mistaken does not alter the nonfictional status of their work, but should they abandon their commitment to their facts in favor of a more purely imaginative account—in favor of deliberate invention—they deserve the epithet liar, at least as much as do poets. Herodotus is accused of lying, I believe, not because he made more errors than other historians, but because he is suspected of deliberately abandoning what he himself believed to be fact in order to report an entertaining story.

Nonfictional writers may make use of fictions from time to time to illustrate a point, but they typically draw clear boundaries around that fiction to distinguish it from factual narrative: "let us imagine," "suppose," "some tell this story." Writers of fiction tend to create a more integrated account. Once within a fiction, there is rarely a need to distinguish fact and invention; the work is typically experienced as a whole. Thus, we may read of the burning of Atlanta and Scarlett O'Hara's reaction to it on the same page without the author's distinguishing her invention from historical fact. History must draw its boundaries more carefully, distinguishing its assertions from its hypotheses, its facts from its inventions. Thucydides' admission that the precise words of his speeches were his own creation is one example of such cautious boundary drawing. The author of fiction does not see any need to draw such boundaries; fact and fantasy mingle indiscriminately. The audience of fiction, in turn, does not normally need to sort out the factual from the fictional, the probable from the merely possible, but only to entertain the story as an engaging construction.

Thus, for their Greek audience, the scenes between Hector and Andromache, for example, may still retain a generally commemorative function insofar as they help to evoke and to suggest the importance of the Trojan War, almost certainly a real event in the mind of both poet and audience, by involving its audience emotionally and imaginatively in the world of that war. But the audience does not need to be concerned, any more than we do, about whether or not the poet's representation accurately commemorates a real conversation. The success of the scene, for them, as it is for us, is measured by the degree to which it moves them. I do not deny that nonfiction may move us and help us to imagine. But I do suggest that whenever the function of Homeric narrative becomes predominantly pathetic, emotive, ox imaginative, the audience and poet may lose interest in the accuracy of the account, and the poet may be implicitly given permission to invent and to fictionalize.

Such a medium is primarily interested not in establishing "what really happened" but in characterizing certain events and individuals and in attempting to reveal more fully their importance. Though nonfictional representation may have this as its ultimate goal as well, nonfictional narrative seems to presume, as fiction does not, that this goal can best be met by attempting to reconstruct what really happened, that knowledge of fact in itself offers the best insight into those events. Fiction assumes that invention can offer equally useful insights into the character of people and events. This is not the only function of fiction, nor is it the only function of Homeric narrative. I am merely attempting to explain how Homeric narrative, without being regarded as consistently truthful, may still fill an important commemorative function in archaic culture.

For this sort of commemorative fiction to work, the poet must share with the audience certain underlying assumptions about the gods, heroes, and events being represented, assumptions that these have a certain value and a familiar character. The poet working in a traditional medium does not need to establish against potential opposition that the Trojan War was an important event or that Odysseus is cunning. Because the audience familiar with traditional narrative in the culture begins with these basic assumptions, the poet has the freedom to explore the importance of the Trojan War from a more complex point of view or to invent a new story that reveals Odysseus' cunning. He does not need to claim that these stories are true (*alethes*), because they are not stories designed to establish facts that might be disputed.[46] The stories may nonetheless commemorate the Trojan War and Odysseus, because they add to the audience's appreciation of the importance and significance of the traditional event or character.

The distance created by the passing of time and the canonization achieved by the tradition may permit this particular kind of fictional representation to work. As Pindar so frequently notes, we are inclined to dispute the worth of our contemporaries, to be embroiled in either envy or partisanship that may demand proof that praise is deserved. In such a context, any suggestion that the poet is inventing may raise the accusation that the poet is a mere flatterer and that the contemporary being celebrated is consequently undeserving. Poets involved in commemorating contemporary events may therefore be held to stricter standards of accuracy, because they are more concerned to establish the importance of the events and characters they commemorate, an importance that may not be acknowledged by the culture as a whole.

The very specter of contemporary partisanship may provoke overt interest in accuracy in the invocation to the Catalog of Ships in *Iliad* 2. There is scarcely any other part of the poem in which the audience would have been more likely to have a vested interest in the information preserved, particularly if, with Nagy, we are to presume a Panhellenic audience for our version of the *Iliad*. The potential for dispute among his contemporaries about their presence at this memorable event may compel the poet to look for authority for the catalog elsewhere. Indeed, the imaginable pressure of such a situation is enough to explain the unusually elaborate invocation with its simultaneous confession of human weakness and boast of divine authority. The poet would not want to be accused of manufacturing information or of excluding it, nor would he want responsibility for the list at all. But this need to claim truth may not be typical, because most of the rest of the *Iliad* would not challenge the audience's basic assumptions about who and what was worthy. The poet must be careful not to treat a particular audience's favorite hero in an insulting fashion, and this is certainly part of the decorum that regulates Homeric narrative, but this is quite different from insisting that all narrative be true.

Though truth (aletheia) may not be necessary to successful, traditional poetry, the canon of appropriate representation will remain a very important one within such traditions. Questions about the appropriateness of certain representations will no doubt arise. Is it appropriate, for example, to depict the king of the gods being deceived by his wife? Is it appropriate to lionize a trickster? Is it appropriate for the most beautiful woman in Greece to abandon her husband and run away with a foreigner? Such questions are endemic in Greek response to poetry. They seem to create the context within which one poet may compete with another by offering an alternate account, an account more appropriate or more pleasing. But this very willingness to reshape the "facts" of traditional narrative, to alter the traditional version to suit this separate and distinct canon of appropriateness, again suggests that archaic narrative is primarily concerned not with aletheia, with gaining certain knowledge of the past through the Muses' eyewitness, but with a kind of representation that can best be categorized as fictional, because it leaves room for the archaic poet to fictionalize.

I might add that our own culture's devaluation of fiction that makes it inconceivable to us that anyone would care about being on a list within a work that was acknowledged to be a fictionalization and to minimize the importance of this kind of legitimation. But we certainly have been willing to acknowledge that this exists in other ancient cultures. No one has ever imagined that the audience of the *Aeneid* thought that it was a nonfictional version of the past, and yet it has often been interpreted as in some sense a legitimation of Augustus' power. Moreover, it would not be surprising that a local tribe might: feel offended by being left off the catalog in *Aeneid* 5; we may value very much such recognitions of our own importance, particularly in a culture where fictive representations may be felt to have an important commemorative function.

Klea Andrôn

In choosing to label their traditional narratives *klea andrôn*, the hexameter poets may suggest not only its commemorative value but the somewhat tenuous relationship of their poetry to what really happened. The phrase *klea andrôn* is typically translated "glories of men." This quite accurately conveys its functional meaning; the traditional stories are important because they preserve the glory of the dead heroes. Nonetheless, like the Latin word *fama*, which originates in the notion of "what is said" (from the Latin *for*, *fari*, "say") about a person and therefore extends to idle gossip as well as to truthful report, *kleos* has an ambiguous status with respect to truth. We have already seen the singular of *kleos* used in the *Iliad* 2 passage to contrast with the Muses' knowledge. Elsewhere in archaic poetry, characters express a similar skepticism about the truth-value of *kleos*.[47] Klea includes "all that is heard" about a person, both true and false. Therefore, in telling klea, the poets take no responsibility for the factuality of their accounts, as they would if they claimed to be masters of aletheia. They might nonetheless insist on the validity of these representations, insofar as they preserve intact the established reputations of the heroes they depict.

DISTANCE AND SELF-INTEREST

The *Iliad* 2 and *Odyssey* 8 passages exemplify in their interest in truth one function that archaic narrative does play: a commemorative one. To this function it may sometimes be useful to claim that the poet does have access to knowledge about the past, particularly if there is a likelihood of giving offense. But elsewhere the poet may be more concerned with creating certain effects that have nothing to do with the truth-value of the narrative, and sometimes he may even wish to call attention to his own inventiveness, as the author to the *Hymn to Dionysus* seems to do. It is therefore neither necessary nor entirely desirable to take the *Iliad* 2 and *Odyssey* 8 passages as programmatic for all of Homeric narrative, certainly not for all of archaic narrative.

In fact, the circumstances of the two passages are not precisely typical of Homeric narrative. Odysseus, unlike the typical audience of Homeric narrative, was actually present at the events that Demodocus narrates. He is therefore in the unusual position of being able to judge the truth of the poet's narrative. The audience of the Homeric bard, in contrast, could not have presumed to judge the accuracy of the events recited. If we were to put Odysseus' words in the mouth of such an audience, they would have an entirely different implication, suggesting not accuracy but vividness and force, not truth but verisimilitude, qualities appropriate to a fictional narrative as well. All of the features Odysseus singles out for praise here might conceivably be found in either a fictional or a nonfictional version of the events at Troy, because the knowledge that comes with being present at a war or hearing of it firsthand may contribute to the verisimilitude of a fictional representation as well.

The language of the passage may put the emphasis of Odysseus' praise on qualities other than simple accuracy. Odysseus praises Demodocus for reporting the story of the war "according to order," "fitly," "appropriately" (*kata kosmon*), not for telling it truthfully (*alethôs*). The phrase has ethical and aesthetic implications that the archaic language of truth does not. Thus,

Achilles' companions spit the meat kata kosmon, and the arms of the Thracians lie on the ground kata kosmon. Both cases suggest that kata kosmon has to do with a sense of propriety, a respect for the way things ought to be done and to appear that is distinct from archaic notions of aletheia. Homer criticizes Thersites' rebukes of the Homeric princes as not kata kosmon. In this case, Homer condemns the ugliness and inappropriateness of Thersites' speech, not its lack of honesty or its falseness. Likewise, when Odysseus castigates Euryalus' insults as not kata kosmon, he is not so much calling attention to their lack of truth, as to their lack of charm, appropriateness, and general attractiveness, categories at once ethical and aesthetic.[48] Odysseus is the master of speech that is kata kosmon, and as readers of the *Odyssey* well know, this includes mastery of both aletheia and certain types of lies. His lies are regulated by the condition of kosmon, and this is what makes them acceptable. (In the next chapter, I discuss further this aesthetic and ethical quality of speech, which governs the content of all varieties of speech in Homeric epic, including poetry.)

When Odysseus praises Demodocus for telling the story kata kosmon, he appreciates a quality of Demodocus' song distinct from its strict accuracy, the appropriateness, for example, of the details that enable him to capture the general characteristics of the war, rather than its specific history. We might compare, for example, the response of a Vietnam veteran evaluating films about the war. A veteran might find that certain representations created more accurate impressions of what went on during the war, without failing to perceive that the narrative contained fictional elements. Moreover, when Odysseus says, "For very fittingly you sing the fate of the Achaeans, / as many things as they did and suffered and all their toils, / as though somehow you yourself were present or heard from another" (*Od.* 8.489–91), we need not be so literal-minded as to imagine that Demodocus' song described every deed, suffering, and toil that took place in Troy. We can imagine instead that he was able to select appropriate details to evoke all those things in a briefer compass. This sort of selectivity, an interest in appropriateness and evocation, distinguishes an artful account from a merely accurate accumulation of detail.

I do not deny that within the context of the *Odyssey*, Demodocus' narration is probably supposed to be a nonfictional one. But this can not establish that this is the only kind of poetic narration Homer or his audience understands. The story of Ares and Aphrodite, for example, also told by Demodocus, certainly could not be praised in the same terms that Odysseus uses, for such praise simply would not make sense: no one in the audience could have been present to verify Demodocus' accuracy. This does not make Demodocus' account of Ares and Aphrodite a worthless song. As has often been pointed out, Demodocus' song illustrates the narrative situation central to the *Odyssey* itself: the underlying fear of adultery, the superiority of cunning to violence. Its function within the narrative, both as entertainment for the banqueters and perhaps also as warning and advice to Odysseus, does not depend on its being accurate commemoration.

Homer creates the encounter between Odysseus and Demodocus, not because this is how he believes all poetry works, but because the dynamics of the situation are interesting: the hero of the deeds hears of his own kleos, as he sits unrecognized in the midst of those who similarly hear of his kleos. He is thus simultaneously known and unknown, recognized and unrecognized. The kleos is known, but the man is not. The various ironies have often been discussed.[49] Within the context of this narrative situation, moreover, Odysseus' interest in the accuracy of the account, or at least in the fairness of the representation, is self-interested: Demodocus' accuracy validates Odysseus' worth. When a poem concerns the distant past, however, the audience becomes less self-interested, and the pleasure given by the tale is much less dependent on its truthfulness. Distance in both time and place give the author greater liberty to invent.[50]

Other audiences within the *Odyssey*, audiences that have greater distance from the events depicted, treat pleasure rather than truth as essential to a song's success. Though Odysseus has requested the song of the Trojan horse, Alcinous stops Demodocus as soon as he sees his guest's sorrow, remarking:

> Hear me, leaders and rulers of the Phaeacians.
> Let Demodocus now stop his keen lyre.
> For in singing these things he does not please everyone.
> Ever since we started dinner and the divine singer began,
> the stranger. has not stopped his bitter mourning.
> Grief has utterly shrouded his spirit.
> But come let the singer halt, so that we might all
> take pleasure, hosts and guest alike, since that is much better.
> (*Od.* 8.536–43)

Here Alcinous suggests that the audience's pleasure is critical to a song's success. (See also 8.90–103, where Alcinous again stops the song when he perceives his guest's sorrow.)[51] Similarly, at *Odyssey* 1.337–46, Penelope asks Phemius to stop his song in favor of one more pleasing to her. Though she is criticized by Telemachus for doing so, her son does not discount the importance of pleasure but suggests that the poet is free to please as he wishes.

The *Odyssey* indeed seems to warn of a certain danger in hearing poetry under conditions that permit one to judge the accuracy of the account. Those who have firsthand knowledge of the events experience pain rather than pleasure in hearing them recounted, as do both Odysseus and Penelope in the accounts above. The dangerous Sirens promise Odysseus a song in which he would have to play a prominent role. Such a song may be enticing, but it ultimately destroys the listener (seemingly because it is a little too engrossing). The poem proposes that when one is too intimate with the facts of a story, the story brings pain or even destruction, (though it may be destruction attended by pleasure), and this pain is not treated as desirable in the *Odyssey*. The poem therefore seems to recommend that stories of uncertain truth are to be preferred. Even Odysseus' lies have a more positive function in the story (see chapter 2). Athenian reaction to Phrynichus' tragedy on the capture of Miletus (Herodotus 6.21) likewise suggests that audiences preferred a certain detachment from the events depicted, that too much reality made the emotions created by the drama intolerable. Our pleasure in fiction comes at least in part from its being part of a world that is removed from our own.

THE MUSES AND POETIC TRUTH

What then of the Muses? Does their omniscience not ensure the truth of all narrative? As the daughters of Memory, do they not ensure that poetry preserves the past perfectly? I suspect that the archaic poets would have looked at it somewhat differently. The omniscience of the Muses was available when the poet needed to claim accuracy for his account, but because an accurate account is not consistently of primary importance, the Muses are at other times present in a less specific way, helping the poet to give pleasure or to create a beautiful song, without necessitating that the narrative be felt as truthful. The Muses' association with knowledge and memory does not mandate that all poetry be true in the sense implied in the model passages. Knowledge is essential to any plausible narrative, to fiction as well as to history; memory to the recounting of any traditional tale, to fairy tale as well as to saga. Though they are prerequisites of truth, knowledge and memory do not guarantee nonfictional truthfulness, because they do not guarantee the speaker's desire to speak this kind of truth. The efficacy of the invocation to the Muses in the *Iliad* 2 passage depends on the assumption that neither the Muses nor the poet wishes to invent or to distort. This in turn demands the assumption that it is wholly desirable to both Muses and poet that the Catalog of Ships be accurate. It is not clear that this desire for accuracy, for nonfictionality, ought to be extended to the epics in their entirety. Once the shared desire for accuracy and precision is gone, the patronage of the Muses no longer guarantees this kind of truth.

Though the Muses could provide the poet with information that was not otherwise available to him, the poet's need for and interest in this sort of specific information seems to have fluctuated. Apart from the Catalog of Ships, there are only a few cases in the *Iliad* where the poet asks the Muse for the kind of specific information that he requests in the catalog, fewer still in other archaic poetry (for the moment, I exclude invocations at the beginning of the poems, which seem to me to have a slightly different function, discussed below). In the *Iliad*, these are all of a specific type, typically who or what was first or best. This may suggest that the poet might wish to turn to the goddesses particularly when the matter of accurate commemoration becomes essential. Elsewhere, however, the poet may not be thinking about commemorating accurately, and so he does not need to request information from the Muses.

A passage from Hesiod supports this impression of a variable dependence. In the *Works and Days*, Hesiod cites the Muses' teaching to provide authority for his advice on seafaring, openly admitting that his own experience is too limited:

> For never have I sailed in a ship on the wide sea,
> Except to Euboea from Aulis,
>
> . . . .
>
> [I omit several lines in which Hesiod describes his victory]
> To this extent I have experience of many-nailed ships.
> But even so I speak the mind of Zeus who bears the aegis,
> For the Muses taught me to sing divine song.
>   (*WD* 650–62)

Hesiod's claim is bold. Despite his limited experience with ships, he can speak with the knowledge of Zeus himself. And the Muses enable him to do so. There is no doubt that the Muses' help is here invaluable and gives the poet knowledge he would otherwise lack. But Hesiod's confession that he has no experience of sailing is unusual in the *Works and Days*. There is no similar attempt to justify his advice about farming.[52] We are left with the impression that Hesiod's advice about farming is based on his personal experience, an impression that this passage, by contrast, reinforces. This implies that the archaic poet's dependence on specific pieces of information that could be provided by the Muses fluctuated, that he might turn to them particularly when the poet felt his own authority and knowledge were weak or insufficient.

I do not mean to imply that the archaic poet ever felt that entirely independent of the Muses. The patronage of the Muses is essential to his success as a poet. But the Muses' specific function as a provider, of knowledge to the poet need not always be essential to that general patronage. The audience's pleasure and the song's beauty are elsewhere named as attributes essential to the success of a poem, and the Muses are just as closely associated with beauty and pleasure as they are with knowledge and memory.[53] Thus, when an archaic poet invoked the Muses at the beginning of a song, he asked them to provide all the various things necessary to a song's success—beauty, pleasure, memory, and knowledge—to aid with all those things to bring to life the theme the poet names. Their aid may enable the poet to speak nonfictionally, if that becomes desirable, but there is no reason the Muses can not help the poet create a fictionalized account of the wrath of Achilles, if such an account can be pleasing and beautiful.

Such a formulation seems consistent with the idea of a bard operating in a genuinely generative oral tradition (as opposed to a tradition that is exclusively concerned with preserving the songs that already exist). Though the skills that enable the bard to create songs at all may be ultimately traceable to the tradition—to the formulae, the themes, the traditional characters, the whole traditional manner of composition— the poet must nonetheless be able to adapt those traditional elements using his own imagination and experience to create a new song. The poet is simultaneously dependent on the tradition (in a general way) and able to subject it to his creativity (in specific innovations).[54] At the same time, the poet might on occasion make use of a piece of information that was wholly traditional and for which he could take no personal responsibility, as Hesiod does when he dispenses traditional advice about seafaring on the basis of one lone sea journey, or as Homer seems to do in the Catalog of Ships. At this point, it might be advantageous to the poet to refer that information specifically to the knowledgeable Muses, to invest it with divine authority.

THE RESPECTIVE ROLES OF MUSE AND POET

I have proposed here a fairly active role for the poet. But it is occasionally argued that the archaic bards conceived of themselves as entirely passive, as mere mouthpieces through which the Muses spoke.[55] The notion of poetry as a gift of the Muses, found several times in archaic poetry, and invocations like that at the beginning of the *Iliad*, in which the poet actually asks the goddess herself to sing, have contributed in particular to the impression that the Muses hold all responsibility for the creation of song.

This conception of poetry as a gift of the Muses need not exclude the poet's being aware of himself as the creator of a poem. When Homer and Hesiod say that a god has given a particular skill to an individual, they single out that person's ability as outstanding. This designation need not imply total passivity on the recipient's part. Just as the god gives song surpassingly to Demodocus (*Od.* 8.44–45), Athene gives excellence in weaving to Penelope (*Od.* 2.116–17) and to the Phaeacian women (*Od.* 7.110–11), Hermes gives the ability to lie to Pandora (*WD* 77–81), and the gods generally give skill at warfare (*Il.* 13.727, 730), music and dance (*Il.* 13.731), and speech (*Od.* 8.167). Such passages need not imply that the human recipients can not feel themselves the creators of their weaving, their lies, their speeches, or their song, or that the god exercises complete control over the recipient's deployment of that gift. Though Alcinous attributes Demodocus' ability to please to the god, he can in the same passage speak of the poet's own spirit (*thumos*), which apparently exercises choice and control over the direction of the song:

> For the god gave to him song beyond others—
> [the ability] to give pleasure in whatever way his spirit urges him to
>   sing
>   (*Od.* 8.44–45)

Likewise, at *Odyssey* 1.347, the poet's mind (*noos*) directs the song, a further indication that the poet had some responsibility for its creation.

That there is no clear distinction drawn in archaic poetry between a god's giving a mortal a gift and a god's teaching a mortal a skill further suggests that the notion of a divine gift does not make the recipient of the gift entirely passive. The recipient is given a skill, not made into a mouthpiece. The incident with the poet Thamyris reported in the Catalogue of Ships (*Il.* 2.594–600) suggests the complexity of the bard's dependence on the Muses. Thamyris feels himself able to compete against the Muses, which would certainly not be possible if he believed that the song came directly from the Muses and that he was not its creator. But his attempt to compete with the Muses leads to his being deprived of their gift altogether. He can no longer sing. The tension here suggests that the bard possesses a general dependence on the Muses, but not necessarily a completely passive role in creating a song on any given occasion. The whole notion of poets competing among one another—mentioned, for example, at *Works and Days* 26—strongly suggests a conception of poetry as a skill possessed by different individuals to different degrees.

Alongside passages that suggest in their phrasing the poet's passivity (like *Il.* 1.1) appear other passages that give the poet a greater responsibility for the song and a more active role in its creation. Only a few lines after the poet first asks the Muse to sing, he again speaks in his own voice, asking who of the gods set the two heroes to fighting. Elsewhere the poet asks the Muse to tell *him*, not the audience ("tell me now Muses"), a given piece of information that the poet will then presumably report in his song. In this formulation, the poet appears more explicitly as a mediator between Muse and audience. At still other points, the poet makes the singer's spirit or mind responsible for the direction of the song, as in the two examples cited above.

Such various ways of representing the respective roles of human and god in the creating of song may seem contradictory to us. Therefore, in these various depictions, some scholars have seen a historical development in which the poet gains autonomy but loses the traditional ability to speak the truth as he becomes less dependent on the Muses.[56] That both modes of expression coexist in numerous early Greek texts including the earliest we have argues against such a conclusion. Even within single passages, the poet may speak of both himself and the goddess as responsible for the song. Thus, the poets themselves apparently saw no contradiction in such formulations.

These formulations must in a certain sense be metaphorical, expressing various aspects of a relationship that is not easily subject to a logical formulation. This does not deny that they are expressions of a real religious belief about the goddesses. But attempting to find nuances of meaning in those passages in which the goddess herself is invited to sing and trying to distinguish these passages from those in which the poet asks the Muses for a piece of information, or separating those passages in which the Muse gives the song to the poet from those in which the Muse teaches it to him, seems futile. Both goddess and singer are at once responsible for song; the poet can represent the creation from either of two perspectives, from the divine or the human. What may seem to us contradictory (though can we explain any better our own tendency to speak of ourselves alternately as willful agents and as objects subject to psychological, historical; or sociological pressures?)[57] is in fact a common way of expressing human action in archaic poetry. Thus, modern readers of Homer frequently find it difficult to determine the degree of responsibility held by human actors, because the gods are so frequently seen plotting and directing the action. The relationship between bard and Muse is like that between other mortals and gods in Homer. Like any human actor, the poet may at one moment view himself as responsible for the creation of the song; elsewhere he may be more aware of his dependence on the Muses.

CONCLUSION

The primary purpose of this chapter was defensive: to raise questions about the evidence for an archaic connection between poetry and truth. Assumption of this connection has become so basic in much of the work on archaic poetics that it seemed necessary to reexamine our sources for this assumption. The evidence is scantier, more contradictory, and harder to interpret than we might assume. Though individual poets stake claims to truth, there is virtually no evidence for a generic association of poetry with truth, with aletheia in particular. The language used to describe poetry and song as a generic category (that is, poetry and song generally, as opposed to this particular song) emphasizes their connection with pleasure and beauty. Thus, if we wish to characterize archaic poetry in terms of a generic function, we should think of it primarily as a giver of pleasure rather than as a giver of truth. Individual poems may still be felt to provide certain kinds of truth or may be believed to contain certain facts. But the predominant function that is consistently identified with poetry is pleasure, and this enables us to contemplate categorizing it with "fiction" (we should remind ourselves that fictional genres do not necessarily exclude fact or truth of various kinds).

Even as they stake their own claim to truth, poets often accuse other poets of lying and expose contradictions in poetic narrative. Consequently, it is difficult to imagine that an audience, even in the earliest period represented by surviving texts, could be convinced of an inherent connection between poetry and truth. Indeed, we have evidence for cultural skepticism about the reliability of poets not only in the historians' responses but in comments like that attributed to the poet Solon: poets tell many lies/falsehoods (*pseudea*). Thus, belief in a connection between poetry and truth could have at most been only partial in the archaic world. But if poetry is not always true, this tends to undermine the basis for a truth claim like that in *Iliad* 2; the Muses can not be consistently relied on to reveal the truth. The inconsistencies in the picture at least raise the possibility that truth claims in archaic poetry are themselves fictional, part of the narrative game.

Nonetheless, before we can comfortably speak of an ancient appreciation of fictionality, we need to have some evidence for a positive valuation placed on narratives that are acknowledged to be made-up, false, or, invented. For this, I now turn to a discussion of lying and tricksters.

NOTES

*Epigraph from Nabokov 1973, 13.
1. The Greek word *pareste*, "you are present," might mean either present now at the occasion of song or present as eyewitnesses at the events being described.

2. The phrase *kata kosmon*, which I have rendered rather vaguely as "rightly," will receive further discussion below and in the second chapter.

3. See Detienne 1960, 1973; Heitsch 1962.

4. See Rösler 1980.

5. The unwillingness to distinguish among different kinds of truth and knowledge is a weakness of Rösler's influential article (1980). Rösler argues that the archaic poets were unable to make the distinction between these separate kinds of truth. But Rösler's own presentation of the evidence fundamentally begs this question. He assumes that all interest in truth is an interest in a nonfictional variety of truth, which is simply not the case. See chap. 5 for discussion of Heraclitus' critique of Homer, which simultaneously assumes the fictionality of the Iliad and demands of the poet gnomic wisdom. In general, modern scholars have had trouble distinguishing between knowledge or wisdom and (nonfictional) truth. But storytelling cultures may believe that stories can provide knowledge or wisdom, without believing that the stories represent real events and are nonfictionally true. See, e.g., LeRoy 1985, 3–14 and passim, on narrative in Kewa tales; Toelken 1976 on Navaho Coyote narratives. The point seems an obvious one, yet it frequently is forgotten.

6. Technically the information that the poet gets from the Muses remains for the poet *kleos*, because after all, he is not an eyewitness but has gotten his information secondhand by word of mouth. This apparent contradiction has led some scholars to suggest that the poet here asks the Muses for a vision of the past (Dodds 1966, 100). This notion of a vision is central to the arguments of Maehler 1963, Detienne 1973, and Vernant 1985. But the language of the passage "tell me" does not at all suggest such a vision. The information obtained by the poet is obtained aurally, nonetheless it has authority, because it is provided by a reliable eyewitness; in contrast, an anonymous *kleos*, of uncertain remove from the events, is much more dubious. Thus, this passage might be used as evidence for an early recognition of the distinction between primary and secondary sources of information. Elsewhere in early Greek literature, the firsthand account of an eyewitness to the author is valued only second to the author's own eyewitness. (See, e.g., Thucydides 1.22) In the Demodocus passage, Odysseus speaks as though there is virtually no difference between Demodocus' having been there or having heard from another (presumably who was). This would seem to be an important distinction. But being one eyewitness from the truth does not seem to be a significant distinction for Greek authors. Any greater distance definitely weakens their confidence in the value of what they are told. It would seem that the anonymity of the source contributes to the unreliability of *kleos*: we do not trust those we do not personally know or interrogate.

7. I say "extraordinary" because the word itself scarcely appears in archaic reflection on the nature of poetry. See n. 26.

8. Detienne does. He argues that the only significant opposition is between aletheia and lethe, not between aletheia and lie or aletheia and the false (Detienne 1973, 27). But the evidence of usage does not support this assertion. See, for example, passages at *Od.* 14.125, *Th.* 27–28, *H.Hermes* 368–69, all of which explicitly contrast aletheia and pseudos. For a critique of Detienne's argument that includes a full examination of the Homeric evidence, see Adkins 1972.

9. Here we have the neuter plural adjective (alethea, "true things") used substantively rather than the singular noun (aletheia, "truth"). In general, scholars have drawn their conclusions based on the use of both adjectives and nouns, as I do here.

10. Even the noun *lethe* may mean something broader than mere forgetfulness. See *Th.* 227, where Lethe appears as the offspring of Eris alongside a whole range of things, notably lies, error, and oath. As a negative effect of *eris*, lethe would seem to be the

equivalent of deception (apate). Indeed, lethe and apate are often linked as related psychological effects. See chap. 2.

11. Chantraine (1983) traces the etymology of the noun *aletheia* through the adjective *alethes* (true) from the verbs *letho, lanthano,* thus there is no reason to take the noun's meaning as the primary one.

12. In the middle voice, *letho* is more like "forget," but I suggest that this is because the primary kind of "hiding" that we do in this middle sense is "forgetting." *Letho* in the middle also includes the "forgetting" of such things as one's battle strength or courage, not necessarily the forgetting of the past. In these contexts, the implied opposition is not to memory specifically but to "full awareness," to "being firmly confident of." Indeed the verbs *mnaomai* and *mimnesko* often seem to denote something more like "to be fully aware of," "to have fully in mind," than they do "to remember" exclusively. Thus, in Greek, an opposition between *mneme/lethe* is broader than the opposition memory/forgetfulness and includes other varieties of consciousness/absence of consciousness.

13. See Cole 1983 and the bibliography cited there, for discussion of different locales for absence of lethe.

14. I agree with Adkins (1972), who argues that notions of truth in Homeric poetry do not differ widely from ordinary-language notions of truth in literate societies.

15. See Krischer 1965.

16. Cf. Thucydides 1.22, where inadequate memory or partiality are the two primary reasons that the truth is so hard to discover, even when dealing with eyewitnesses.

17. *Aletheia* and *alethes* are virtually always used in Homeric diction as the object of a verb of speaking. Cole notes that in Homer *aletheia* is never used to describe divine speech, only human (1983, 27). And Homer does not use it to describe a poet's or prophet's words.

18. For an example of this kind of argument, see Walsh 1984, 11–16.

19. Griffith 1990, 185–207. On the agonistic context of early poetry, see Martin 1989. Early evidence for poetic competition includes Eris among poets (*WD* 26), Thamyris' competition with the Muses (*Il.* 2.594–600), and *H.Aphr.* 19–20.

20. *Pseudomenoi* means to speak falsehoods. It does not necessarily mean to tell a falsehood deliberately. I choose to give it the most contentious translation, which seems to reflect the spirit of the passage best.

21. Nagy (1990b, 57) attributes the awareness of variant myths to the poet's mobility, which brings him into contact with a range of local versions of different myths. He suggests that for the poet the truest version of the story is the one least tied to local traditions and most Panhellenic. But, although this seems psychologically possible as a way of explaining how the poet determines what the true version is, it is harder to understand the psychology of the audience. Why should it listen to the poet who comes from outside with a new Panhellenic tradition that challenges its local myths?

22. See also Nagy 1990b, 52–81. Nagy argues that the concept of *aletheia* represents "Panhellenic truth-value." By this argument, the passage could be interpreted as an attempt to get rid of partisan, local versions of Dionysus' birth in favor of a nonpartisan version that favors no particular locality. Dionysus is said to be born far from all men (Nagy 1990a, 45). By Nagy's interpretation, this version would have to prevail as the "true-ist," because it is the least partisan and the most Panhellenic. But this version does not seem to have supplanted the canonical version of Dionysus' birth to Semele at Thebes. See Griffith 1990.

23. Something similar seems to be going on in Stesichorus' *Palinode* and in *Olympian* 1. See chaps. 4 and 5.

24. Austin 1960. As Pavel has pointed out (1986, 18–27), Austin's characterization of this opposition between ordinary and fictional discourse as "serious" and "nonserious" does not work consistently, because there can be no question that some fictions may be taken very seriously by their culture. One of the problems, I suspect, in modern reading of archaic poetry is in understanding how they possibly could have taken poetry as seriously as they did. This "seriousness" of Greek response seems to indicate for modern scholars the nonfictionality of poetic discourse for the culture. But perhaps we simply do not take fiction seriously enough.

25. A large number of such priamels have nothing to do with narrative but are statements of various opinions, capped by the poet's own opinion, in striking contrast to those that have gone before. Sappho provides a well-known example in fr. 16: "Some say an army of horsemen, others one of footsoldiers, / others an army of ships is, on the black earth, / the most beautiful thing, but I say / she whom one loves." As in the *H.Dion.* priamel, the structure seems designed to set off the poet strikingly from others rather than to convince the audience of the certain truth of Sappho's opinion. Sappho's opinion may win the audience's assent, but it need not do so to make for striking poetry.

26. This characterization is compatible with the poetics of *muthos* discussed by Martin (1989). Martin's discussion does not confront the more traditional evidence for Iliadic poetics, i.e., the *Il.* 2 passage and the sorts of claims it seems to mount, nor does he discuss the function of the Muses. Instead, he uses evidence from the *muthos*-speeches of the heroes themselves to construct a poetics of myth.

27. There is a tendency to think that humans develop in their religious attitudes from fundamentalism to a more figurative understanding of traditional narratives. But this is a crude characterization. See Toelken 1976 and chap. 3 for further discussion of the way assumptions about "primitive" narrative may misinform scholars' response to such narratives.

28. That the gods may take pleasure in hearing human lies is indicated by Athene's response to Odysseus' lies at *Od.* 13.291–99. See chap 2. The notion that lies and acts of deception are entertaining as pure performances, as something to watch, seems clear from the numerous and detailed portrayals of them in archaic literature (Ares and Aphrodite; the *Dios apate*; the numerous elaborate lies in the Hymns, particularly in the *Hymn to Hermes*; Odysseus' behavior in the *Odyssey*; etc.). But the whole notion of a lie as something to be enjoyed as performance strongly urges us to think in terms of fiction.

29. See, e.g., Tlepolemos' suggestion at *Il.* 5.635 that those who say that Sarpedon is the son of Zeus lie/speak falsehood (*pseudomenoi*), because the hero is much worse than those men who were engendered by Zeus among former generations. Notably, questions about Sarpedon's worth give rise to questions about the validity of the traditional genealogy. Homer's account supports the traditional genealogy of Sarpedon, but the possibility that it might be false is raised.

30. For an early example, see Herodotus 2.116.1. Willcock (1964) argues for deliberate inventions in composing paradigmatic stories. See also recent work on competing traditions, which strongly suggests awareness of variant versions on the part of both poet and audience of all periods. Martin offers the interesting suggestion that the story of Thamyris' being deprived of his art when returning from Oikhalia is "a claim that the Herakles' tradition is faulty" (Martin 1989, 228–30). Nagy (1979, 19906) and Edwards (1985a, 1985b) also have interesting things to say about competing traditions.

31. The epithets for song [ὕμνος οτ ἀοιδή], for example, reflect its sweetness, its beauty, its divinity, and the piercing quality of its sound—γλυκερός: *Il.* vii 59, *Il.* xix 18; ἡδύς: *Od.* 8.64; μελίγηρυς: *H.Apollo* 519; καλός: *H.Apollo* 164, *Th.* 22; ἱμερόεις: *Od.* 1.421,

18.304, *Il.* x5, *Th.* 104; χαρίεις: *Od.* 24.197–98; ἀθέσψατος: *Th.* 22, *WD* 662; θεσπέσιος: *Il.* 2.599–600; θέσπις: *Od.* 8.498, *H.Hermes* 442; λιγυρός: *Od.* 12.44, 12.183, *WD* 583, 659. The adjectives καλός, ἱμερόεις, and ἐρατός/ἐρατεινός also frequently qualify other words that occur in the context of music and song. See, e.g., *Il.* 1.473, 18.570; *H.Hermes* 423, 426, 455; Th. 65, 70; *H.Apollo* 515. See also *Theognidea* 15–17. Less frequently, an epithet may refer to the emotion roused or expressed in song—λυγρός: *Od.* 1.340–41; στονόεσσα: *Il.* 24.721; στυγερή: *Od.* 24. 200.

32. *Il.* 1.472–74, 9.186, 9.189; *Od.* 1.421–23 = 18.304–6, 8.429, 17.605–6, 12.188; *Th.* 37, 51, 917; *H.Apollo* 149–59, 204.

33. This is not a minor point, given that the word aletheia specifically, and its etymological relationship with lethe, rather than a familiar concept of truth, has frequently shaped discussion of truth in Homeric poetics. But *aletheia* specifically is actually named in connection with poetry in only two places in all of archaic poetry: in Hesiod's proem to the Theogony, hardly an unambiguous context (see chap. 3), and in connection with victor praise in epinician. But surely victor praise has a very different status from mythical narrative (on truth in epinician, see chap. 4). All other evidence for truth in archaic poetry uses a different vocabulary, the words *etumos* or *etetumos*, for example. Or such passages may condemn poetic lying or seem simply to imply truth (as do the *Il.* 2 and *Od.* 8 passages). If we are to argue that aletheia is not the same as our notion of truth and even that the opposition of aletheia and pseudos is not relevant in archaic thought, as Detienne does, we can not use this kind of evidence to support a widespread connection between poetry and aletheia. That poetry does have a connection with memory and therefore may be opposed to one variety of lethe, forgetfulness, is an important point, but though memory and truth are certainly categories that are related in important ways, this does not make them perfectly homologous in Greek any more than it does in English. Agamemnon's not forgetting the words of the lying dream in *Il.* 2 does not make the dream itself alethes.

34. I find unpersuasive Walsh's arguments that pleasure or aesthetic shape overlap with truth in Homer to such an extent that the one may be sufficient proof of the other. See Walsh 1984, 6–9. Pleasure and truth are found both together and separately in Homer. Odysseus' lies may bring pleasure, Demodocus' truths pain. The figure of Pandora in Hesiod unites pleasure with falsehood, as do any number of female seductresses. For further discussion of this point, see chap. 2.

35. Hope Simpson and Lazenby 1970.

36. See Thucydides 1.10.3, where he raises questions about whether one ought to trust Homer's poetry as a source or not and acknowledges that, in any case, since he is a poet it is likely that he exaggerated. See also Thucydides 1.21.1, where he uses virtually the same expression to characterize poetic reports of the past. For poetic invention, see Herodotus' comments on the river Ocean at 2.23, which he attributes to the invention of Homer or some other poet.

37. Interpretation of the *Ion* has often led scholars to think that Homeric poetry was supposed to preserve technical information on such diverse arts as prophecy, medicine, and charioteering. But this seems to me to be based on a misunderstanding of the types of argument Socrates employs. Ion himself concedes that the rhapsode has no special expertise in these areas. Ion's inability to define where precisely the rhapsode's special area of expertise lies contributes to the misunderstanding. Socrates uses the arguments only to establish that the rhapsode does not possess any identifiable body of knowledge or skill (*techne*), such as that represented by medicine, fishing, charioteering, and the like; without a defined body of knowledge, there can be no special rhapsodic *techne*. His arguments can

not be used to establish popular notions of what poetry was supposed to do. See chap. 5 for further discussion of the *Ion*.

38. See, e.g., Pavel's characterization of the reader's response to modern fiction: "During the reading of *The Pickwick Papers* does Mr. Pickwick appear less real than the sun over Goswell Street? In *War and Peace* is Natasha less actual than Napoleon? Fictional texts enjoy a certain discursive unity; for their readers, the worlds they describe are not necessarily fractured along a fictive/actual line" (Pavel 1986, 16). This does not mean that we do not draw a distinction outside the fiction between Napoleon as a historical figure and Natasha as a fictional one, but that as we are engaged in reading the text, we may not find such distinctions pertinent. To follow the narrative, to entertain the fictional propositions, we must pretend that it is all real, even though we may know perfectly well that it is not. This double perspective of the audience to fiction has been nicely described by Newsom 1988, see esp. 127–28.

39. Dégh and Vázsonyi (1976) offer a useful account of the range of audience reaction to legends. Their account suggests that the level and type of skepticism varies widely among members of the audience.

40. This does not necessarily mean that it will not be felt to provide any kind of knowledge or wisdom, or that there is a complete absence of factual material in the poetry. See Pavel 1986, 81, for a discussion of a similar kind of fictionality in medieval romance.

41. See Bauman 1986, 9, and bibliography cited there.

42. I am speaking here of an early stage of development, before the works become more or less codified, when the tradition is still a generative one—Nagy's stage 1: "At a phase of the tradition where each performance still entails an act of at least partial recomposition, performer 'L' publicly appropriates a given recomposition-in-performance as his or her own composition" (Nagy 1989, 38). Later, the performer of the works is no longer the composer. Nonetheless, the notion of fiction is still relevant, because the conception of the "author" still exists in the mind of audience and performer. To its audience the poem is by Homer; it is his fiction. Cf. Nagy's stages 2 and 3 (Nagy 1989, 38).

43. Veyne also compares the *Iliad*'s status to a historical novel, but he argues very differently, suggesting that, though the reader knows that the author of such a work invents certain details, he does not view the story as fiction (1988, 21). But, in English, at least, we do designate the genre as a fictional one.

44. Some historical fictions may contradict established facts, while other kinds seem to attempt to contradict nothing that is actually known, but only to fill in detail. Feelings about what kind of invention is permissible in such mixed genres as historical fiction, the "new journalism," and other fictional representations of the presumed-to-be-real (e.g., a film version of the life of Jesus) can run very high, and there are apt to be strong differences of opinion.

45. Aristotle draws a related distinction between poetry and history in the *Poetics* when he says that history deals in "what happened" and poetry deals with "what could happen" (*Poetics* 1451a.36–b.7). Aristotle's distinction is broader than mine. The sorts of things that could happen include not only "what could have happened" in the past but the sorts of things that might happen in the present or even in the future. But I am talking only about one particular type of fiction, historical fiction, a subcategory of all the various types of fiction that there are.

46. Unlike epinician, where the poets' claims to truth seem to be directed against the potential slanderer. The epinician poets are attempting to establish the worthiness of the victor, and to this function, truth claims may be essential. See chap. 4.

47. See, e.g., *Il.* 17.142–43, where Glaucus suggests that Hector has a false kleos; *H.Hermes* 276–77 = 310–11 where Hermes denies all knowledge of cows, claiming that he has only heard kleos.

48. For the difference between *kata kosmon* and Homeric notions of truth, see Adkins 1972.

49. See esp. Segal 1983 and bibliography cited there.

50. I suggest that this assumption may also operate in historical narratives. See Livy *Praef.* 6 and Plato, *Republic* 382d for statements about the acceptability of invention when there is distance in time from the events under discussion.

51. Walsh argues that the Phaeacian response of unmoved pleasure is as peculiar as Odysseus' excessive sorrow: "The *Odyssey*, then, contains at least two distinct kinds of audience, and both seem a little odd according to modern notions, too deeply touched by the singer's performance or too serenely pleased" (1984, 2). Walsh is right to call our attention to the excesses of both audiences, but wrong, I think, in failing to consider fully that neither audience is the real one, which may be much more like the audience that Ion describes, an audience that takes pleasure in its tears. Homer's audience can be neither as removed as the Phaeacians (who live in an unreal world untouched by war) nor as excessively given over to sorrow as Odysseus (intimately familiar with the events described), but it is at once capable of sympathy and detachment. In that detachment; caused by the distancing of time, the Homeric audience also loses both Odysseus' interest in and his ability to recognize the accuracy of poetic narrative. Perhaps, in its greater knowledge of the world outside, it also loses the naïveté that, by Walsh's interpretation, causes Alcinous to be confident that Odysseus' account of his fantastic adventures is entirely true (for another interpretation of this passage, see chap. 2). Walsh argues that there is no third audience, but many other audiences, of many different kinds, seem implicit in the *Odyssey*. Eumaeus is an audience capable of both sympathy and detachment, of simultaneous pleasure and pain. He thus makes a much better audience to fiction. See chap. 2.

52. We might see a certain artifice in Hesiod's mention of that lone sea journey, which happens to be one during which he won a prize for his singing. Is the passage fulfilling its ostensible function as a helpful exposition of Hesiod's life experience with ships, or is it more correctly a boast, designed to call attention to the poet's supremacy? It would certainly be wrong to think of archaic poetry as completely absent of artifice, and I suspect that if Hesiod ever had two journeys on ship, he would not necessarily have bothered to mention the other one here. See Rosen 1990 for an interesting interpretation of the passage as programmatic for Hesiodic poetics.

53. There could have been a time when the function of the Muse was more purely mnemonic. It is interesting how often requests for specific information in Homer involve catalogs and lists organized by rank (who was the best? who was the first?). It is possible that epic originates in a need to keep this sort of record, something like a victor list. But Homeric and even Hesiodic poetry, whatever its origination in and close ties to catalog poetry, has advanced beyond this to imaginative re-creation, and the Muses' function seems to have kept pace with such a change.

54. I am aware that one of the great problems in Homeric scholarship is defining the relationship between tradition and originality in Homeric poetry. I am not claiming here to solve this problem in any profound way, only to suggest, as many others have, how such a relationship is loosely comprehensible.

55. For an elegant formulation of this argument, see Svenbro 1976, esp. 16–45, also 193–212.

56. E.g., Accame 1963.

57. I do not attribute this to a "naive psychology," as Walsh suggests this would have to be. One disturbing feature of language is that it forces us to make ourselves either subject or object, active or passive, when, depending on the perspective, both may be equally appropriate ways of configuring our relation to a given event.

AHUVIA KAHANE

Hexameter Progression and the Homeric Hero's Solitary State

TEXTUAL AND NONTEXTUAL PROPERTIES

The poetry of Homer as we have it today is a highly *textualized* verbal artifact. In other words, we come into immediate contact with the *Iliad* and *Odyssey* as fixed sets of graphic symbols that are independent of any particular performance event, rather than as time-bound sequences of sounds that are unique to their performance context. Many aspects of this *text* are indeed unchanging regardless of whether we speak out, or hear the poems, or read them silently. At the same time, we are increasingly aware of what we might call the *nontextual* aspects of Homer, that is, of the *Iliad* and *Odyssey* not as fixed texts, but as reflections of a broad repository of themes, motifs, scenes, word-groups, and so on, as the manifestation of a potential that we sometimes refer to as an *oral tradition*. As a consequence, we are also increasingly aware that a simple dichotomy between "oral" and "literate" is somewhat restrictive.[1]

But perhaps, the most immediately obvious *nontextual* element of Homer's poetry is its meter, or what is better called its rhythm.[2] Paradoxically, writing seems to preserve perfectly the hexameter's *dum-da-da-dum-da-da-dum-da-da-dum-da-da-dum-da-da-dum-dum.* Furthermore, even in writing this rhythm remains an event: it calls for a speaker/reader/hearer; it is not a hexameter unless complete (sequential,

From *Written Voices, Spoken Signs: Tradition, Performance, and the Epic Text,* edited by Egbert Bakker and Ahuvia Kahane. © 1991 by the president and fellows of Harvard College.

unbroken) and in the right order; it is a time-bound, linear "beginning-
movement–end" sequence, and as such it is a performance.

THE FUNCTION OF RHYTHM

Let us now ask, what is the function of rhythm in Homer?[3] Does it facilitate
memorization of the poems? Perhaps not. Or at least not directly. Oral
traditions normally display a degree of *mouvance*, as Paul Zumthor has called it:
each performance is one manifestation of an otherwise flexible tradition.[4] But if
the very thing we call "oral poetry" is flexible, that is, if full verbatim repetition
(in our literate sense) is not in fact achieved, what is the purpose of rigid
metrical/rhythmic form, of formulae, type-scenes, and other "oral" devices?
Would such devices not thus be a burden on memory, rather than, as is
commonly assumed, an aide-mémoire? Would it not have been more
convenient to transmit the contents" or "message" of the tradition, for example,
as nonmetrical folktales? Why, then, the use of metrical/rhythmic structure?

One possible answer is that the hexameter rhythm and its technical
apparatus, the metrical structure, formulae, and perhaps also type-scenes, are
symbols of fixity and "sameness," and hence *symbols of cultural continuity*.[5]

In literate cultures the written *text* ("the Book"; the Bible, the Koran)
is the most common symbol of fixity and "sameness."[6] However, a society
that knows no writing, or that knows writing only in a very limited sense, will
by definition not know this symbol. Oral societies must rely on other means
to satisfy their need for fixity and continuity.

To those who know no writing, our literate notion of verbatim, *objective* "sameness" over thousands of lines is meaningless. Indeed, no two
performances can ever be fully coextensive. However, if during different
performances an identical rhythm is used, and if diction is inseparable from
rhythm, then a *semblance* of fixity is achieved.

It is easy to identify the fixed entity we call hexameter. If a particular
proper name, for example that of Odysseus or Achilles, is used repeatedly at
different times during a performance and/or during different performances
but always "under the same metrical conditions" (as Milman Parry would
have it), then a "sameness" is easily and immediately affected, even though
there may be many real differences between the verbatim contents of one
version and another; this is what I mean by "a semblance of fixity." In
manifestations of traditional poetry like the *Iliad* and the *Odyssey*, whose
stated purpose is to preserve the *kleos* "fame," "glory," "hearsay" (a
manifestation of fixity and continuity) of the past, such fixity is essential. Let
me, however, stress again that this version of fixity does not restrict the
inherent flexibility of the tradition.

Two other features of hexameter rhythm should be noted here: first, the rhythm's ability to mark epic as "special" discourse, and second, its ability to indicate that the tradition is always broader than any individual performance.

The hexameter progresses regularly for six feet, then pauses at the verse-end,[7] then repeats itself, then pauses, and repeats itself again more or less regularly for many lines. This manner of controlled, cyclic progression contrasts hexameter discourse to ordinary parlance and hence to our "ordinary" everyday verbal experiences. While all discourse has rhythmic features, almost no form of everyday parlance displays such extended, cyclic regularity. The hexameter rhythm is thus a performative act: its very utterance is the making of "special" discourse.[8]

Furthermore, each hexameter verse/unit is by definition not unique; it is but one of many similar units within larger poems. However, the size of these poems themselves is not regarded as a fixed unit.[9] The implication is that each utterance of a hexameter is a manifestation of a body of hexameter discourse of undetermined scope that is, as it were, "out there."

The point is this: Homeric poetry sharply distinguishes between the heroes of the past and the men of today.[10] By speaking of such special characters in "special discourse," their special nature is thus enhanced. By allowing each line to represent a broader body of hexameter discourse, we allow the shorter, performed utterance to function as an elliptic representation of the greater tradition.[11]

THE SEMANTICS OF RHYTHM

Let us try to apply the preceding to a concrete example. Perhaps the most widely recognized manifestations of rhythmicized regularity in Homer are noun-epithet formulae describing the heroes, such as *polumêtis Odusseus*, "many-minded Odysseus," or *podas ôkus Achilleus*, "swift-footed Achilles." As John Foley suggests, such formulae invoke "a context that is enormously larger and more echoic than the text or work itself, that brings the lifeblood of generations of poems and performances to the individual performance or text."[12]

These common formulae are concrete "symbols of fixity." They are easily recognized as words that are "the same" as those uttered in other places, at other times, in other performances, by other poets singing about Achilles and Odysseus in hexameter, hence they are "traditional," hence they are also far more "echoic."

Noun-epithet formulae do not simply refer to a character. Rather, they invoke an epic theme, creating what we might call "an epiphany." As one scholar has recently put it, "If an epithet is a miniature-scale myth, a theme summoned to the narrative present of the performance, then, like any myth, it needs a proper (one could say, 'ritual') environment for its reenactment."[13]

The ritual summoning of a hero is a very practical matter: in order to reenact "Odysseus" we must, literally, *say the right words*, that is, repeat the *same* words that we know have been used before for the same purpose, for example, *polumêtis Odusseus*, "many-minded Odysseus." But of course this, and most of the other formulae invoking the central characters of epic, are also fixed metrical sequences, for example *da-da-dum-da da-dum-dum* (*po-lu-mê-tis O-dus-seus*). Furthermore, this sequence is not a freestanding semantic-rhythmic unit. *It is meaningful only when embedded and localized in the proper rhythmic/metric context, at the end of a line of hexameter*. Odysseus is thus "recognized" and invoked not just by the words but also by the rhythm—which is a distinctly hexametric, distinctly epic and heroic medium.

LOCALIZATION, SILENCE, AND REALITY

It can hardly be unimportant that common formulae such as *polumêtis Odusseus* and the very idea of the epic hero are localized at the end of the verse,[14] or that others, such as the emotional *nêpios* ("fool," "wretch"), the speech introductory *ton d'apameibomenos* ("to him answered *hôs phato* ("thus he spoke ..."), and many others are anchored to the beginning of the verse. The beginning and the end of the hexameter are its most distinct points, the points at which the flow/pause opposition and the cyclic nature of the rhythm are most clearly marked. As we have suggested above, this cyclic rhythm can mark epic as "special," "extra-ordinary" discourse. The hexameter, like other contexts of *mimetic* activity such as the stage and amphitheater, like the darkness of a cinema-hall, creates a "distancing" effect; it is an artificial context that indicates to us that what happens "out there," the events described/presented, are an imitation, that they are part of a different reality, and not directly a part of our own here-and-now. No matter how elaborate the tale, the modulations of gesture and voice, or for that matter the animatronics (as they are known in Hollywood), we know that epic heroes, tragic personae, Jurassic dinosaurs, and the like, are not real. No self-respecting Greek ever rushed down from his seat to prevent murder on-stage. No hearer of epic, no matter how enchanted or moved by the song, ever mistook the poet's imitation for the real thing.[15] As we hear, say, a speech by Odysseus, we are never fully allowed to forget that this is an imitation, an artificial reconstruction of "Odysseus" and specifically of "what Odysseus said." The most immediate reason for this, of course, is that no character in real life, except poets who are by definition the mouthpieces for "other worlds," ever speaks in hexameters.

The conclusion to be drawn from this is as inevitable as it is central to our argument: as we hear the rhythm of epic, it must be that we are both "here" and "there." We are ever conscious of two (paradoxically) overlapping realities or planes: on the one hand, the plane of our own time-present and of the here-and-now performance, and on the other hand the plane of the fiction and of heroic *temps perdu*.[16]

But now briefly consider cinema again: our sense of the reality on-screen depends heavily on a continuous, rapid flow of what are otherwise still images. Stopping the projector means "stopping the show." Slowing down the projector may produce a flickering sequence in which the world of the narrative is still "out there," but now more markedly "punctuated" by split-second interstices of real-life cinema-hall darkness. Such interstices (as in early, particularly silent, cinema) bring "fiction" and "reality" into a sharper contrast. They have the power to affect what we might call the *deictic* balance between the reality of the narrative and the real world.

The case of cinema and the flow of images is a useful (if somewhat contrastive) analogy when considering the flow of words, and in our case, the flow of epic. A pause in the performance of discourse, if it is long enough, affects the balance between our perception of the fiction "out there" and of the here-and-now reality around us.[17] At the same time, as Wallace Chafe says: "The focus of consciousness is restless, moving constantly from one item of information to the next. In language this restlessness is reflected in the fact that, with few exceptions, each intonation unit expresses something different from the intonation unit immediately preceding and following it. Since each focus is a discrete segment of information, the sequencing of foci resembles a series of snapshots more than a movie."[18]

While the hexameter has several conventional points at which a pause in the rhythmic flow can occur (for example, caesurae),[19] the pause at the end of the line, and consequently at the beginning of the next, is the one that is most clearly marked.[20] It coincides with a word-end without fail, and it coincides with sense breaks more often than any other pause in the verse.[21] It is affirmed by special prosodic features, such as the license of the final *anceps* syllable,[22] the lack of hiatus, of corruption, of lengthening by position, and it is in the most immediate sense the boundary of the hexameter (the very name "hexameter" defines this boundary). I would suggest, therefore, that the beginnings and ends of the verse, its *onset* and *coda*,[23] are those points where the potential for "interstices of silence," and hence for creating ripples in the flow of epic fiction is greatest. They are the points at which the poet can begin or end his song, hence affecting a full *deictic shift*.[24] More significantly, they are the most convenient (although not necessarily the only) points where, in the midst of song, a poet may pause for an instant, affecting what we might term as deictic fluctuations, situations that contrast more sharply the heroic reality of the past, and the (arguably more humble) here-and-now reality of the performance.

Although I would not hazard a more precise definition of this mechanism without considerable further research, the general function of the hexameter's pause/flow nature is, I believe, sensible to most readers and audiences of Homer. As the poet says the much repeated hexameter line ending with the name of Odysseus *ton d'apameibomenos prospehê polumêtis Odusseus* (answering him, said in reply many-minded Odysseus), he pauses, as surely he must, not only because the hexameter unit has come to an end, but also because a sense unit (the grammatical sentence) has terminated, and because a discourse unit (the narrative section) has ended, and we are about to begin a different type of discourse (direct-speech), which requires the poet notionally to change his person (from "narrator" to "Odysseus," and, of course, no physical change takes place in the here-and-now). An epiphany of Odysseus, the hero of the past, is thus invoked at the end of the speech introductory line, but immediately there follows a pause. This interstice of silence, brief as it may be, does not break the "flow of fiction"; but I would suggest that it momentarily alters the balance between the narrative reality "out there" and the time-present reality of the performance, contrasting the past and the present in a more vivid, concrete, experiential, rather than cerebral manner.[25] And of course, this is more or less what ritual is meant to do: it summons something from "out there" to the reality of the here-and-now, creating, as it were, a complex warp. This effect is also a practical manifestation of *kleos aphthithon*, "undying fame," a process of preserving events outside of their "normal" spatio-temporal boundaries. Furthermore, *kleos aphthithon* is precisely what epic strives to generate. We may thus describe our poems as a type of event that stitches together the past and the present, as an *enactment* of *kleos*, as a special type of *performative* speech-act.[26]

What follows is a specific example of the workings of this mechanism, centering on the verbal presentation of the epic hero's solitary state.

OIOS, MOUNOS, AND THE EPIC HERO

The hero is a basic paradigm of epic, and one of the hero's most important properties is his state of being alone, that is to say, his existence as a heroic one-of-a-kind. Achilles, for example, is unique both in his military prowess and in his greatness of heart. This idea of isolation, of being unique and/or alone, is implicitly embedded in many Homeric scenes. However, it is most directly expressed by the use of two words, *oios* and *mounos*. These words have different roots, in that *oios* is probably a numeral,[27] and *mounos* an adjective describing a state, but our lexicons do not suggest any difference in the functional semantics,/of the terms,[28] which raises the question of why two words are used.[29]

In *Iliad* 24.453–456 we find the following lines:

".. the gate was secured by a single beam
of pine, and three Achaeans would close (epirrêsseskon)
and three would open (anaoigeskon) the huge door-bolt; three
other Achaeans, that is, but Achilles could close (epirresseske) it,
        alone (oios)."

This important description of a mechanism for opening (*anaoigeskon*) and closing (*epirrêsseskon/-ske*) the door of Achilles' hut is very significantly positioned: it opens the closing scene of the *Iliad*. The lines are also a situational definition[30] of Achilles as a hero separate from all others. The three long iterative verb-forms emphasize that this is not a one-time event but instead a matter of long-term significance.

The passage commenting on Achilles and the door is a digression, a form of narratorial comment not strictly required for the flow of narrative time.[31] The climax of this digression, both in "meaning" and in "form" is the verse-terminal word *oios* "alone," "on his own" in 456.[32] *Oios* is emphatically positioned at the end of the line, the end of the long sentence (453–456), the end of the passage, and the end of the whole narrative unit that is the introduction to the concluding section of the *Iliad*. It is thus the verbal focus of the narrator's amazed admiration for his hero's singular, larger-than-life abilities. In addition, as we have suggested, line-ends, especially those that are likely to have longer pauses (interstices of silence) after them, are points of potential *deictic fluctuation*, where the narrative reality can be contrasted with the reality of the performance. This, I suggest, is what actually happens here. Through the use of the localized, verse-terminal word *oios*, Achilles in his capacity as a hero of singular ability has been brought as close as possible to the surface of our own "here and now." Rhythm has generated a situation in which we, through the poet, are most sensible to the contrast between Achilles, the singular hero of the past, and ordinary men.

This reading of the *nontextual* function of *oios* cannot, of course, be based on a single example. In fact it relies on a tightly woven rhythmic-semantic network comprising many other examples of the word, the usage of *mounos*, and ultimately, the usage of other words and types of words, and thousands of individual examples.

Consider three further passages that present us with prominent situational definitions of an Iliadic hero as existentially "alone." In all, *oios* is positioned at the end of the verse (this is linked, of course, to the use of formulae, on which see further below), at the end of the sentence (which is usually long), the end of the passage, and at the end of the narrative unit. In *Iliad* 5.302–304 the poet describes the larger-than-life (as in *mega ergon* "a great deed") abilities of Diomedes:

> "... But Tudeus' son in his hand caught
> up a boulder, a great deed, which no two men could carry
> such as (hoioi) men are now, but he lightly hefted it, alone
> (oios)."

These lines are repeated word for word in *Iliad* 20.285–287, except that the name of Aineias is substituted for that of Diomedes. Terminal *oios* is the focus of the narrator's amazement, or, shall we say, of his emotionally charged awareness of the sharp; opposition between the qualities of the heroic past and the humble present.

Consider further the example of *oios* in *Iliad* 12.445–451:

> "Hektor snatched up a boulder that stood before the gates
> and carried it along; it was broad at the base, but the upper
> end was sharp; two men, the best in all a community,
> could not easily hoist it up from the ground to a wagon,
> such as (hoioi) men are now, but he lightly hefted it alone (oios).
> The son of devious Kronos made it light for him.
> As when a shepherd lifts up with ease the fleece of a wether
> (*oios*)."

These examples allow rhythmic functions to generate yet more complex effects. In 5.302–304, 20.285–287, and 12.445–451, not only is *oios* verse-terminal, but in fact, at the beginning of the verse, just after the preceding interstice of silence, a word highly similar in sound occurs, *hoioi*, which is the plural of *hoios*, "such a ... / what a ..." Furthermore, if we recall expressions such as *eu de su oistha*, (...) *hoios ekeinos deinos anêr*, "for you know well, what a mighty man he is ..." (*Iliad* 11.653–654, Patroklos to Nestor about Achilles), we shall realize that the word *hoios* is a key element of Homeric expressions of amazement. Indeed, its function, on many occasions, is *expressive*, not *directive* (in speech-act terms). The common phrase *hoion eeipes*, for example in Zeus' words to Poseidon *o popoi, ennosigai' eurusthenes, hoion eeipes* (*Iliad* 7.455) is best translated "o my, o mighty lord of the earth, I am amazed by your words!" (literally "what kind of thing have you said?").[33] Once we accept this, the alliteration of "o-o-o" sounds in 7.455 takes on special significance: it replicates and extends the archetypal exclamatory Greek utterance "o,"[34] whose meaning, or rather whose *function*, is central to the verse as a whole.[35]

I am suggesting that within the specific discourse of Homeric hexameter there are significant pragmatic links between the word *oios* (alone, on his own) and the word *hoios* (such a ... / what a, as an expression of emotion), and that these links are strongly marked by basic rhythmic properties (that is, by prominent localization).[36] This idea need not surprise us. What Milman Parry termed *calembour* (more serious than a "pun") is a recurrent feature of Homeric poetry: *aütmê //* and *aütê //*; *omphê //* and *odmê //*; *dêmos //* (fat) and *dêmos //* (people) are some well known examples, all localized (like the rhyme in later poetry) at the end of the verse.[37] Finally, if any further emphasis on this phonetic and rhythmic marking is needed, we may note the verse-terminal *oios* (of a wether) in our last example (12.451), which echoes yet again the link between *oios* and *hoios*.

Like 24.453–456, these passages are not, strictly speaking, narrative; rather they provide narrator comments. In our very first passage, 24.453–456, the narrator comments on Achilles' abilities without openly acknowledging the reality of the performance. In the stone-lifting passages the normally reticent narrator makes unambiguous verbal reference to the present, to the performance and the audience *hoioi nun* "[the men] such as they are today." Regardless, in all passages, the contrast between past and present is the very essence of the words. And it is precisely this contrast that the extremities of the verse bear out, indeed *enact* so well.

To sum up my point so far: the preceding examples are condensed, highly memorable concrete images, effective situational "definitions" of the epic hero, in which the word *oios* in verse terminal position is a codified element of ritual, an enactment of the epic hero as the possessor of singular abilities unmatched by the men of today, and a marker of the narrator's amazed reaction to these abilities, and his consciousness of the wide breach between past and present.[38] Terminal position, being a point at which the world of fiction and the real world can be effectively contrasted, allows the contents of the definition—the contrast between the epic hero and the men of today—to be enhanced by the cognitive features of performance mechanics. In the three stone-throwing passages we saw how terminal *oios* is further emphasized by the contrastive *calembour*, using verse-initial *hoios*, a word close in phonetic value to *oios* and having an exclamatory force.

It is widely recognized that "unmarked" terms are semantically more general, or even "neutral," compared to their "marked" counterparts.[39]

Terminal *oios* is clearly a "marked" term. Almost two thirds of the nominative masculine singular are localized at the end of the verse;[40] other grammatical case-forms are hardly ever used at the verse-end;[41] usage of the apparent synonym *mounos* at the verse-end would have provided a convenient metrical alternative (and hence formulaic "extension" in the Parryan sense), but in fact it is all but avoided.[42] Unmarked (non-terminal) *oios* does seem to be used in a less focused manner,[43] but virtually all other examples of terminal, nominative usage of *oios* can be read, sung, heard, or in general, *enacted* in accordance, with the interpretation suggested here.

Here are a few more examples: first, passages that convey the essential idea of "walking alone" and that employ the terminal, nominative singular *oios*.[44]

In *Iliad* 10.82 the surprised Nestor demands to know the identity of an addressee who is walking about the camp at night (10.82–83):

"Who are you, who walk through the ships and the army alone
(oios)
and through the darkness of night when other mortals are
sleeping?"

In *Iliad* 10.385 Odysseus interrogates Dolon about the latter's nocturnal perambulation (10.385–386):

"Why is it that you walk to the ships, away from the army, alone
(oios)
through the darkness of night when other mortals are sleeping?"

Comparable use of *oios* may be found also in *Iliad* 24.203 (Hecuba to Priam about his visit to the Greek camp); in *Iliad* 24.519 (Achilles to Priam about the visit); and in *Odyssey* 10.281 (Hermes to Odysseus on Kirke's island). These five passages are another node in the nexus of exclamatory, heroic, verse-terminal *oios*.[45] All imply that the addressee is doing something exceedingly bold, something that we would have called heroic but for the fact that the addressee is, or is assumed by the speaker to be, a nonhero. The speaker construes the actions as reckless and/or abnormal, indicating his awareness of the discrepancy between character and circumstances.[46] In each one of these examples, heroic isolation is enacted in an inappropriate context, with the result being that it is construed as "madness." The speaker's understanding of the situation, and no less our own, relies on a contrast between "heroic" activities and "ordinary" abilities. And this, of course, is precisely the kind of contrast that can be marked by the interstice of silence at the end of the verse, where *oios* is positioned.

The last example is *Iliad* 1.118: Agamemnon, having heard Kalkhas' explanation of the plague, agrees to send Khruseis home, but adds (118–120):

> "Give out to me forthwith some prize, so that I shall not (mê) be
>   alone (oios)
> among the Argives without a prize, since that is unseemly;
> for as you can all see, my prize goes elsewhere."

This passage of direct discourse is an emotive request. If my interpretation is correct, then here too *oios* is marked as an exclamatory echo and may be enhanced by the effects of a *deictic fluctuation*.

The king's speech is preceded by a long and intensely visual display of anger (a "heroic" emotion ...). Agamemnon is the *far* ruling (102) raging (103) *black* hearted (103) *burning eyed* (104) evil *staring* (105) overlord. Remarkably, over the course of just fifteen lines his rage simmers down to a whimper: "Give out to me forthwith some prize so that I shall not be alone among the Argives without a prize, since that is not seemly. For, *as you can all see*, my prize goes elsewhere." And yet, as the assembled Greek host can *see*, the person speaking is not a feeble priest begging for his child or an ancient king begging for a corpse. Indeed, the speaker is not anyone resembling men as they are "now," but a mighty hero and far-ruling king, a point stressed by the repeated visual vocabulary.

But there is more. We the audience also see the raging Agamemnon in our mind's eye (the reality within the narrative), but we no less see in front of us, with our real eyes (in the reality of the performance) a humble bard (helpless? blind ... like the poet Demodokos in the *Odyssey*? Like "Homer" himself?). To the assembled Greeks the discrepancy between sight and sound to Agamemnon's audience spells out a message: the humbler the plea, the bigger the threat. The contrastive falsity of Agamemnon's words is also, I suggest, directly reflected by the mimesis itself, and no less by verse-terminal *oios* (indeed me *oios*, "not" *oios*), a word that pretends to speak of a uniquely wretched and dependent state (as are the men of today ...) but that enacts, at the point of *deictic fluctuation*, the violent, larger-than-life hero who does not depend on the consent of their peers but who acts "alone."

Consider now more closely the use of *mounos*. First let us note that although *mounos* itself contains the "*o*" vowel (the word derives from *monwos*) there is in our extant text far less alliterative play on the exclamatory sounds, and, of course, *mounos* cannot echo the exclamatory *hoios* ("such a ..."). In the one example of *mounos* we have seen so far (our first passage, *Iliad* 24.453–456 above) *mounos* was used to describe the beam securing the door of Achilles' hut, but the word was verse-internal.

The beam, we assume, is unique in size among door-bolts, and as such is an important matching accessory for the great hero. It is not, however, a discreet element of the lost, heroic past. Neither ritual song, nor a singer are essential for its reenactment. An ax, a steady arm, and a big tree might easily produce a real object that is "bigger and better" than door-bolts of the past … By contrast, no amount of woodwork will summon Achilles to the present. My point is that *mounos* in 24.453 is an important word in the context, but it is not rhythmically marked in the manner of *oios* in line 456, and it is not the focus of a verbal reenactment ritual.

It is, nevertheless, easy to find examples of *mounos* that are formally marked and that relate significantly to examples of terminal *oios*, both in terms of their localization and in terms of their discourse functions. By far the most prominent cluster of attestations of *mounos* in Homer appears in *Odyssey* 16.113–125, where Telemakhos is speaking to the disguised stranger, who is his father:

"So, my friend, I will tell you plainly the whole truth of it.
It is not that all the people hate me, nor are they angry,
nor is it that I find brothers wanting, whom a man trusts for
help in the fighting, whenever a great quarrel arises.
For so it is that the son of Kronos made ours a line of only sons
    (mounose). Arkeisios had
only one (mounon) son, Laertes. And Laertes had
only one (mounon) son, Odysseus. And Odysseus in turn left
only one (mounon) son, myself, in the halls, and got no profit of me;
and my enemies are here in my house, beyond numbering."

The idea of *mounos*, of being alone, here in the sense of "an only son" is repeated four times in as many verses. In three consecutive lines *mounos*, or rather the accusative masculine singular form *mounon*, is verse-initial.[47] As in the case of Achilles and the beam, and also the stone-throwing passages, these lines too are a situational definition. They too describe not one particular moment in time but a permanent attribute of the main characters of the *Odyssey*. Previously, this permanence was effected by iterative verbs; here it is effected by (rhetorical) anaphora and by the idea of a genealogical chain put together by Zeus.[48]

The word *mounos* here is not uttered in amazement and admiration for the abilities of some singularly great character ("what a …!") as in the case of terminal *oios*. And as just stated before, it carries none of the phonetic echoes of exclamation. Being *mounos* as Telemakhos clearly explains, is the state of having no brothers *hoisi per anêr // marnamenoisi pepoisthe* "whom a man trusts for help in the fighting" (115–116), that is, it is a state of helplessness. He speaks of Laertes, an old man, of Odysseus, a great hero but presumed dead, and of himself, a boy too young to resist his enemies. Furthermore, this hereditary helplessness has been ordained by the most powerful of the gods, the son (...) of Kronos, whose will is supreme. So *mounos* here does not mark amazement at the larger-than-life heroic abilities of a hero but rather the very opposite, a reaction to isolation as a state of weakness that is beyond mortal control.

Mounos in this passage is an element of exposition. This, says Telemakhos, is how Zeus decided that our family should be: [interstice of silence] "*mounos* my grandfather" [interstice of silence] "*mounos* my father" [interstice of silence] "*mounos* I myself ..." The word *mounos* is physically the first word of each verse. It may be difficult to determine the precise length of the pauses (which in any case are likely to differ from performance to performance), but such precision is not needed. The threefold repetition of *mounos* at the beginning of the hexameter unit stresses the cyclic nature of the utterance. To reject a pause at the beginning of these lines is to reject the very rhythmic essence of epic, which is impossible. Three times we face a member of the family at the point of the *deictic fluctuation*. Each time we meet not an epic hero who is *oios*, not "bigger and better" than ourselves, but a supposedly helpless *mounos*, someone more like "the men of today." Our empathy and pity almost fully overlap Telemakhos' anguish. This, I suggest, is where epic is *enacted*, as the past and the present are placed side by side. And of course *mounos* is localized in a position that is formally the opposite of *oios*: *after* the pause, not *before* it.

Many examples of verse-initial, "emphatic," "weak" *mounos* can be found in Homer. They suggest that *mounos* and *oios* function as complementary/opposing rhythmic-semantic terms. At the same time, several important clues indicate that among the two words, *oios* is the more-specific, marked term, while usage of *mounos* covers a broader, more loose range. We have noted how distinctly *oios* is used at the verse-end, how *mounos* is excluded from the verse end, and how *mounos* does not replicate the exclamatory sound "o." Furthermore, judging by the extant remains of ancient Greek literature, usage of the word *oios*, and especially in the nominative masculine singular, is commonplace only in Homer and ancient commentaries on the *Iliad* and *Odyssey*(!).[49] Usage of *mounos* in authors other than Homer is much wider,[50] and in Homer verse-initial usage varies between nominative *mounos* and accusative *mounon*. All this makes good sense: conceptually *oios* is the more "special" term (describing "special" heroic abilities), *mounos* the more "ordinary." Inasmuch as these two are a pair, *oios* is the marked term.[51]

In *Odyssey* 2.361–365 Telemakhos' plans to sail in quest of information upset the nursemaid Eurukleia:

"So he spoke, and the dear nurse Eurukleia cried out,
and bitterly lamenting she addressed him in winged words:
'Why, my beloved child, has this intention come into
your mind? Why do you wish to wander over much country, you,
an only (mounos) and loved son?'"

The *deictic fluctuation* at the beginning of the verse has the potential to provide concrete illustration to the contrast between a weak Telemakhos, who is more like the men of the present, and the dangerous reality in which he is situated, that calls rather for the unique abilities of a hero.

In *Odyssey* 16 the poet breaks the narrative in order to comment on Eumaios' greeting of Telemakhos by use of a simile (16.19):

"And as a father, with heart full of love, welcomes his son
when he comes back in the tenth year from a distant country,
his only (*mounon*) and grown son, for whose sake he has undergone
   many hardships
so now the noble swineherd clinging fast to godlike
Telemakhos, kissed him even as if he had escaped dying."

Closely related is the example of *Iliad* 9.481–482, within Phoinix' speech to Achilles:

"and [Peleus] gave me his love, even as a father loves his
only (mounon) son who is brought up among many possessions."

The love of fathers for their ("only") sons in the reality of the present and in the world of the narrated heroic past is doubtless identical; here we encounter this emotion, centered on the word *mounos*, precisely at a point that itself allows the poet to enhance our consciousness of *both* realities.

In *Odyssey* 20.30 the narrator describes the thoughts of Odysseus as he wonders how he should take revenge on the suitors (*Odyssey* 20.28–30):

"So he was twisting and turning back and forth, meditating
how he could lay his hands on the shameless suitors, though he
was alone (mounos) against many."

The beginning of book 20 describes Odysseus' deliberations. The passage kicks off with the active, wild and reckless thoughts ("let's jump and kill them all at once!" 11–13) of a barking heart (14–16), through a transitory stage of rational reflection and restraint (17–18), to a simile, in which Odysseus tossing to-and-fro is likened to entrails roasting in the fire—a powerful image, but one of passivity and helplessness, not of singular heroic ability and resolve. The dog imagery and entrails simile are externalized representations of an internal transition: from "that which bites/kills/threatens" to "that which has been killed/is screaming in agony/is about to be bitten." By the end of the transition the polytropic hero is hardly feeling ready to perform astonishing deeds.

Again we have no means of measuring the precise duration of the interstice of silence preceding *mounos*, but its potential as a concrete enhancement of the contents of the situation is clear. Verse-initial *mounos* presents us with the hero at his weakest, at a moment when he is least like the *oios* hero. Interesting comparable usage may be found, in fact, in *Odyssey* 20.40 and in *Iliad* 11.406.

In our next passage the poet describes the death of the unsuspecting Antinoos at the hands of Odysseus (*Odyssey* 22.9–14):

"He was on the point of lifting up a fine two-handled
goblet of gold, and had it in his hands, and was moving it
so as to drink of the wine, and in his heart there was no thought
of death. For who would think that a man in the company of
     feasting men,
alone (mounon) among many, though he were very strong,
would ever inflict death upon him and dark doom?"

The omniscient narrator is here voicing the thoughts of one who is oblivious to impending doom: Antinoos has no grasp of reality.[52] Indeed, the whole section relies on the tension between heroic characters who *can* stand up to the many (more or less) alone, and helpless characters, marked by the word *mounos*, who *cannot*. This, again, is also the essence of the distinction between the heroic reality and the weaker reality of the performance (the "men of today") which interstices of silence bear out.

Finally, consider the case of *Iliad* 17.469–473. Alkimedon is here wondering that Automedon is about to enter battle alone:

"Automedon, what god put this unprofitable purpose
into your heart, and has taken away the better wits,
so that (hoion) you are trying to fight the Trojans in the first

shock of encounter
alone (mounos), since your companion has been killed, and
    Hektor
glories in wearing Aiakides' armour on his own shoulders?"

Automedon is charioteer to both Achilles and Patroklos (a man
professionally inclined to fighting in pairs, not "alone"), and not thus of
equal heroic rank to the great warriors. He has just been deprived of his
companion Patroklos, is thus in a passive state of isolation, but has also
chosen to fight alone. *Mounos* is used in its familiar verse-initial position, but
the very preceding line speaks of insane, valorous action, perhaps
reminiscent of the *oios*-type hero.[53] Indeed, line 471 begins with the word
hoion (in this case adverbial) and thus immediately contrasts, both
semantically and thematically, with the following *mounos*. Two lines later,
Automedon in his reply to Alkimedon says (17.475–480):

"Alkimedon, which other of the Achaeans was your match
    (homoios)
in the management and the strength of immortal horses,
were it not Patroklos, the equal of the immortals in counsel,
while he lived? Now death and fate have closed in upon him.
Therefore take over from me the whip and the glittering guide
    reins
while I dismount from behind the horses, so I may do battle."

Automedon the charioteer, the man whose fighting role is "incomplete"
without a partner, a *mounos* type character, undergoes a transition and
becomes more of an *oios* type hero who can and does fight successfully alone
(cf. 17.516–542). The passages are rich in echoes and melodies. And yet part
of their complexity is set within an ordered rhythmic, hexametric framework.
The central poetic opposition of this section—the contrast between
helplessness and heroic abilities, between pity and amazement, is firmly
linked to usage at the extremities of the verse (*hoion, mounos, homoios*), which,
we have seen elsewhere, mark important examples of *mounos* and *oios*, and
which can emphasize the contrast between the larger-than-life past and the
present. How far do these echoes extend? This is a difficult, if not
impossible, question to answer. But to assume that so many repeated
attestations of such significant words at such prominent positions in the verse
are due to mere chance or to mere technicalities, is to assume a poet whose
indifference to the sounds of his words is almost complete. And of course,
soundless words, if they exist at all, exist only on a written page.

THE EXTENT OF RHYTHMICIZED SEMANTICS

We have seen some examples of a system of rhythmicized semantics/poetics in Homer that relies on the basic pause/flow nature of the hexameter. Two types of solitary states were noted: isolation as the mark of larger-than-life heroic abilities, which is the "special" attribute of Homer's heroes, and isolation as the mark of "ordinary" mortal helplessness. The two opposing notions were formally marked by use of two otherwise synonymous words, *oios* and *mounos*, employed in notable examples with repeated localization at opposing verse extremities. This formal opposition helped mark the contrastive, but perhaps no less the complementary, nature of the two terms. The relationship between the two terms was made even more significant by the fact that they correspond to a conceptual opposition central to Homeric epic: the contrast between the larger than life reality of epic past, and the more humble reality of the present and the performance. I have tried to argue that the very cognitive functions of the pause/flow rhythm at the points where these two words are prominently localized embody this contrast. Localized usage of *oios* and *mounos* at the extremities of the verse allows an almost literal *enactment* of *kleos*, "fame": a juxtapositioning of past and present.

But have we been using a sledgehammer to crack a nut? After all, *oios* and *mounos* are but two words in the Homeric lexicon, and in order to explain their usage, we have argued for the existence of a mechanism that endows every verse with the potential for emphasizing *deictic* fluctuations. How often, then, is this potential realized?

I have elsewhere argued for statistically significant and hence also semantically significant localization tendencies of lexical/semantic/ grammatical items, largely single words, at the ends of the verse, for example theme words of the epic, such as *andra* (man), *mênin* (wrath), and *noston* (return), vocative proper names, nominative proper names.[54] These tendencies apply to thousands of individual examples, and there are other obvious candidates for the further study of rhythmical semantics (for example, *nêpios* "wretch!" at the beginning of the verse[55]). While the localization of many words, grammatical types, and so on, clearly relates to, indeed overlaps, "formulaic" usage, it extends well beyond the use of formulae, as they are presently defined, and it cannot be explained in terms of simple metrical convenience. Now, the mediation between past and present is not simply one among many motifs in the poetry of Homer. It is arguably the most important aspect of the poems, their very raison d'être: the poems are exercises in the preservation of *kleos*. Any device that can emphasize the contrasts and/or similarities between the realities of past and present could be of use in a very wide range of Homeric contexts and would have the ability to imbue many epic words with specifically hexametric, "performed" significance,[56]

ONE MORE WORD, AT THE END

In worlds such as our own, that rely so heavily on texts, and especially in the even more highly textualized world of scholarship, vocality risks being construed as a flourish. Many will admire the voices of an Auden, an Eliot, or an Angelou, and still feel that the performance is in essence a fleeting thing, an ornament to the "real" artifact, an object that "does not change in time," an object that can be held in our hands and possessed.

Auden, Eliot, Angelou, and many other "literate" poets rely heavily on voice, but a full understanding of their poetry always assumes a book. They require a close, leisurely (that is, not monodirectional, time-bound) contemplation of the *text*. But if access to a *text* is limited or even nonexistent (either in the production or in the reception process), if words must flow at a constant pace, how can there be contemplation? Approaching Homer with this problem in mind has led on the one hand to implicitly (or explicitly) *textual* readings, and on the other to various degrees of denial of precise shades of meaning (for example in formulaic discourse). More recently, phonology, discourse analysis, pragmatics, and the study of orality (indeed, the work of many of the contributors to this volume) have shown that epic words do allow us to reflect. Epic words relate to and recall, not so much this or that fixed point elsewhere in a text, rather they activate a whole "theme," a "myth," a "node" in the tradition.

Thus, essentially, one line of "ritual" of epic verse opens the same kind of window to the epic world as do a hundred lines. "The Movie" of a television series and the shorter network "episodes" are in a deep sense "the same." Likewise, it is "the same" if we are shown the world of epic heroes "out there" either for part of an evening or for three whole days. A thousand-line epic poem about Achilles is in this sense "the same" as a poem fifteen times in size.[57] Paradoxically, writing, the very medium that seeks to preserve "sameness," converts a long and a short version of "the same" song into two "different" *texts*: writing results in two objects that can be placed side by side at a single point in time and hence shown, in a literate sense, to be "not the same." But if two poems are nothing but fleeting streams of words and if each is performed at a different time, how would we ever know that they do belong together, that they are both parts of "the same" world? It is because key elements of this world are repeated, again, and again, and again: *po-lu-mê-tis-O-dus-seus, po-das-ô-kus-A-chil-*

leus, chanted ever in a fixed position within a short, repetitive pattern we call the hexameter. At this point vocal, rhythmic properties become the key to sameness, to continuity, to "authority," to "*nontextual* contemplation." We can transcode vocal similarities in two hexameter sequences using graphic signs, but the moment we do so, we have produced two *different* verses, and in a concrete sense two *different* texts! Inasmuch as the poetry of Homer is traditional, and inasmuch as traditional implies "sameness," Homer's poetry is not, nor can it ever be, *textual*. However, this does not mean that it cannot be written down. It can, it has (how, and when, I dare not here say), and furthermore, as I have tried to show, the written voice does "sound" the same.

NOTES

Translations are based on R. Lattimore. Some license is taken with English word order so as to reflect a word's original position in the verse.

1. Especially Oesterreicher and Schaefer in this volume.

2. I use the term "meter" to refer to the formal framework of sequencing and segmentation, syllabic in the case of Homer. I use the term "rhythm" to refer to a much broader and less formal range of sequential/segmentational phenomena. See Devine & Stephens 1994:99–101.

3. "Literate" hexameter authors (Apollonius, Quintus, etc.) use a meter almost identical to Homer's (O'Neill 1942; Porter 1951), but they do not link their rhythm and their diction in quite the same way as Homer. Use of formulae is a case in point (see Edwards 1988:42–53; Sale 1993).

4. Zumthor 1990a:51, 203.

5. Perhaps a kind of *sphragis* ("seal"). Compare Nagy 1990a:170.

6. Many poststructuralist approaches (hermeneutics, reader-response criticism, deconstruction, etc.) strongly suggest that even the *text* is a symbol of fixity.

7. See Daitz 1991; Wyatt 1992; Daitz 1992. I would suggest that this "pause" can be a cognitive entity, rather than an actual silent duration.

8. Ordinary parlance can display "phonological isochrony" (Hogg and McCully 1987:222–225), but not large-scale repetition of formally identical (e.g., 6 beats) units.

9. Unlike, e.g., the sonnet.

10. See Griffin 1980:81–102.

11. On ellipsis in this sense see Nagy, in this volume.

12. Foley 1991:7.

13. Bakker 1995:109.

14. See Kahane 1994:114–141.

15. Siren songs (*Odyssey*; Göethe, *Lorelei*) are deadly exceptions. For drama and epic see Greenwood 1953:124: Greek drama "did not attempt to produce in the spectators' minds any sort of illusion, any feeling, however temporary, that they were seeing and hearing what, in the distant past, actually took place ... in epic ... illusion was plainly impossible and was in no way attempted [but epic] could nevertheless cause the hearer to

imagine vividly the scene and the various persons acting and speaking, so drama could do this."

16. See Chafe 1994:33 ("Conscious Experiences May Be Factual or Fictional"); Bakker, in this volume ("near," "far"); Schechner 1985:117–150 ("Performers and Spectators Transported and Transformed"); Lada 1993–1994.

17. See Devine and Stephens 1994, ch. 3. Our sense of rhythm depends on patterned temporal sequences, in which stimuli occur regularly: "8 to 0.5 events per second." "Slower stimuli tend to be perceived as discrete events not joint to each other in a rhythmic pattern." Estimates vary as to the duration of rhetorically significant pauses (see Deese 1980). Actual duration values do not, however, affect our argument.

18. Chafe 1994:29–30.

19. Caesurae also affect the flow, but verse ends/beginnings are more prominent. For the internal metrics of the hexameter see Ingalls 1970; Kahane 1994:17–42 on relative prominence of pauses.

20. See Daitz 1991; Wyatt 1992; Daitz 1992. 21. See Ingalls 1970.

22. The last full position in the hexameter may be occupied by either a single long or a single short syllable. With a few exceptions in "irrational" hexameters, no other position enjoys such privilege.

23. See e.g. Gimson 1994, ch. 4.

24. Compare codas at the end of narratives, which bring the narrator and listener back to the point at which they entered the narrative (Labov 1972:365).

25. See Toolan 1988:162–163.

26. For speech acts see, e.g., Searle 1968.

27. See Linear-B (PY Ta 641): O-WO-WE, TI-RI-O-WE, QE-TO-RO-WE (*oiwowes, triowes, qetrowes*, one-eared, three-eared vessels; etc.).

28. *Oios* from Indo-European **oi-*, "one"; *mounos* (<*μόνϝ ος) perhaps associated with *manos*, "rare, sparse," and *manu* = *mikron*, "small." See Chantraine 1968–1980; Frisk 1960–1972; Boisacq 1938; *LSJ* with verbal communications from P. G. Glare. Waanders 1992 (on origin and etymology of numerals) is silent on *mounos*.

29. *Oios* and *mounos* are metrically identical, but the former begins with a vowel; the latter with a consonant, i.e. these two apparent synonyms are metrical variants. See following notes.

30. Oral cultures tend to classify items "situationally" (i.e. by linking them to a situation), while literate cultures stress abstract, decontextualized properties (Ong 1982:49–54; Olson 1994:37–44).

31. Narrative is a description of events along a time axis: "John got up (a), brushed his teeth (b), had breakfast (c), and left (d)" = $T^0 \ldots a \ldots b \ldots c \ldots d \ldots T^n$. Although the narrative's presentation of temporal events is not always linear (flashbacks, visions, etc ...), we can generally separate between "narrative foreground," elements that directly push the plot forward in time, "John got up," "he had breakfast," etc., and "narrative background," elements that do not: "He [i.e. John] was an ornithologist." See Fleischman 1990:15–51. For the narrator's comments in Homer see (S.) Richardson 1990:67, 177; de Jong 1987:19, 44.

32. After which the main, "objective" narrative picks up again *dê ra toth' Hermeias...* "then did Hermes ..." (457ff.).

33. *Hoios* is an indirect interrogative pronoun (Chantraine 1963:238–239), but we cannot paraphrase "Poseidon, what are the contents of what you have said?" (since Zeus has just heard his brother's words). The rest of Zeus' speech makes it clear that he is not seeking an answer and that he has not really asked a question: technically (as in Searle 1968) an *expressive* rather than a *directive* speech act.

34. See Frisk 1960–1972 for comments and bibliography.

35. The alliteration is common. Compare *Odyssey* 17.248: *ô popoi, hoion eeipe kuôn olophôia eidôs* "o my, o, what has the dog said, this thinker of destructive thoughts."

36. The formal antithesis of *Iliad* 5.304 is enhanced by the plural/singular antithesis *hoioi/oios*.

37. See Nagler 1974: 1ff. and his note 1, p. 1; Parry 1971:72. On phonetic/semantic relationships see, e.g., Geiger 1958.

38. Compare *Iliad* 12.379–383, where the stone's size is more modest: *oude ke min rea kheiress' amphoterêis ekhoi anêr...* "a man would not easily lift it up in both arms."

39. Comrie 1976:111; also Nagy 1990a:31–34.

40. 17 out of 26 examples (65%). This is not the result of simple metrical tendencies. Disregarding semantic, lexical, grammatical, and context-specific considerations, the tendency for words with metrical values – ∪ and – – to be localized at the end of the verse is 35.9% and 41.3% respectively (*Iliad*), 34.3% and 41.7% respectively (*Odyssey*) (data: O'Neill 1942:140).

41. There is no metrical reason to prevent terminal usage in any grammatical case. Dat. masc. sing. 4x verse-terminal (*Odyssey* 9.160, 10.524, 11.32, 21.146); acc. masc. sing. 1x terminal (*Iliad* 16.340); gen. and voc. masc. sing. not attested in any position; nom. fem. sing. 1x terminal (*Odyssey* 9.207); dat., acc., and gen. fem. sing. never terminal.

42. Terminal localization of *mounos* is metrically possible and occurs elsewhere in epic (e.g. Apollonius Rhodius, *Argonautica* 1.197, 732; 2.112; Oppian, *Halieutica* 2.571; Eumelus, *Corinthiaca* (in Dio Chrysostom. *Or.* 20.13)), but never in Homer except for a single example *mounê* (feminine) in *Odyssey* 23.227.

43. In *Iliad* 6.403 Hektor is the only hero of Troy (*oios* as the mark of heroic isolation): (*Astuanakt'.*) *oios gar erueto Ilion Hektor.* "(Astuanax—lord of the city;) since Hektor alone (*oios*) saved Ilion." But also in contexts where no heroic element is discernible, as when Tudeus kills everyone except Maion (*Iliad* 4.397) *pantas epephn', hena d'oion hiei oikonde neesthai* "He killed them all, except that he let one man alone (*oion*) get home again."

44. These examples are clearly formulaic. But this "system" is not linked, in formulaic terms, to our earlier *kai oios* examples: localization of *oios* may be related to formulaic composition but is a much broader phenomenon.

45. The examples are not statements, but questions (rhetorical, or otherwise), and hence more specifically expressive elements of direct speech.

46. The shrieking Hecuba *kôkusen* (24.200. Pucci 1993:258: *kôkuein* normally in mourning for a *dead* husband) says to Priam: "Where has your mind gone?" (24.201–202). Achilles, in saying "ah, wretch ..." (24.518) implies that Priam has lost his senses through suffering. Agamemnon says "I fear terribly for the Danaans, my heart is unsettled, I wander, my heart flutters outside my breast, my limbs tremble ..." (10.91–95). Dolon's first words of reply are "Hektor caused me to lose my senses" (10.391). Priam explains that his motivation is divine (compare 24.220–224) and thus possibly a variety of madness. In his reply to Achilles Priam totally ignores everything in his interlocutor's words (553–558).

47. The choice of *mounos* in verse-initial position rather than *oios* or the accusative *oion* is not affected by meter.

48. (Rhetorical) anaphora in Homer is often localized at the line's extremities; and particularly its beginning, as for example in 14–15 in our example, //*oute* ... //*oute* ...; *Iliad* 2.671–673, //*Nireus* ... // *Nireus* ...; *Iliad* 10.227–231, *hoi d'ethelon* ... //*etheletên* ... //*ethele* ... //*ethele* ... //*ethele* ... Compare the rhyme in later poetry.

49. For example, *TLG* (#D) lists total 370 attestations of nominative masculine singular: Eustathius' commentaries on Homer (81); *Iliad* and *Odyssey* (66); scholia to Homer (64); remaining 159 attestations are dispersed among 57 authors/collections.

50. The variant form *monos* is virtually universal. The forms *mounos/mounon* are found mainly in hexametric contexts (incl. scholia), but usage is far less markedly Homeric. For example, TLG lists total 340 attestations of the nominative masculine singular *mounos*: Nonnus (60); Greek Anthology (26); Herodotus (26); Gregory Nazianzenus (19); scholia to Homer (18); Eustathius (15); only 14 in Homer.

51. Comrie 1976:111; also Nagy 1990a:31–34.

52. Even in death Antinoos' rowdy "feasting" continues: he casts away his cup, kicks the table, blood, bread, and meat gush out (17–21). Confusion here is part of the wider matrix of Odyssean disguises and late recognitions. As Antinoos collapses, the suitors rush about in disarray (21ff.), and their thoughts are described in a highly unusual manner (Griffin 1986:45, on *Odyssey* 20.31ff).

53. Some elements of this speech may be comparable to Hecuba's address to Priam (see earlier), where *oios* is used.

54. Kahane 1994.

55. On *nêpios* see also "Bakker, in this volume.

56. The semantic functions of rhythm as described in this article may be more difficult to trace in later, "literate" heroic epic. But this requires separate study.

57. On the magnitude of the Homeric epics, see Ford in this volume.

ANDREW FORD

Epic as Genre

T o call the *Iliad* and *Odyssey* 'epics' today can evoke two quite different sets of comparable works. The first grouping would put Homer at the head of a Western tradition of literary epic that runs from Apollonius of Rhodes through Vergil, on to the Renaissance and beyond.[1] The second, with equal justice, would view Homeric poetry as one instance of a type of traditional oral narrative to be found the world over, including cultures far outside the influence of the West.[2] For all their divergence, these two classes of 'epic' are not unrelated: the traditional oral art embodied in Homer was, after all, what Aristotle took as his exemplar when he laid the groundwork for the theory of Western epic in the *Poetics*. Between these two aspects of epic is yet a third way of defining the genre, in relation to the other forms of song that were named and recognized in Archaic Greece. This chapter will attempt a definition of Greek epic in such terms, asking how Homer's poems were presented to and accepted by contemporary audiences as instances of a particular kind of singing. Defining the genre in historical and culturally specific terms may offer an enriching perspective on the works, and may make clearer the connections between Homer the oral poet and Homer the father of classical epic.[3]

We do not know when the Greeks began to sing what we now call epics, for the *Iliad* and *Odyssey* derive from oral traditions reaching back to

From *A New Companion to Homer*, edited by Ian Morris and Barry Powell. © 1997 by Koninklijke Brill.

the Bronze Age (see Horrocks, this vol.; Bennet, this vol.). Because the
Myceneans did not write their songs down, we can only conjecture that they
may have had songs about notable ancient kings which they distinguished
from cult songs or praises of living men.[4] It is in any case generally agreed
that the Greek 'Dark Age' was crucially important for developing the themes
and the special style we see in the Homeric poems.[5] By the end of the eighth
century, the Ionian version of this ancient art had triumphed over all others
as *the* way to sing the exploits of heroes and gods. This style, entailing formal
features such as a characteristic meter and dialect as well as larger narrative
patterns, amounted to a distinct genre in the sense that it could be expected
of a certain class of singers when they performed certain themes, no matter
where they came from or where they sang.

This genre appears to have had at first no particular name, though
Greek critics eventually named it 'epic.' When the Western critical tradition
was founded in Plato and Aristotle, Homeric poetry was popularly called
ἐποποιία, meaning something like 'verse composition' or 'hexameter
composition.' Although Aristotle objected to naming kinds of literature
according to the meter used,[6] he recognized that trial and error had
established the dactylic hexameter as the only proper vehicle for heroic
narratives, and he took account of meter in defining epic.[7] His conception
of ἐποποιία as a distinct genre, however, also includes historical, 'natural,'
and thematic considerations: epic was the ancestor of tragedy, each genre
satisfying a human impulse to imitate the actions of serious or elevated men;
the shared themes and aim of epic and tragedy distinguished them from
such genres as mock-epic and comedy, while they were distinct from each
other in formal terms: epic was longer and greater in scope; it used a single
meter throughout which was intoned without the full musical range
employed in tragic odes or other songs such as the dithyramb; epic could
not dispense with an element of narrative. For Aristotle, these features and
the genres they marked were far from arbitrary conventions; on his view,
literary genres were rooted in natural aptitudes and appetites but evolved
historically as poets discovered the kinds of representations that most fully
and efficiently achieved their particular aims. (Aristotle notoriously
specified the aim of tragedy as a catharsis of pity and fear; some ancestral
form of this is often assumed to have been the aim of epic).[8] Aristotle's
teleological outlook disposed him to view epic in relation to tragedy, and
indeed to rank the later-arising form higher for its intense and economically
achieved effects (ch. 25). Yet he influentially singled out the *Iliad* and *Odyssey*
as paradigms of the epic art, and his acute observations on these poems[9]
came to have prescriptive force as canons, future poets would be wise to
observe: the most effective epics had been predominantly naturalistic

representations of the deeds of notable figures from legend; the stories were framed within a third-person, past-tense narrative, though the speeches of characters could be given in the first person; the plot, which could begin *in medias res*, normally progressed in a linear sequence, subsuming many episodes under a single main topic; large size, scope, and a relative degree of unity were valued.

Literary conceptions of genre clung to the poems when they entered Rome, where Homer remained a staple of liberal education and the proper approach to a classic work (the *praelectio*) demanded an understanding of its genre. By the time the poems had come to dominate Roman literary practice, Greek critics were speaking of 'epic poetry,' and Roman schoolmasters and littérateurs of *epicum poiema* and *epicus poeta*.[10] When Vergil subsumed the Greek models and critical ideas of epic in his *Aeneid*, Homer's name and the idea of epic were ensured a lasting place in the literary traditions of the Latin west. The rich and multifarious tradition of classical epic achieved its greatest prestige and most rigidly defined form in the seventeenth century, but it is worth remembering that a now canonical exemplar like *Paradise Lost* challenged that form as much as it continued it. The decline in the prestige and practice of formal epic after the eighteenth century did not entirely extinguish the genre, since Romantic long poems or modernist epic novels implicitly invoke the classical mold if only so that their departures from it may have snore force. Hence Aristotle's analysis of epic may be said to have shaped much of Western theory and literary practice from the fourth century B.C. through the present.

In the twentieth century the epic corpus expanded exponentially to accommodate traditional narratives from other cultures ranging from Bosnia, northern Russia, and Asia to the Americas and Africa. Interest in non-canonical epics can be traced to the eighteenth century, but the researches of Milman Parry and Albert Lord into how oral poems are composed and handed down gave a deeper understanding to the formal dynamics of such works. For example, Aristotle explains Greek epic's predilection for archaic and exotic words as a matter of choosing diction 'appropriate' to its dignified meter and themes (*Rhetoric* 1406b3; *Poetics* 1459b35); oral formulaic theory adds that many such forms were retained in the poetic language through centuries because they were ready to hand, metrically convenient, and inseparable from the tale as heard and performed. The study of epics as products of oral composition in performance has also made it possible to specify a further array of formal patternings which were, even if executed unthinkingly, so frequent as to have been hallmarks of the form: the paratactic style, composition by type-scenes, the use of formulaic expressions, extended similes, and ring composition.[11]

The comparative study of epic conceives of genre not as a series of texts linked in a conscious literary tradition but as a cross-cultural type or kind: in part because Aristotle had defined the form so influentially, the definition of oral epic is not substantially altered from his (a lengthy recitation, usually sung or chanted, which treats the quasi-historical exploits of notable heroes from the culture's past); but the sample from which such a definition is drawn makes it clear that each of its terms (length, recitation, history, heroes) is relative and is only fully significant in relation to specific cultural norms. Hence defining Homeric epic may include asking how the archaic Greek version of this kind of singing was conceived by its poets and understood by its earliest audiences.

An inquiry into the early conception of epic cannot confine itself to descriptive analysis. Terms that might be adequate to sort written texts into classes are not necessarily sufficient or even relevant for an oral culture in distinguishing kinds of songs (cf. Bynum [1976]; Rosenberg [1978]). Aspects of performance, for example, are less evident in a text than its formal properties, yet in Archaic Greece the social context in which songs were performed played a major role in determining their formal requirements. Outlining the sorts of considerations that went into classifying kinds of singing in Homer's time suggests that epic and all archaic Greek poems were defined in relation to four major categories: (1) the context of the song, (2) its 'form' or the ways it marked its language, (3) its 'contents' or themes, and (4) the relations between the poet and the audience. Let us consider these categories in order, devoting most attention to the latter two which will prove the most significant.

Like any complex society, Archaic Greece organized its singing along with the rest of social life, recognizing only certain kinds oh speech, rhythm, melody, and movement as appropriate on certain occasions. Thereby particular contexts generated corresponding types of song, with social and religious notions playing as large a role in their definition as formal and aesthetic criteria.[12] Most of the named kinds of songs in Homer are tied to particular ritual or communal occasions, such as the hymenaios (*Il.* 18.493) for weddings, the *threnos* (24.721) for funerals, or the *linos* song (18.570) for harvesting (see Diehl [1940]). But epic performance was confined to no particular settings, times or places. The poems suggest that such songs were particularly at home at banquets (*Od.* 8.99; cf. 9.2–11, 13.7–10), but other evidence makes it likely that epic poetry was also performed in the marketplace or at contests held in connection with funerals and national religious festivals (Kirk [1962] 274–81). The only contextual requirement for epic performance, then, appears to have been leisure, a break from normal business sufficient to hear a long account of ancient deeds.

The context of Archaic song also determined its formal requirements, for the kinds of music and rhythms favored in particular contexts depended both on the actions to be accompanied by the song (e.g., dancing, processions, pantomimes) and also on how performing roles were to be distributed among participants. *Threnoi*, for example, not only required suitably lugubrious themes and music, but also restricted solo singing to select participants based on their age, gender, and status relative to the deceased: in *threnos* described by Homer, women kin offered a short song to which the larger group responded antiphonally (Alexiou [1974]). This pattern in which a single performer 'leads' the rest of the group was used in other types of song as well and was marked with a particular word for 'leading'.[13] A different formal pattern folded all participants into one homogeneous choral group singing in unison: in Homer this is exemplified in the soldiers' paean, a collective prayer to Apollo: provided it expresses group solidarity, the paean is equally suitable in situations of distress (*Il.* 1.472–73) or of triumph (22.391–94). Epic performance would appear to represent the other extreme from these practices, to judge from the singers Homer represents: they perform solo, accompanying themselves on a stringed instrument;[14] there is normally no dancing, and the audience is specifically designated as still, seated in rapt silence (*Od.* 1.325–26). Although the music of epic performance can only be guessed at, the vocabulary for 'singing' indicates that it was a sort of recitative, felt to lie above plain speech but below fully melodic singing.[15] This mode of performance would have distinguished epic from the melodic songs the Greeks called μέλος (including most of what we call 'lyric' poetry), but not from solo recitatives in other stichic meters such as iambics and trochaics.

Neither performative contexts nor their formal requirements, then, gives us more than the most general definition of archaic Greek epic: we can only say that already for Homer it was a traditional kind of non-melic poetry, adaptable to many situations but identified with none and so without a particular name. What most obviously set epic apart from other non-melic forms in iambo-trochaic meters was the themes it treated. To turn to the contents of epics, the invocations offer important evidence.

Evidence from Homer and other early epics shows that the narrative proper was regularly announced with an invocation, a prayer that the Muse 'sing' or 'tell' a certain story; the invocation could be repeated later in the song to make a transition to new themes or inset pieces.[16] Invocations had a relatively set form: an imperative, vocative ('sing, Goddess,' 'tell me, Muse'), and a brief naming of the theme which would have served as a kind of title for the song: 'the Wrath of Achilles,' is Homer's title for what was called the *Iliad* in the classical period, and 'the Man of Many Turns ...' his title for the

Odyssey.[17] Other songs mentioned within the poems are identified in the same format (Ford [1992] 18–23): 'The Baleful Return of the Achaeans' (*Od.* 1.326–27), 'The Quarrel of Odysseus and Peleus' son Achilles' (8.75), 'The Destruction of the Achaeans / As much as they wrought and suffered and as much as the Achaeans toiled' (8.489–90), 'The Fashioning of the Wooden Horse' (8.500–501), 'The Destruction of the Argive Danaans and of Ilion' (8.578). Invocations next regularly emphasize the great scope of the action, its pathetic quality, the nations involved, and the presence of the gods throughout. At the end of the invocation the poet specifies from what point the tale is to begin: the *Iliad* is to be sung 'from the time when the son of Atreus and Achilles first stood apart in contention' (1.7–8); the poet of the *Odyssey* asks the Muse 'of these things, starting from some point, tell us now' (1.10).

The first seven lines of the *Iliad* and the first ten of the *Odyssey* promise a kind of poem that Bowra (1925) has well described as 'heroic epic.'[18] The poet's 'sing' or 'tell' means the song is fundamentally a narrative, as Aristotle noted (1462a16–17), although Homeric poetry is half dramatic speeches. The narrative will concern the actions of great men and women from the nation's past who suffered and strove beside the gods; it will be a large and complex story, but only a part of a much larger story that might be told. With the recognition that the Muse is taking up the story from a certain point, the poet reminds us, as Aristotle noted too (*Poetics* ch. 8), that any particular epic is carved out of a notionally larger whole. In Lord's words ([1960] 123), 'a song in tradition is separate, yet inseparable from other songs.' This larger story, even if only an abstraction, is significant because it would appear to constitute the theoretical limits of the epic repertoire, and limiting content is a major component in defining this genre.

To delimit the themes of epic for Homer means in the first instance describing the kinds of songs that the Muses inspire professional singers to sing. For among the many divinities (*Il.* 1.604; *Od.* 10.254) and mortals (*Il.* 1.473; *Od.* 14.464) who 'sing' in Homer, some are singled out as professional singers with the title ἀοιδοί. The word is only used of professional singers in Homer and Hesiod, those who may be listed among the society's itinerant craftsmen along with carpenters, seers, healers, and heralds (*Od.* 17.382–85).[19] The professional singers in Homer are masters of 'singing and dancing' (*Od.* 1.152) for any occasion: Priam summons *aoidoi* to the palace to 'lead' the threnos for Hector (*Il.* 24.720–22), and Odysseus can require a song to accompany a wedding dance from Phemius, the *aoidos* on Ithaca (*Od.* 23.133 ff.); Phemius seems to play and sing a *molpê* while the suitors sport (1.150–55), and the Phaeacian Demodocus can accompany acrobatic dancing by troops of young men (8.261–64) or perform a burlesque hymn in the agora (8.266 ff.). Nevertheless, to infer from this picture that the epic performer in Homer's time was a jack-of-all-songs may be erroneous. For it seems reasonable to suppose that poets would have had to specialize to produce epics of such length and complexity, and no melic poems were ascribed to Homer in Greek tradition.

Homer seems aware of a distinction between the singers' heroic narratives and the other kinds of song they provide when he describes Phemius' 'Return of the Achaeans' (*Od.* 1.328) and Demodocus' 'Destruction of the Achaeans' (8.498) with the formula, 'singing filled with the words of god.'[20] The epithet is also applied to professional singers, who are the only mortals said to be 'filled with the words of a god'[21] referring evidently to the central role the Muses have in defining this kind of poetry. For the modern observer, what made a professional epic poet was a long apprenticeship in learning its themes and style; in Homer's terms, it is the Muses who make some singers *aoidoi*, and presumably make their singing superior to that of amateurs.

The search for a Homeric term that would describe in general what poets sing has focused on the phrase κλέα ἀνδρῶν, as when Achilles sings 'the fames of men' to a lyre (*Il.* 9.189). The dedication of a kind of poetry to conferring 'fame' on its subjects derives from chic's very ancient connection with Indo-European praise poetry (Schmitt [1967] 61–102). Preserving and disseminating 'fame' was especially the concern of poets: *aoidoi* are said to 'confer fame' upon their subjects by celebrating them in song (*Od.* 1.338; cf. Hesiod *Theogony* 32; *Works and Days* 1); Hesiod speaks of an *aoidos* 'the servant of the Muses,' who 'celebrates the fames of earlier men' (*Theog.* 100; cf. *Hom. Hymn* 32.18–20). Although κλέα ἀνδρῶν is clearly a traditional term for oral heroic traditions, other uses of κλέος in Homer show that professional epic poets claimed to present these traditions with an authority unavailable even to Achilles.

The *Odyssey* offers valuable evidence for the way poets regarded their repertoire when Homer describes a poet beginning a heroic theme:

> the Muse then stirred up the singer to sing the fames of men
> from that *oimê* whose fame at that time reached broad heaven,
> the Quarrel of Odysseus and Achilles, son of Peleus,
> how they once contended with each other at the rich feast of the gods
> *Od.* 8.73–76

An individual story a bard might perform, such as 'the Quarrel of Odysseus and Achilles,' is here given the quasi-technical name οἴμη, possibly understood metaphorically as a 'path' of song.[22] A professional poet like

Phemius knows many such stories: 'the Muse has made οἶμαι of every kind grow in my heart' (*Od.* 22.347–48; cf. 8.479–81). The aggregate of οἶμαι are the κλέα ἀνδρῶν (8.73). The κλέα ἀνδρονῶν, however, include any account of earlier men of note, not just those purveyed by poets. Κλέος basically means 'what is heard,' and κλέα include whatever is handed down from mouth to ear. Indeed, simply as 'what is heard,' κλέος may be casual talk, second-hand report, or mere rumor (e.g., *Od.* 3.83; 4.317; 16.461; 23.137).[23] Phoenix tells, without 'singing' and without invoking the Muses, an old story about Meleager which he ascribes to the 'fames of men': 'so we hear tell of the fames of men of long ago, the heroes' (*Il.* 9.524–5). Genealogies may circulate in the same way, and are identified with κλέα when Aeneas compares his lineage with Achilles':

> We know each other's lineage, we know each other's parents
> from hearing the sayings that have been heard before among
>   mortal men;
> but as for actually seeing them, you have never seen my parents,
>   nor I yours.
>
>   *Il.* 20.202–204

Oral genealogical traditions arise as each generation 'hears' from the one before, and not particularly from singers, the names of ancestors. But Aeneas significantly contrasts such knowledge (202) as mortals may have of their past with the first-hand knowledge an eye-witness might have (204). This opposition is significant because Homer uses it at a key point to distinguish his own inspired poetry from humanly transmitted κλέα ἀνδρῶν as a source of knowledge about the past.

In his extended invocation to the catalogue of ships Homer distinguishes the account his Muses inspire from the general run of oral tradition: 'For you [Muses] are goddesses, and are present, and know all / but we hear only and do not know anything' (*Iliad* 2.485–6). The Muses 'know' these things in the root sense of that word, they 'have seen' them and so bring the authority of eye-witnesses to the events of which the poet wishes to speak. The poet and his generation do not 'know' the past in this way; for them, as for Aeneas, knowledge of the past without the Muses is mere report. These same distinctions are deployed in the *Odyssey* when the hero praises a heroic singer: 'very rightly you sing the destruction of the Achaeans ... as if you had been there in person or had heard about them from someone who was' (*Od.* 8.489–91). The implication is that the blind bard has an eyewitness' knowledge from the Muses.

Among the functions of the Muses, then, is to underwrite the claim by professional poets that their songs about the past are superior to the many other accounts available in the society. The Muses' favor and assistance make the difference between 'mere' κλέος and θέσπις ἀοιδή. Although the poet and the gentleman hero may share an interest in the fames of men, the poet's status depends on confining 'true' epic to what the Muses give. Accordingly, the range of epic is the range of songs that Muses inspire *aoidoi* to sing. Bowra's notion of 'heroic epic' well expresses the ethos of these poems, but a comparison with the Hesiodic corpus suggests that the range of 'heroic' song should be interpreted broadly.

Although the preeminence of the *Iliad* and *Odyssey* may incline us to identify θέσπις ἀοιδή with heroic poetry, the range of themes the Muses inspire is in fact wider. After all, Hesiod also invokes the Muses, and much of the poetry that went under his name shares the diction, meter, dialect, and legends to be found in Homer. A consideration of Hesiodic poetry shows that the repertoire of the Muses' singer extended beyond the doings of 'heroes,' and that it is better defined, in Homer's terms, as 'the deeds of gods and men that singers celebrate' (*Od.* 1.338) or, in Hesiod's terms, as 'the fames of men of former times/and the blessed gods who hold Olympus' (*Theog.* 100–101).

It used to be common to distinguish between an Ionian (Homeric) 'school' of heroic epic and a Boeotian (Hesiodic) school of didactic or catalogue poetry. But the opposition of epic to didactic is wholly inapplicable to the Archaic period,[24] and such a gross dichotomy obscures important conceptual affinities that Homer's poetry had with at least some of Hesiod's (Thalmann [1984] xi–xiii, 75–77). The epic singer, after all, must be knowledgeable (*Od.* 1.337–39), and later Greece put Homer on an equal footing with Hesiod as a teacher.[25] Moreover, the *Theogony* at least (I postpone discussion of *Works and Days*) is closer to Homer's poems than a strict epic/didactic dichotomy allows. In its proem Hesiod appears very much like a Homeric singer: he learned the art of singing, from the Muses (*Theog.* 22; cf. *Od.* 8.481; 488) who breathed into him a 'voice filled with the words of a god' (*Theog.* 31–32). He initiates his theme in much the same fashion as Homer, invoking the Muses to 'celebrate the holy race of the gods' and bidding them to 'tell me these things... from the beginning' (*Theog.* 104–115). Hesiod's theme is undoubtedly sacred history, but it is also a narrative of noteworthy deeds, and deeds that are far from unconnected to heroic history.

A bridge between the Hesiodic *Theogony* and Homeric epic is provided by his *Ehoiai* or *Catalogue of Women* which is blended into the end of our *Theogony*. After the ascendancy of the Olympians is secured, the *Theogony* changes its theme with a transitional invocation at 963–68: 'sing the tribe of goddesses ... who lay with mortal men and produced godlike children.' Another invocation at 1019–22 switches to the converse of this theme, asking for the 'race of [mortal] women' who consorted with gods and the heroic descendants of these unions. With this latter invocation a transition is effected to the *Catalogue of Women*.[26] What we may call Homer's 'heroic' tales follow logically and chronologically on this *Theogony–Catalogue* continuum: one divine–mortal union that was recounted in the *Catalogue* (at some length and with a dramatic speech) was that of Thetis and Peleus (Fr. 210–211 M-W), but the union of Achilles' parents is equally an epic theme, as in the cyclic *Cypria*. From this perspective, epics appear not as secular stories about heroic mortals as opposed to gods, but as later stories in a single continuous history. The same comprehensive vision informed the epic cycle, which not only filled in the prologue and aftermath of the Trojan war but reached back to describe the Titanomachy and perhaps too the birth of the gods.[27]

Firm distinctions begin to become perilous here, for one may usefully describe the catalogue poem as a separate genre, a type of poetry that may be paralleled in Greece and elsewhere.[28] Even on such a view, however, catalogue poetry will often function as sub-genre or narrative mode within epic: the catalogue style, for example, is also at home in telling tales of Troy (e.g. *Il.* 2.484 ff., 1.2.89–104), and Homer no less than Hesiod may need to list a number of rivers (*Il.* 12.17–23; cf. *Theog.* 337–45) or Nereids (*Il.* 18.37–49; cf. *Theog.* 240–64). Even the characters within heroic narratives may have reason to list their ancestors at some length (e.g. *Il.* 6.150–211, 20.200–258). In a notable passage from Odysseus' account of his visit to the underworld (*Od.* 11.225–332), the hero catalogues for his audience the noble women he saw there, thus taking up the themes and much of the manner of a poem like the *Catalogue of Women*.

Whether one wishes to view catalogue poetry as a distinct genre or as a mode of heroic narrative, Hesiod's *Theogony* and *Catalogue of Women* suggest that theogonies were not set apart as distinctively didactic poems but were, like Homeric epic, narrative and sometimes dramatic accounts of earliest history. In the repertoire of the Muses, the κλέα ἀνδρῶν were connected to theogonies, and the whole embraced a discrete mythic epoch beginning with the birth of the gods and ending when the Trojan war resulted in a breach of the close intercourse between gods and mortals (Hesiod Fr. 1.6 ff. and Fr. dub. 264; cf. *Od.* 7.201–203). Although some nobles at epic performances may have claimed descent from the great dynasties mentioned, their world was irretrievably cut off from that age, most obviously because the gods no longer mixed as freely with mortals on earth.[29]

Archaic epic, then, was significantly defined by the themes it could treat. The Homeric and Hesiodic conception of Muse-inspired poetry was based on this mythic age and not on a division between poetry about mortals versus poetry about gods (which is essentially, and perhaps originally, a Platonic way of dividing poetry).[30] The restriction of epic to themes from this imaginary time held force for a very long time in Greece; as far as we can see, it was not breached until the fifth century when Choerilus of Samos, with much fanfare in his proem about innovation, gave epic treatment to Greece's wars with Persia.

Other poems attributed to Hesiod appear to have been Muse-inspired narratives of ancient times, such as the *Marriage of Ceyx*, *Descent of Pirithous*, and *Aegimus*. Yet to call all of Hesiod 'epic' may be reductive: if we consider the fourth respect in which archaic poetry defined itself, the poet's relation to the audience, we will realize that Greek epic also involved a quite distinctive rhetorical stance of the poet toward his audience.

Hesiod's *Works and Days* begins with an invocation and so might be immediately taken as a form of Muse-inspired epic. But this invocation is in fact the reverse of those in Homer and the *Theogony*, and it establishes a relationship between poet and addressee that differs vastly from that of epic's to its audience. Hesiod bids the Muses to perform, but not to perform the *Works and Days*. They are asked to tell of Zeus and celebrate his justice (1 ff.): at the end of the proem, the poet turns to a certain Perses and proclaims that 'I would tell [you] true things' (10). The actual poem will thus be Hesiod's speech to his brother, not the speech of the Muses.[31] This is not to say that the poet wished to sever his own song form from the true and authoritative song of the goddesses, but it does mean that *Works and Days* will not be a narrative, a fact reinforced by its many subsequent addresses to Perses. Hesiod will relate parts of divine and heroic history (such as the stories of Pandora and Prometheus), but always as a particular speaker advising a particular auditor, in order to draw lessons about what Perses should do in this morally ordered cosmos.[32] By contrast, Homer's epics and Hesiod's extended narratives present stories of the past in the first instance as coming from the lips of the Muses, and never explicitly indicate how to apply these tales to their auditors' lives.[33] Whereas the *Works and Days* establishes a highly individualized persona for both poet and addressee (as, presumably, the *Precepts of Cheiron* did also), the epic narrator's relation to his audience is far less specific: its projected audience is a nameless collectivity, a weaker and more ignorant generation of mortals living long after the heroes (e.g., *Il.* 5.302–304; 12.380–83).

These differences in the way the poet orients himself to his audience suggest that the *Works and Days* is less close to the *Theogony* than to other hortatory, non-narrative Hesiodic poems such as the *Precepts of Cheiron, Bird Divination*, and *Astronomy*. Slicing up genres is particularly perilous here, but much as these poems may share with epic in diction, meter, dialect, legends, and morals, the personas of poet and addressee are quite different, and their themes could hardly be summed up as ἔργ᾽ ἀνδρῶν τε θεῶν τε, τά τε κλείουσιν ἀοιδοί. When Greeks wished to draw a clear distinction between Homer and Hesiod, the latter's poetry is exemplified with *Works and Days* as forming a clear contrast to Homer: Aristophanes' list of useful ancient poets includes Hesiod who taught 'working the land, seasons and harvests and farming' and Homer, the teacher of 'battle formations, courage, and armor.'[34] Whatever name or status one may wish to give these Hesiodic works, they clearly derive from a different tradition than epic, one that may be called 'wisdom poetry' (M. L. West [1978] 3–25). To be sure, the hortatory mode of wisdom poetry may appear in epic too: Phoenix is giving instruction through heroic legend when he recounts the Meleager story to Achilles (9.524605). Once incorporated into the *Iliad*'s hexameters, the Meleager tale may look like an 'epic within an epic'; but the whole is preceded and followed by direct, second–person instructions to Achilles on how to apply the story to his situation (9.513–23, 600–605). In a somewhat subtle variant, Nestor tells Patrochis one of his own youthful exploits (*Il.* 11.670–761): this Pylian cattle raid is recounted with typically heroic form and structure (see Hainsworth [1991] 22); but it is presented as the personal reminiscence of an elder warrior to a youth, and it is framed with pointed remarks contrasting Achilles' present behavior (11.663–668, 761–63).[35]

Archaic Greek epic must thus be defined in formal, thematic, and rhetorical terms. It was a long, solo song performed in a rhythmical recitative; it narrated on the authority of the Muses the deeds of gods and early heroes. The themes epic treated, the 'paths' it could take, were extensive but firmly circumscribed by a mythic conception of a long-lost golden age. The stories were presented dramatically and without explicit cues for how to apply them to their auditors' lives. This discreet attitude toward its audience and its lack of a fictional addressee distinguished epic from exhortative recitatives such as the *Works and Days*; it also would have distinguished epic from such melic poetry as offered extended mythic narrative but explicitly applied the stories to the present ceremony and community.[36] The combination of this limited range of themes, the poet's discreet way of rendering them, and the solo recitative was sufficient to distinguish epic formally and thematically from all contemporary lyric songs and from all non-narrative recitations.

Having achieved this much of a definition of epic in Archaic terms, it remains to add that manipulating these shared conventions offered the poet possibilities for subtly expressive effects. A simple but resonant example is Odysseus' deliberate misapplication of the rules governing wedding songs. After the slaughter of the suitors, Odysseus commands Phemius to produce a wedding song so that passersby might infer that Penelope has at last decided to marry (*Od.* 23.133 ff.). By applying a specific kind of song to the wrong context the hero strategically miscommunicates what has gone on in the palace. A wedding song is hardly what one expects to follow a blood bath, and yet such a song is ironically appropriate when the hero is about to be reunited with his wife.

In a more subtle example Homer discreetly evokes the Archaic genre of maiden's songs (later called *partheneia*) to provide a background to the scene of Odysseus' first meeting with Nausicaa. When the hero first spies the princess, she is amusing herself by playing a ball game with her maids and leading them in an antiphonal song and dance (*Od.* 6.101). The narrator does not tell us the song's theme but gives the performance a specific coloration when he compares it to the virgin goddess Artemis sporting with her nymphs in the wild (6.102–109). Such a conceit was typical in maiden's songs, which could be performed antiphonally and for which Artemis and her chorus provided a divine archetype.[37] The tableau moves Odysseus to make the same comparison and to venture how well Nausicaa must dance in choruses; he adds that his only comparable experience was on Delos, which was famed for its women's choirs (6.151–63). Once again these subtle intimations of non-epic song are particularly appropriate to the scene, for the partheneion ceremony functioned as a kind of 'coming out' ball in which well-born women might attract the amorous glance of a spectator (cf. *Il.* 16.179–83), and the possibility of taking this princess to wife will soon present itself in the story.

The *Iliad* exhibits a particular versatility in exploiting another non-epic genre, the *threnos*. In drawing to a close, the poem modulates from epic narrative to first-person women's lament with a protracted presentation of the threnodies for Hector (24.723–776). It exploits this genre both for its themes of pathos (a tone also borrowed for the speeches of Andromache and Hecuba in *Iliad* 6) and for its antiphonal structure which allows Helen herself, as the final threnodist, to reflect on the war being fought for her sake. But the conventions of the *threnos* are significantly evoked throughout in the *Iliad*, especially in connection with the death of Patroclus. At Patroclus' lavish funeral in book 23, his comrade-in-arms Achilles 'leads' laments while the Myrmidons in full panoply respond (23.1–17). The verb suggests that Patroclus is being given a formal *threnos*, at least insofar as the battlefield allows. Earlier uses of the word place this male *threnos* for Patroclus in a series of more or less spontaneous laments which anticipate, albeit imperfectly, the final ceremony of 23. When Patroclus' body was being prepared, Achilles embraced the corpse and 'led' lamentations for the Achaeans who groaned in response (18.314–17, 354–55). This spontaneous lament resembles a *threnos*, though it is not formally constituted as one; and Achilles promises Patroclus another lament, that women will mourn him (18.338–42). This comes true in an unforeseen way: Briseis catches a glimpse of the body and 'leads' a lament to which her companions respond with groans (19.282–302). The multiplication of these scenes (also 19.314–39) dramatically emphasizes the loss Achilles feels rather than reflecting any precise set of funeral practices (M. W. Edwards [1986]). Two further quasi-antiphonies which begin the series suggest that the poet keeps returning to the form as a way of exploring how raw suffering may be transmuted into artistic structure. When news of Patroclus' death is first announced, Achilles falls to the ground in an orgy of grief, groaning, and self-defilement. These sounds arouse the captive women in his tent who come running and collapse around him beating their breasts (18.22–31). The actions are perfectly comprehensible in themselves even as the tableau suggests an antiphonal lament; it is as if the poet is deliberately superposing on the elemental and impassioned expression of grief its most proper and ceremonious form (its genre). That form is soon repeated when Thetis hears the cries and comes with her Nereids to comfort the hero. Taking Achilles' head in her arms, in another conventional gesture of mourning (18.72; cf. 24.712, 724), she 'leads the groaning' for the nymphs who beat their breasts in response (18.50–51). Her ensuing complaint (18.52–64) thus becomes at once highly pathetic and a generic anomaly: a god's lament in prospect for the son she knows will die. The *threnos*, then, serves the poet of the *Iliad* as a source of pathetic themes, as an evocative pattern for structuring action, and as a way to intimate the great pathos of an event that lies beyond the limits of the story he has to tell.

Generic conventions offer no less suggestive material when the genre being represented is epic itself. The *Iliad* does not show us epic singers performing; Priam has professional singers summoned to Hector's funeral, though their singing is not subsequently described (24.721–22). Their presence, however, suggests that epic's noble pedigree reaches back even to praises offered heroes at funerals, an idea that may contain a grain of truth.[38] The *Odyssey* offers more extensive representations of epic singing which dramatize Homer's definition of epic, affirming the distinction drawn above between epic and non-inspired accounts of the past.

The *Odyssey* twice suggestively juxtaposes epic song to nonpoetic accounts of heroic deeds: in book 1, Phemius sings about the return of the heroes while Telemachus privately discusses the same topic with a well-traveled guest (in reality, a disguised Athena); on Phaeacia, Odysseus praises

Demodocus as a nonpareil epic performer, their goes on to recount his own adventures in a kind of 'prose' sequel to the poet's Trojan tales. In both cases the unique access that the Muses give to the past for Homer's generation is ironically reaffirmed: if epic poetry was once an entertainment worthy of heroes, it will be all the more valuable in a post-heroic age when gods do not so readily appear on earth bearing news, and heroes no longer give their own accounts of their actions. The contrast between song in a heroic context and song in Homer's own day is further underlined by the response of the audience. Penelope's tears at Phemius' song are set against the pleasure taken in the same song by the suitors, and Odysseus' repeated sobbing at songs of Troy provokes the curiosity of the pacific and music-loving Phaeacians (1.325 ff:, 8.83 ff.). For non-heroic mortals, pleasure is the normal response to epic: when a man hears songs about earlier men, 'straight away he forgets his sad thoughts and does not think about his cares' (Hesiod, *Theog.* 102–103); even an embittered Achilles finds pleasure (*Il.* 9.189) in the κλέα ἀνδρῶν because the men in question are of former times. Because Penelope and Odysseus are not of the generation of later mortals, but are personally involved in the actions described in song their response differs heroically from the norm.[39]

A final outstanding example of Homer manipulating the conventions of his own genre is Odysseus' apologos in *Odyssey* 9–12. In a tour de force the poet assumes a persona which liberates him from three fundamental conventions of epic narrative: he narrates the story in the first person; as a vagabond sailor, he incorporates fantastic and supernatural tales otherwise out of place in Homeric poetry; finally, he boldly flashes back to tell at length events that preceded the beginning of the poem. But we are not quite allowed to forget the epic narrator who has modulated his own voice into that of his character. Odysseus too casts a singer's spell over his audience (*Od.* 11.333–34 = 13.1–2; cf. 1.337–40), and King Alcinous explicitly compares him to a singer (11.363–69). If the *apologos* reveals to the Pheacians that the apparent vagabond is really a hero, it also reminds Homer's audience that behind this hero stands a poet no less skilled in disguising himself.

Our ability to appreciate the ways in which Homer relies on and exploits his contemporaries' notions of genre rests on a very limited sample of Archaic songs. Although there is much we cannot know, nonetheless we may claim that a notion of epic genre helped the poet to guide the expectations of his audience and helped the audience place new songs in relation to ones it had heard. If at times the conventions of epic were pressed to their limits, the result would still be an epic, a tale of the vast but not infinite past delivered by the Muses to the skillfully recreative singer.

118   Andrew Ford

NOTES

1. Valuable overviews of the classical epic tradition are Newman (1986); Hainsworth (1991).

2. For an introduction to the vast and ongoing research on oral poetics, see A. B. Lord, 'Oral Poetry' in *The New Princeton Encyclopedia of Poetry and Poetics*, ed. A. Preminger and T. V. F. Brogan (Princeton, 1993), 863–66.

3. A. Fowler (1982) argues powerfully for the continuing usefulness of genre criticism in these terms.

4. Cf. Webster (1953) 91–135.

5. Kirk (1976) 19–39; M. L. West (1988).

6. Because the poet's essential task is not versification but imitation: *Poetics* 1447a28–47b23; cf. 1451a37–b5, 1451b27–29.

7. *Poetics* 1459b31–60a1. Cf. Aristotle's brief formulas for epic: 'the mimetic art in hexameters' (1449b21) or 'the art of narrative imitation in recited meter' (1459a17).

8. On Aristotle's notion of genre, see Rosenmeyer (1985).

9. Surveyed in Hogan (1973).

10. Cicero, *de Opt. Gen.* 1, 2; Quintilian, *Inst.* 10.1.51, 62 (where the broad range of 'epic' poets is noteworthy). The Greek phrase is first attested in Dionysius of Halicarnassus, *On Composition* 22 (where it is a very probable emendation); on ἔπος as a name for the genre (e.g., Horace, *Satires* 1.10.43), see Koster (1970) 86–91.

11. For a full description, see M. W. Edwards (1987) 29–123.

12. R. P. Martin (1989) 43–44 argues that 'social genres' are primary and that literary genres vary according to a society's ideas of performance.

13. E.g., *Il.* 24.723 (Hector's mother 'leads off' the laments for her son); *Od.* 4.15–19 (a musician and tumblers lead a wedding song); Archilochus leads the Dithyramb and the 'Lesbian Paean' (120, 121, M. L. West, ed., *Iambi et Elegi Graeci*, Second edition [Oxford 1992]). Further varieties in *Lexicon des Frügriechischen Epos*, ed. B. Snell et al. (Göttingen, 1979–) s.v. ἄρχω, B I 2e and B II 2 (Hereafter, *LfgrE*).

14. On musical instruments in Homer, see Barker (1984) 4–17, 25. By the Classical period, epic performers had dispensed with the lyre altogether; how early this occurred is unclear: see M. L. West (1966) on Hesiod *Theog.* 30. G. Nagy (1990b) 21–24 cautions that the portrayal of poets in Homer may not directly reflect contemporary practice in every respect.

15. For a musical reconstruction of epic recitative, see M. L. West (1981), who also discusses the terms for singing.

16. In addition to *Il.* 1.1–7 and *Od.* 1.1–10, cf. Hesiod *Theog.* 104–115; *Thebais* fr. 1, ed. M. Davies (1988); Antimachus; *Thebais* fr. 1 Wyss. Transitional invocations: *Il.* 2.484 ff:, 2.761–62, 11.218–20, 14.508–510, 16.112–13; Hesiod *Theog.* 965–68, 1021–2. See especially Fränkel (1975) 6–25.

17. Cf. Lord (1960) 99: 'When one asks a singer what songs he knows, he will begin by saying that he knows the song, for example, about Marko Kraljevic when he fought with Musa, or he will identify it by its first lines.'

18. Cf. Hainsworth (1993) 32–53.

19. *LfgrE* s.v. ἀοιδός and ἀοιδή.

20. Cf. *Il.* 2.600, *Od.* 12.158; *Hom. Hymn Hermes* 442.

21. *Od.* 17.385; cf. Hesiod fr. 310.2 R. Merkelbach and M. L. West, *Fragmenta Hesiodea* (Oxford, 1967), hereafter M-W.

22. On the meaning and etymology of *oimê*, see Ford (1992) 42 n. 78 and the literature there cited; a different view in Nagy (1990b) 28.

23. Cf. Redfield (1975) 32–34.

24. The most influential formulation was the fourth-century grammarian Diomedes: E. R. Curtius, *European Literature and the Latin Middle Ages*, tr. W. R. Trask (Princeton, 1973) 440. Cf. W. Kroll, 'Lehrgedichte,' *Pauly-Wissowa Realencyclopädie der classischen Altertumswissenschaft* 12.2 (1925) 1843.

25. For Homer as teacher: Xenophanes B 10 DK (H. Diels and W. Kranz, *Die Fragmente der Vorsokratiker*, 6th ed. [Berlin, 1952]); Heraclitus B 56. Xenophanes paired Homer with Hesiod in denouncing their portrayal of gods: B 11, A 1.18 DK; Herodotus joined them as the source of Greek ideas about the gods (2.53).

26. Hesiod fr. 1 M-W. On these transitions, see M. L. West (1985) 49, 126–27.

27. Bernabé (1988) 8; against any recoverable cyclic *Theogony*, see Davies (1989) 13.

28. M. L. West (1985) 3–11.

29. M. L. West (1985) 9–11, 29–30, remarks that early Greek catalogue poems are relatively unusual among other genealogical traditions in concentrating on the heroic age and not continuing lineages up to the 'present' time.

30. The differentiation of 'hymns' for gods from 'encomia' for mortals is found first in Plato (*Republic* 607a, etc.); see Càssola (1975) x–xii.

31. The gnomological *Theognidea* also opens by addressing the Muses and other deities before the poet resumes the first person to direct advice to a certain Cyrnos (esp. 27 ff.).

32. Because the story of the *Theogony* involves the founding of the moral order of the world, it too sometimes briefly comments on the present effects of past actions, as when Oath is characterized as 'the one who most vexes perjurers on earth' (231–32). But even in lengthier excursuses on why the world works as it does now (e.g. the moralizing that follows the Prometheus–Pandora story, 590–616), the *Theogony* avoids appealing to a 'you' and quickly resumes its narrative thrust (cf. 612).

33. De Jong (1987a) shows the many ways in which the epic narrator may to move away from the impersonal voice of the Muse and closer to his audience, but always to a degree of involvement that falls far short of direct exhortation.

34. *Frogs* 1033–36; Hesiod wins the *Contest of Homer and Hesiod* (233.207–210 Allen) on the grounds that he calls the people to 'farming and peace' whereas Homer urges them on to 'war and slaughter' (see Rosen, this vol.).

35. The dramatic situation of this moral instruction suggests, again, the *Precepts of Cheiron*, and even more strongly Hippias of Elis' 'Trojan Oration,' which he performed (at schools) as a prose sermon from Nestor to the young Neoptolemos (Plato, *Hipp. Maj.* 286B).

36. On the generic relations between epic and lyric narratives in the Archaic period, see Burkert (1987).

37. See Calame (1977) II, 90–91; Ford (1992) 118–19.

38. Reiner (1938) 62–67, 116–20; Bowra (1952) 8–10.

39. A related ironic reversal of a fundamental epic norm is Telemachus' defending Phemius' heroic theme on the grounds that men love best the 'newest' song (*Od.* 1.350–52). Only in a heroic age can epic be 'new.'

RICHARD GOTSHALK

The Homeric Transformation of Bardic Poetry

Although the later Greek tradition knew a difference of opinion as to when Homer lived, and indeed, knew little with assurance about him, it is without suspicion of a Homeric problem as this has come to be defined in modern times. I shall only mention in passing that controversy, which is focused on such things as whether the two poems which the Greeks attributed to a man named Homer were indeed the work of one man, and what the original forms of the poems were. For my purposes, it is enough simply to state what seems most plausible to me: that a bard named Homer flourished in the last half of the 8th century,[1] that he was Ionian (born, perhaps, at Smyrna or on Chios, and at least closely associated with them both), and that he composed the two monumental epics attributed to him (the *Iliad* and the *Odyssey*).[2] As works of oral poetry, the two were of colossal length.[3] A bard working within an extended tradition of shorter poetry would have occasions for performance which also offered the opportunity for longer works; such were the religious festivals like those at Mykale (the Panionia) and on Delos.[4] But judging from the dramatic unity and coherence of these long works, the reason for their creation must lie not simply in some opportunity but more importantly in the poet himself,[5] in the desire and need to express a broad and coherent vision of life which he felt to be of significance for his contemporaries. The advantage taken of the opportunity

From *Homer and Hesiod, Myth and Philosophy*. © 2000 by University Press of America.

to create long works seems to have been unique to this one poet, and its effect likewise unique. If Homer flourished in that transition time between a pre-literate and a literate society, and if the poems he made are later saved—and relatively fixed—by being written down,[6] his is a work which bears its greatest fruit in a society which is becoming literate, without its being a literary work itself. The text which we have coming in, the end from Alexandrian sources, was written down in Athens at the instigation of Pisistratus and in connection with his attempt to give to the local festival to the goddess Athena a more 'national' appeal. The poems (in both their oral transmission after Homer and in their written forms up until their reconstitution and fixation in Alexandrian times) have undergone some modification (changes, interpolations) but of a minor and (for the most part) readily detectable sort. Their basic character and structure, and their overall internal unity, remain intact.[7]

What is the transformation wrought by Homer with these two poems? And what are the basic issues set by them, for one who would understand the beginnings of philosophy among the Greeks?

A. The Transformation: Monumental Epic

The basic transformation is made manifest in two features of the poetry.

One is the amplitude of the scope of the story-telling as well as of the length of the poem.

The other is the development of a main story-line which involves a complex of agents, events and deeds, but which centers on the inward transformations which the central figures (Achilleus and Odysseus) undergo in the course of what they achieve in their participation in such events and deeds.[8]

Through their scope and length, the poems celebrate a whole world—that of the heroic protagonists of the past, and of their gods. That celebration lays emphasis upon life's splendor and variety, the ambivalence of human mortality, an ordered working of divine powers,[9] and a peculiar closeness of human and divine interlinking in the tension of kinship and difference.[10]

In the main story line of each poem, the heart of the drama concerns something inward to the heroic assumption of life.[11] In particular, life in its heroic realization is an adventure, participation in which is the medium for a growth and maturation in the mortals involved. But it is growth in an individual humanity through which, on the basis of their commitment to an aspiration to reach for the highest, human beings are to become established in a community with each other. More fully and accurately: it is a community

not simply of human beings with each other but also with the gods, in which
community justice is to be honored and hold sway and recognition of high
achievement is to be accorded by the highest and best (of human beings and
gods) to the highest and best. One must grow capable, individually, of being
such a human being as can assume responsibility and share in such a
communal realization of human life in such a world.[12]

In two poems with such features, Homer transforms bardic narrative
concerning the human past into a vehicle for expressly bringing the existence
which is problematic for human beings to the fore in its wholeness and for
offering a coherent vision—or more precisely, a re-visioning, a re-vision of
the traditional vision—of that existence in its meaning. Wholeness here does
not mean completeness; there are facets of life and experience, aspects of
things, forms of knowledge and achievement, which are ignored. Wholeness
means the inclusive unity of an ordered universe of diverse powers in whose
life and existence something is at stake. In that universe the problematic of
meaning for human life and effort is not intelligible apart from a reference
to the inclusion of the human in the whole and to the manner of achievement
of this inclusion. It is this embracing vision of reality and meaningful life in
it that is offered by Homer to his contemporaries—to all Greeks caught up
in the resurgence of 8th century life and involved in the formation of new
interconnections with each other. It is this vision that is to be educative for
them concerning the way in which, with the help of their efforts, the promise
of the future may—indeed, is meant to—be brought to pass.[13]

The accomplishment of this transformation involves certain further
striking structural and stylistic features which not only point into the overall
meaning of the narrative but enable a contemporary Greek audience to find
it coming home to them more pointedly and forcefully than otherwise.

As for the structural features: Both poems could be formed as
narratives which unfold in straightforward chronological order. But neither
is. Each involves a temporal dislocation which points to the drama as Homer
would have his audience hear it and keys the listener to that transformation
of the bardic legend-telling which he is effecting.

In the *Iliad*, a ten-year war together with some of its antecedents is
brought into view in the course of the narration of the main story-line, which
unfolds in a fifty-four day sequence somewhere toward the close of the war.
It is not out of the ordinary that important events or conditions
chronologically located in times before and after the sequence being narrated
are alluded to in the course of narration. But it is unusual, and awkward, that
the events within the sequence itself include matters that would,

chronologically, have happened before the main sequence starts; yet they are brought forward as if they were happening within that segment. And thus in the account an affair which involved most of the known world, and which preceded and succeeded the main drama temporally, is placed in a dramatically subordinate position to deeds and sufferings (the wrath of Achilleus) which, in fact, are relatively small affairs within the larger affair. A straightforward chronological narration would risk being dispersed among the many events, and in any case would not convey what Homer wished to convey. That emerges only in the register of this peculiar dyschronological counterpoint of larger event and what is at stake in it as regards the larger world, with the lesser event of the wrath of Achilleus and the sufferings which he brings on himself and others through it. On the background of the effort to uphold the norms of the heroic world and to enforce respect upon Paris and the Trojans, Homer would focus his audience upon Achilleus himself becoming educated in the meaning of honor and respect (*aidôs*). More specifically, he would display the manifold ways in which diverse individuals take their own lives upon themselves and participate in the embracing world, with that manifold both highlighting by contrast this matter of how a mortal human life may become invested with meaning, and being highlighted in return by light out of the depths of what happens to Achilleus.

In the *Odyssey*, there are two chronological dislocations which again point into the heart of the story as Homer would have the audience attend to it. The first: the nine-year return journey of Odysseus is not brought into view in straightforward narration, but in a retrospective account by Odysseus himself, given at a time close to its end. The second: there is the account of what is happening to Telemachus as he is coming of age, given first place in the order of narration despite the dyschronology this entails and despite the initial focus upon the much lesser figure that placing this narrative first involves. And yet, as the narrative brings together the two, father and son, middle-aged man and youth entering upon manhood, to join in tine final deed through which Odysseus arrives home, it has thereby brought them forward as each entered upon a crucial turn in life's unfolding, and at crucial places in the process of discovering what it means for a mortal human being to dwell at home on earth.

The temporal dislocations to which I have just briefly pointed are not simply unusual narrative devices, but are also pointers into the way Homer is transforming the content of the legendary, bringing the deeds and heroes into a distinctive deeper focus, and inviting his audience to discover and share a vision contemporary and futural in its bearing. They not only disappoint our expectations of straightforward chronological narrative but they do so in such way as helps bring our attention to this matter of time in another reference, that of our growth as human beings.

As for stylistic features: Both poems utilize a multitude of modes of holding together diverse broad features and elements in the world and pointing to them in their unity yet contrast: past and present, war and peace, older and younger, earlier and later generations, gods and human beings, and others. More precisely, they utilize modes of integration which help to link the audience in the present with events in the past and to strengthen the pressure to reflect upon this matter of human life as a temporal affair in which something of ultimate importance is at stake.

One of the most significant modes, more extensive in the *Iliad* than in the *Odyssey* because of the relatively limited and intense sphere of action involved and the relatively greater need for contrast by some device subordinate to narrative, is the use of similes.[14] Illuminating the heroic by likenesses which draw on the contemporary world, Homer not only brings the past alive for his hearers with the help of the present, but subtly strengthens the invitation to respond to the drama reflectively in focus on the likeness and contrast of past and present.[15]

This linkage of past and present, and the call to reflection on the meaning of the difference, ranges more widely than the use of similes.[16] There is some modernization in regard to various things. In the *Iliad*, it may concern the depiction of a city, or of warfare and weapons, for example. References to Ionia, or the Anatolian littoral, in and beyond similes, are common; and indications of interests beyond battle are colored by Ionian experience.[17] In the *Odyssey*, it may concern sizing up land as suitable for colonization, or the discovery of an expanding world with novel things to experience distant from the past. In both poems, it may involve numerous small points of dress, work, trade, and custom, in which the past is clothed in present-day garb.

The linking of past and present is given a further color and emphasis by the way the other contrasts I noted above bring forward the major dimensions of life on earth with a peculiarly temporal tenor. War and peace not only embrace the major alternative conditions of collective human existence, but call such existence to mind as involving something at stake. Older and younger, earlier and later generations, call to mind the temporality of the existence: in which that stake is to be gained or lost. And the contrast of gods and human beings, of 'immortals' and 'mortals', not only brings home the limited time which one has for gaining what is at stake, but something of the mixture of the scrutable and inscrutable, dependable and unreliable, the potent and the impotent, which marks existence and human participation in it. Moreover, through the privy connection of the poet with the divine, what is otherwise remote to human beings in their normal involvement with things is brought forth as intimately linked with what happens and with a destiny at work in affairs; thus the narration of unfolding events can be reliefed by anticipations, the larger dramatic movement at the heart of each poem can be kept recurrently in mind, and a dwelling on the unfolding itself by which gradually (through delay and obstacle) what was anticipated is brought to pass is made possible.

In the use of these structural and stylistic devices to reinforce awareness of the temporality which is crucial to the heart of each drama, the poet helps bring the audience, in a way difficult to avoid, into the presence of the problematic of existence, and with it, the question of meaning which invests temporal human existence. The central thematic of both poems, emphasized and colored by these supporting devices, precisely concerns this condition which we all find as our own, and brings it home in a way that reinforces the need for reflection which attends our awareness of that condition.

The distinctive educative force of the two monumental poems derives then not simply from their power to touch and claim the audience at the core of their being where death and aspiration lie counterposed, but from their bringing forward for the attention of the reflection naturally called forth in such self-awareness a wholistic vision of human existence as able to find resolution to this problematic in which it is caught up. To the audience of Greeks of his own day, Homer's poems thereby offer a sense of the past according to which the future lying before his audience members depends upon human effort which, aligned with an aspirational reaching for the heights, can operate within the meanings of Moira and with the co-working of the gods and find meaning, even if not always happiness. And they invite those audience members, even as they are recognized as standing in a decline from those who are celebrated in the poems, to take that glorious past as their own and, in venturing under its inspiration, to realize a capacity for a higher future than the present.[18]

The depth of the resonance of these poems in the Greeks of Homer's time and thereafter was profound. Carried by Ionian singers to the mainland and throughout the Greek world, the effect of his monumental rendering of life and life's meaning was to crystallize in a 'modern' but heroic form a sense of themselves as Greeks which was already emerging in his audience, but which for the most part was inchoate yet.[19] The poems thus functioned effectively to assist in the defining of the self-consciousness with which the Greeks in their ongoing present not only connected themselves with the past but dedicated themselves to the future. If response to the inspiration of the poems was soon to issue in a lyric poet like Archilochus, biting in his rejection of the heroic and honor as irrelevant to what really matters in real life in the present, such fostering of opposition (here, to the future as a perpetuation of the past), was in keeping with the Homeric summons to responsibility. For human beings of the present were to make of the future a realization of aspiration whose directions for venture, though searched out under inspiration and encouragement from the past, need not therefore form a repetition of the past. It is to be as human beings were, to do as they did, but in the present, within the range of the possible harbored in it, that Homer urged his contemporaries. In that way, they could venture, learn, grow, become, and achieve, as participants in the continuing of this ongoing tradition whose 'beginning' was celebrated in its character in the legends and, in transformed shape, in his poems. In fact, his urging to this effect was heeded, and so well heeded that, as the later Greeks recall him, Homer was *the* poet and educator of Greece.[20]

B. THE BASIC ISSUE: TRUTH

Despite the fact that epic soon died as a living art,[21] the impact of Homer increased with time, the poems being transmitted eventually by the reciter-rhapsode instead of the singer, and finally, being transcribed into a written text. With their encompassing vision of the problematic of meaning and their pointer into an answering that would be adequate to that problematic, the two monumental poems transformed epic poetry in such way as implicitly to offer a challenge to Greek religion and myth. The matter at issue in that challenge was truth.

Truth is a mark both of reality and of a disclosure of reality, being the self-manifestation of the real and being what is revealed in the undistorting apprehension of reality as it is. Such disclosure arises for us in our involvement with an existence which is marked by a pervasive problematic, that of meaning. Within a traditional society such as that of the Greeks of the 8th century, the fundamental horizon within which the truth of such existence was collectively disclosed was to be found in religion, and more specifically, in the primordial myths which represent the deepest and broadest speech which religion can provide addressed to that matter. We have considered at some length the symbolic character of primordial myth, its disclosive function in the ceremonial story-telling-and-listening, and the possible confirmation of the truth-claim of the narrative in the occasion itself of the ceremonial telling. We have also contrasted such myth and myth-telling with epic poetry and bardic singing, and considered the poet-singer as maker composing under divine inspiration, as making a story that calls back to mind past events and deeds of human beings and that adumbrates some perspective on the problematic of meaning that is worth recalling to his audience, and as thereby bringing forth for his audience to respond to the truth of a past which is irremediably gone but whose truth has a continuing interest to the present and into the future.

In bringing home the contrast of myth and epic poetry in this matter of truth we have spoken of the two as if they were complementary. Myth-telling opens up truth concerning ultimate matters, the creational character of existence, whereas bardic song, developing stories within the general horizon offered by myth, brings intelligibility to the particulars of the movement of human existence in time which are not a focus for myth. And under the latter sense of the poetic endeavor, we paused briefly over the problem of how the truth of the poetic construal of the past might be confirmed or rejected, in contrast with the way this might happen with the truth of myth.

In thinking through the Homeric transformation of bardic narrative, we need to reconsider some of these thoughts, and developing them and making some distinctions, to more carefully formulate what is involved in this matter of truth as Homer's poems would disclose it. Let us do this in three steps: first, by considering the inspired character of the poetry; second, by considering its representation of human affairs; and third, by considering its representation of the divine. Then we will return to this matter of the challenge to myth offered by Homeric poetry.

1. THE MUSE AND TRUTH

The *Iliad* and the *Odyssey* both begin with an invocation to the Muse. The *Iliad* opens:

> Sing, goddess, the anger of Peleus' son Achilleus and its devastation, which put pains thousand-fold upon the Achaians, hurled in their multitudes to the house of Hades strong souls of heroes, but gave their bodies to be the delicate feasting of dogs, of all birds, and the will of Zeus was accomplished since that time when first there stood in division of conflict Atreus' son the lord of men and brilliant Achilleus. What god was it then set them together in bitter collision?

The *Odyssey* opens:

> Tell me, Muse, of the man of many ways, who was driven far journeys, after he had sacked Troy's sacred citadel. Many were

they whose cities he saw, whose minds he learned of, many the pains he suffered in his spirit on the wide sea, struggling for his own life and the homecoming of his companions. Even so he could not save his companions, hard though he strove to; they were destroyed by their own wild recklessness, fools, who devoured the oxen of Helios, the Sun God, and he took away the day of their homecoming. From some point here, goddess, daughter of Zeus, speak, and begin our story.[22]

In these beginnings, and in the occasional kindred invocation here and there in other places in the poems, we find internal to the poetry itself a reflexive pointer to the narratives for the listeners. The story in each case is being offered as having its source not simply in the human poet but, in a co-operative fashion, in a divine power as well.[23] The fictive 'world' which is the main connecting link between poet, audience, and the past being recalled through it, is itself something which the poet, in his initial invocations, tells us is not simply of his own contrivance.

About this matter of the source of such a 'world', the poet in the *Odyssey* himself speaks further (but indirectly) through the bards Phemius and Demodocus, who are figures in the drama he recounts.

In Book XXII (345–7) of the *Odyssey*, Phemius beseeches Odysseus to spare him because he is a singer who sang for the suitors only under compulsion. As one who sings, Phemius speaks of himself to say: "I am self-taught but the god has implanted in my wits song-ways of every kind" (*autodidaktos d'eimi. Theos de moi en phresin oimas pantoias enephusen.*). He is self-taught in the sense that while he stands within a tradition and has learned from others stories and techniques, in his singing his song is not something which he has learned from others and which he is simply performing.[24] Instead, it is his own work, coming out of himself in an act which takes him beyond such learning. Yet his composing various poems involves a finding of the "song-ways" which are his own under the inspiration of the divine. The 'making' is thus a co-operative, a joint, effort, in which the singer transforms what he may take over from others in the tradition, but does so on the strength of a working of the divine which enables it, which supports it, which invests it with power and authority. There is no sense here in which the involvement of the Muse removes or derogates human effort; it is rather that the Muse raises human effort—presumed and presupposed in this case as a self-help affair (thus, not an affair of simply *repeating* what has been learned from others)—beyond what it could achieve by itself alone.

Then again, when Odysseus is praising Demodocus (a singer whom the Muse stirred to sing: VIII/73; thus presumably one of those singers whom the

Muse has taught song-ways: VIII/480–1), he says: "Surely the Muse, Zeus's daughter, or else Apollo, has taught you, for all too fittingly (*kata kosmon*) you sing the Achaians' venture (*oiton*), all they did and had done to them, all the sufferings of these Achaians, as if you had been there yourself or heard it from one who was" (VIII/488–92: Lattimore modified). What the Muse would seem also to enable, then, is a kind of authority and truthfulness to the story being told such as bespeaks a first-hand witnessing, a first-hand knowing of the reality being brought into speech. In this particular case, the authority can not stem from the poet himself; for not only was he not there, but even had he been, since he is blind he could not have seen what he portrays in his song. It remains that he could have heard it from someone who was there,[25] but Odysseus[26] suggests that it was grounded in the working of the divine (the Muse, or perhaps even Apollo, who of course was there[27]) and that it was this which enabled the 'making' to have such a character.

What would we find if we applied to Homer himself and to the two poems in which they appear these suggestions concerning the Muse, being self-taught, finding one's own song-ways, and singing true stories? We would understand him as breathing a distinctive life into traditional language and stories by the development of his own capacities for vision and by his finding of the song-ways that enabled him to bring his understanding of what was involved in the stories to an apt dramatic rendering. Yet this transformation would not be something simply arbitrary because it came not simply out of himself in his ordinary selfhood but out of himself inspired by the Muse, out of a self which was self-conscious to his own poetic creating as involving the forming of ideas which "came to him" and were worked out in song by him in ways that also "came to him"—but with a "coming" that betrayed the working of the divine in their origination. It is not as if he were simply a passive receptacle to fully formed ideas and speech; he is, rather, a 'maker'. But the work that issues is not the work simply of an individual, nor was it the work simply of a god. It was the work of an individual inspired by a god, the individual being released in that inspiration into powers and capacities for work which were normally unavailable to him though they were his capacities, and being supported in the exercise of those powers and capacities by that same liberating divine presence. But more: it was a work integrating a tradition also, a tradition of language at the very least, but with it also, a tradition of ideas and stories. More specifically: in each invocation the poet-singer himself proposes the story to be told—a well-known story, it seems—, and calls upon the Muse to sing/tell the story starting from that time when .... Thus for the creating of the work, the poet gives over his singing/telling of a self described and self-focused story to the working of the Muse, so that in their working together an account may emerge which has an authenticity and veracity which it could not have because Homer was eye-witness since the events happened far before his own time. Those events have been brought to speech in story long ago, and maintained in the sustaining of the stories through the generations. But Homer calls for the Muse to sing/tell through himself, that is, he calls for her guidance in his singing/telling. He is not simply repeating traditional stories on his own, but recasting them under her inspiration. Thus the poetic work has, in a definite sense, a three-fold "source".[28]

It is as such works that the *Iliad* and the *Odyssey* claim truth. How does that claim have substance? Substance is provided by the three sources working together in the making of the story; each contributes to the shaping of a truthful story. The Muse, bearing the divine witnessing to the past into its inspiring of the poet, enables the functioning of the poet-singer's capacities in ways not otherwise possible and enables that functioning to reach a discernment of truth not otherwise open to the poet. But this functioning is the poet-singer's own, and that discernment which the poet reaches through his own capacities and functioning concerns the truth of a past which is maintained in the heritage of legend which derives ultimately from human beings who were there as well. About these matters, there is much we would like to ask, in the absence of anything further in the two poems themselves. How is the poet changed by this inspiring presence, how ingathered differently than otherwise? And how is he enabled to see? Is the change, the ingathering, the enabling, different for different poets, even though in every case these involve a working of the Muse in her presence? Then again: What sort of discernment, and what sort of truth, is opened up to such a concentrated story-maker? Is it different for different poets, and if so, in function of what? How does the poet-seer see beyond the variousness of legend to discover the truth of the past? Finally, accepting that the Muse is also at work in the poet's bringing to speech the truth he is being enabled to discern, and keeping in mind the oral-aural character of the story-telling and that the communication of truth is only effected in participation in the ceremonial occasion, we would also like to ask: By whom is that truth-being-conveyed actually received? Is the listener, simply because he/she hears the words, being made privy to the truth they convey; or does his/her listening have to become ingathered and 'inspired' for the disclosure to be consummated?

2. TRUTHFUL REPRESENTATION OF THE HUMAN

Under its Homeric transformation, bardic poetry speaks of the whole, of gods as well as human beings, and of the interaction of these diverse beings which is part of the coherence of the whole. Now the human beings being recalled in the poems belonged to the past of Homer and his audience, and to a past sufficiently long ago that there was no way of assessing and resolving any claim to truth relating to that past by a direct confrontation of it in its actuality or by the testimony of any present (human) witness.[29] What alone gave the poet access to that past actuality was two-fold: the legends which claimed ultimately to have stemmed from the time, and the Muse under which his capacities for seeing and singing were convoked and employed. Now attending to his works as meant to function disclosively in a ceremonial-telling-and-listening, what sort of truth do we find that the inspired poet was enabled to discern and convey in his poems when he availed himself of legend?[30] And how do the poems convey such truth?

The Homeric poems function disclosively by creating in their words a 'world', with places, events, figures, deeds, and the like, and by claiming that the past is truthfully represented by this fictive world. But "truthfully represented" means what? How is 'what was' being brought back into mind and its truth being made accessible by the poet in and through this fictive world?

To the extent that the representation in the poems is of the past simply in its publicly discernible factual character, then one can ask: Was there ever in fact a Trojan war? or an Achilleus? or an Odysseus? Supposing that there was such a war, did it take place in the manner represented? Did the participants speak and act as they are reported to have done? "Truthfully represented" would then mean accurately depicted, portrayed precisely as it actually was, in its factual character. It would mean that the fictive 'world' was an accurate image of that past reality. In that case the truth would be what a chronicle of the past sought to convey in descriptive statements, but what the poet 'images' in the 'world' he creates.[31]

But the poems do not limit their representation to the publicly discernible facts. And indeed, they would not have been capable of disclosing human being and human affairs as they *are* or *were* if they had so limited themselves. For the factuality of such beings and affairs does not lie in the publicly discernible facets of them. Indeed, if as human beings we *are* in a venturing in which something is at stake and we ourselves are at risk, the factuality of such a being in the undertaking of this or that includes all that was actually involved in the forming and carrying out of such undertaking: not only the actual motivations, thoughts, feelings, and decisions, of the agent, including how he or she was actually taking (and perhaps mistaking) them to be, but also for example the situation as it actually was, the possibilities actually latent in it, and the stake as it actually was, however the agent was taking these to be. Now even if something less than omniscience could truthfully disclose such factuality, is that what the poetic representation seeks? At the very least, to maintain a clear and intelligible story it would simplify, omit, and emphasize. But is that simply indicative of the inability of a poetic story to live up to a standard appropriate to it if it is to be a truthful disclosure? so that all stories would be at best incomplete, if not also false in many regards due (if for no other reason) to that incompleteness?

The factuality of human being and human affairs involves something even more essential than the elements of actuality and possibility just mentioned. For at the heart of our being we are implicated in a destiny (a meant-to-be), and more narrowly, in meanings to be realized somehow in our doing what we do. And indeed, the Homeric presentation of Achilleus makes central such destiny and meanings as effectively involved in the factuality of his being and doing. Suppose that it is such matters—destiny and meanings—which are of fundamental significance in the factuality of human being, and that the poetic representation of the past would truthfully disclose that being. How could such representation convey that factuality in keeping with the fundamental place of destiny and meanings in it? I have already pointed to the inescapable presence of simplification and emphasis in the representation even of 'the facts', let alone of the factuality of human beings and affairs. Could it be that because of the centrality of the realization of meanings to our being, representation of what actually was would require not merely simplification and emphasis, but even the distortion of factual elements, that the essential might come out more clearly? If so, then the representation would not be an image in the mode of reproduction, whose truthfulness would amount to its exact correspondence with the facts. It would rather be an image in the mode of adaptation, which adapts and fits facts together and integrates them with what is not fact in such way as enables the *effective narrative representation* of the *factuality* of the being of human beings *as this factuality centers in* a realization of meanings and is not merely a miscellany of complex factual elements. Truthful representation in such a case would not amount to exact correspondence of image with all the facts; indeed it might involve and even require for its narrative execution some misrepresentation of facts. Truthful representation would rather consist in the disclosure of what was but a disclosure in the light of the destinies and meanings which were actually involved in the past being brought to speech. The fictive 'world' which is the word-formed image functioning in this mode then would *signify* actuality in its *essential factuality*, it would not simply mirror 'facts'.[32]

If Homer created such signifying images by sifting out the truth of the past which legend held and doing this through ingathered capacities functioning under the inspiring presence of the Muse, then through those images he first and foremost conveyed as truth the meanings he could discern being concretely realized in the particular segment of the past which legend held still some memory of. His transformation of the bardic thereby involved a signifying representation of the human past which claimed to carry its truth in the sense just characterized. And what ultimately authenticated his representation of truth was the combination of the inspiring Muse, enduring legend, and amplified capacity.

3. TRUTHFUL REPRESENTATION OF THE GODS

To the extent that the poems introduce divine figures they do not represent realities which no longer exist and access to which is only through traditional story and the working of the Muse. It is true, so far as the specific activities of such gods in the human past are concerned, there is the same distance and lack of immediate access as obtains in the case of the realities of the human past. And to that extent their representation would be subject to the same conditions as the representation of the human. But because the gods are immortals, because they are enduring presences who still exist in the present of the poet, because they are realities directly accessible to the poet in the time of his making of the poems, the question of the character of their representation takes a different turn. All the more is this the case for the fact that the poet's 'making' claims the inspirational presence of the Muse who is daughter of Zeus, the major god involved. What are we to make, then, of the anthropomorphic character of the representation of those powers? Let us begin by considering the kind of anthropomorphism involved, the features of the image itself.

At least at the top of the hierarchy of divine powers (and that upper echelon is almost all that is represented in the poems), the gods are figured forth as aristocratic betters to human beings, deathless in their being whereas human beings are mortal, and powerful in ways to which a human being can not stand up in successful opposition (unless supported by another god, in which case it is not human but divine power that prevails). Yet just as with the best of human beings, these 'aristocratic' powers are limited in their efficacy and action, and judged from the point of view of the 'lower-class' (which is that of human beings in this representation), they seem strong-willed agents, relatively independent of each other in their functioning so that human beings are liable to get caught up in their conflicts. Since for the most part these 'aristocratic' powers are subject to passion and favoritism and are liable to capricious action on behalf of what their passion and favoritism for the moment leads them to support, they are not allies one can depend upon to act as one would like them to. Operating often without human cognizance of their activity, even when they manifest themselves to human beings they do not fully and openly disclose themselves in their being or purposes. Indeed they seem not to make such disclosure of their actions and purposes even to each other.

What these 'aristocratic' powers ask of human beings is, above all, acknowledgement, respect, honor, an *aidôs* to be shown mainly in a service which is carried out for the most part via sacrifice. In return they honor excellence in human beings; or at least, Zeus among them can be counted on for this, even if he may not show this in ways and with the timeliness human beings would like. With this acknowledgement of excellence, however, they impose no embracing code of conduct upon human beings, although there are expectations in certain situations, stemming not simply from Zeus (thus e.g. the hospitability to strangers as something he enforces) but from the other gods, given their particular concerns. The gods respond to this lower and inferior being which human beings are in a variety of other ways as well as in their acknowledgement of excellence. Occasionally they become captivated with human beauty, and respond in love; occasionally they become moved when human beings face death, and respond in pity; occasionally they respond in anger or hatred, when human beings they love or honor or things which they desire for their favorites are threatened by other human beings. Similarly in other regards, the gods become drawn into the ongoing of human affairs and exert themselves actively, as 'aristocrats' with some interest at stake. But in no case do they consider human beings as on the same level of being as themselves, and because that interest does not set at risk their own existence, their concern is a limited one. There is one exception, namely, Zeus, when what is at issue is the realization of moira and its justice. Only then is the divine concern something approximating to an absolute one.

The Homeric rendering of the divine in such an anthropomorphic figure is distinctive, but it is only one inflection to a widespread tendency toward use of the human being as figurative representation for a divine power. That tendency is common in religion as well as Homeric poetry, and more particularly, in the myths which are integral to religions. Now what is at issue in general in myth is bringing the problematic of existence to appropriate disclosive speech, and in particular, bringing into presentationally symbolic speech a universe which is dramatic in its essence. That means: bringing into speech a creational movement in which existence is so shaped as to involve something at stake for the powers and agents which compose it. The divine power potently at work in the 'beginning' back to which myth-telling takes participants manifests itself in, yet beyond, many facets of the created world itself—the heavens, the earth, various places and forces, and so on. These creaturely presences are powers active out of themselves, and the divine, as manifesting itself in them, is to that extent an active power among others. The human being, given in particular the inflection of human activity by will and purpose, and given the inward access to that being provided to each of us, is a readily available figure to re-present the divine in these particular manifestations as well as in its creational working. For the sense of something at stake, and of a directionality in the movement of things, are capable of being pointed to under such a figure. And the particular manifestations of the divine, in the 'beyond' belonging to their manifesting, may also become developed under an anthropomorphic figuring-forth into a distinctive personality who can be active (because not limited to the 'in') in other spheres and references, as well as in other ways, than the primordial 'in'.

If the presentational symbolism of myth avails itself of the human figure as a potent element in itself, it remains that in the ceremonial rediscovering first-hand of the divine power at the 'beginning' a participant encounters that power in its own being, and knows it beyond the symbol. In the case of the Homeric poems, however, we are involved with a rather different kind of speech altogether, and a different functioning of the human figure than as presentational symbol.

Thus to begin with, regardless of what in the way of the depth of time is opened up in the experience of the listener, the bardic representation of the divine in epic poetry focuses that listener's attention not upon presences out of that present depth but upon the divine as in time past it disclosed itself as functioning in the course of ongoing affairs and as having a bearing on that ongoing. In the poetic signifying, then, the depth of time as a creational affair is ignored, disregarded, in favor of such depth as might have obtained in a past[33] which is being regarded not only in its onward movement but also as harboring agents already existent and caught up in the problematic of existence concretely. It is a limited range of the depth of time, then, that is being brought to speech in the poetic signifying.

But secondly, the Homeric anthropomorphization of the divine is entered into a story whose focus is upon human affairs in the ongoing of time, and not upon the divine. The anthropomorphization concerns the divine in its 'beyond', and thus under a figure which can be developed all the more readily in its human elements. Since the story focuses on the human and introduces the divine as it impinges and bears upon the unfolding of the human, such a full development of the anthropomorphic figure could help in the dramatic development of the story. And indeed, the Homeric portrayal of the divine involvement in the two stories works quite effectively to that purpose.

How, then, does Homer's anthropomorphic representation of the gods function, if it is representational image and not presentational symbol, if the poetic signifying in which it operates does not recall the participant in the story-telling back to the divine as effectively functioning and manifest power in the past but leaves that power in the same 'gone by' distance as the human figures and thereby leaves the meaning of the figurative sign *ungrounded in immediate presence*?

In its function as a signifying figure in such poetry, the human signifies a presence which is divine, and more, is in its own being 'beyond' all that is manifest phenomenon. In particular, it signifies a presence which is not human, yet is intimately interlinked with the human in (much of) its functioning. The two-sidedness of the signifying—that it is not really human, although its figure is, and that it is nonetheless closely linked with the human—is visible in the very representations themselves.

The one side is carried by the anthropomorphism itself, through which the kinship and close interlinking of divine and human is attested. In this side of the image the gods show a measure of concern for human beings, they recognize and acknowledge excellence in human being and achievement, and they support human endeavor that is aligned with the measure immanent in the whole of things and that establishes for human beings who measure up a significant place in that whole. To this extent, the divine reality which is crucial to the unfolding of events within the whole and in the course of human life itself is signified as kindred to human beings, and apt to be kind to those who are of its kind.

The other side is focused in the upper-class rendering of the 'human' figure of the gods, to mark the gulf, the differentiation, between divine and human, and more specifically, the superiority of the divine in power and standing and being within the whole. Included under this rendering of a higher class itself multiple in constituent powers but ordered hierarchically and headed by Zeus, are the elements of secretiveness, of independent initiative, of passionate and biased action, of limited and undependable concern except as Zeus may bring some dependability out of the chaos of active powers, and so on. To this extent, the 'kindred' divine reality is being signified as not working (or able to be brought to work, through coercion of any sort) in ways anticipatable and/or controllable by human beings, and indeed, as not working simply or primarily for human good, even though in some assured fashion the divine does honor humanity at its best (doing so in its own way, however, and not at the behest of or upon the terms set by human beings).

Seen in this way, the Homeric rendering of the divine in the anthropomorphic figure of the gods (especially the Olympians) has a definite religious sense.[34] It means the divine power as beyond all other presences in power and functioning, and yet as concerned in the latter for (at least) human beings. Nonetheless, because the signifying figure leaves the powers being signified at an experiential distance, because in the disclosing effected in the story-telling they remain unexperienced first-hand, what meaning such figuration has for the participants in the story-telling must come from somewhere else than the immediacy which the story-telling fosters in the ceremonial getting. The divine powers that are part of the story thus function for the audience in that same limbo as regards immediacy as do the human figures—Odysseus and Achilleus, for example. And to the extent that Homer's rendering of the presence and functioning of the divine powers within the poems skillfully adapts these to fit smoothly into the human drama, to that extent it is for the most part as if these figures were simply further human beings. Even if the religious significance of these figures is never altogether removed, the gods are nonetheless so like to real aristocrats and fit so readily into an ongoing drama focused on real aristocrats that that significance is somewhat muted, with incalculable consequences in the times to come.

4. HOMERIC POETRY AS RIVAL TO MYTH

While continuing the bardic tradition of a focus on the human, the Homeric transformation of narrative poetry struck such a strong and widespread responsive chord as to make it stand out from the rest of the bardic tradition. Something novel was being entered into the Greek world here, and something with broad appeal. Because in the poems Homer conceived of the divine in such close connection with the human and made of the active presence of the divine in the affairs of the human world such an important factor, the appeal of his poetry meant a wide audience responding not simply to his engaging portrayal of the human but also to his vivid rendering of the divine. The latter—the representation of the gods in particular—had an enormous impact on the way the Greeks came to conceive the divine powers which were central to the definition of their religious horizon, the Olympians in particular.

This coming to the fore of a poet in the refining for a people of the way the divine powers central in its religious horizon were conceived as presences at work in human life, is quite unusual. It seems to have had several roots.

One root lies in the variegated character of Greek religion. It is easy to be misled by the phrase "Greek religion", and think that one is speaking of a single thing, like Christianity. Even in the latter case, where there is a fixed reference point back to which to relate the various manifestations of the religion, namely, the Bible, there is considerable variety and profound divergence. The Greeks lacked any such written focal point, and also any unifying organization like the Church. For there were not simply the different groups who were Greek, but there were manifold expressions of religion, at the level of family, at that of the *polis*, and at levels in between, and in groupings not directly related to either but (say) ethnic in character. Theirs was also a religious horizon marked not only by its oral articulation, but also by the diversity of the sources of such articulation. There was indeed some kinship in the myths that constituted the horizons established in these various expressions of religion. But the diversity in the threads of traditional legend, the complexity and overlap and modification found as over time those threads became interwoven or separated out, is to be found at the level of religion as well. At no level of religion was there a priesthood which, by the sheer power of being organized and dedicated to the sustaining of the religion the priests were functionaries in, could work to bring, throughout the Greek world, something like a uniformity in religion.[35] But just as, in Mycenaean times, a political diversity seems to have endured while a cultural integration and assimilation developed and brought what approximated to a uniformity in some aspects of culture, so in the time of Homer and on through classical times, the Greek is closest to unity at the level of culture. Yet it is a 'one' which is not a uniformity but a set whose members show close family resemblances, so to speak. Thus in the religious background of Homer's voice was to be found no uniform voicing of "Greek religion" but rather a diversity of voices, all Greek and yet speaking with significant difference in emphasis and focus on one god or another. In the coming together of Greek with Greek, a vehicle which reached across the differences and gave to Zeus, say, a clear character for all could contribute to the growing sense of being Greek as well as to the feeling of the distinctiveness of the Greek in contrast with the 'barbarian'. Homer created such vehicles.

A second root lies in the thrust of the religiosity that was fostered within the varied but kindred religious horizon. At least so far as we know it apart from poetry and in its own right, and so far as the reception of the Homeric vision of the heroic itself suggests, when Homer placed the reaching for the heights at the center of his vision of the human he was being faithful to an important element of that religiosity. In an unusual twist, the emergence of a poet as voice who could profoundly affect the vision of the divine which entered into the ultimate horizon of a people's religious understanding of things was quite in keeping with the character of the religion itself. For that reason, the Homeric poetic refinement and ordering of the religious visions of the varied Greek peoples was not felt as a threat, especially not to any orthodoxy. The bardic performance of the two poems gained a place in festival occasions which were religious in nature. And the profound appeal and impact of the poems, among the upper classes in particular, and the degree to which their vision of the human and the divine became influential in the self-definition to themselves of the Greeks in their own being as Greek, would seem to attest not simply their consonance with the religious spirit generally but their capacity to meet a broad need unfilled by religion in any of its forms on any of its levels but able to be met by this poetry with its striking human appeal and its comprehensive vision of divine and human, of life and life's meaning.

A third root lies in the creativity of the poet-singer, not simply as regards his treatment of old stories but also as regards the transformation of the bardic achieved in his monumental poetry and as regards his discernment of and response to the need just mentioned. His was a time of change and revival, a time when previously settled arrangements of life were being replaced and when a new spirit was beginning to animate Greeks from all parts of the Greek world. Another sense of themselves was emerging, and Homer's seizing the opportunity and creating the vehicle through which this sense received an apt public voice was timely and consequential.

If those were the roots for Homer's emergence as a unique and powerful poetic voice, it may seem odd—if not perverse—to speak of him as a "rival" to the myth-maker and as "challenging" the established religious (mythical and ritual) self-definition of the Greeks, especially when any such rivalry and challenge, if they existed, were only implicit. Yet the ensuing course of events would seem to warrant at least this, that his poetry opened the way to a challenge. And our preceding discussion, especially of this matter of truth, can help us understand the character of what happened.

First, while bardic poetry was nothing new among the Greeks, and its spread in Homer's time reflected a burgeoning need and interest that many bards could address, Homer's poetry addressed more deeply, more comprehensively, and more directly, the problematic of existence that that need and interest were rooted in. In him an individual assumed the burden and responsibility of speech that would effect, on the reflective level, an integration of the Greeks through a vision of what it meant to be human that was Greek in inflection.

Second, with the emergence of opportunities for story-telling on occasions like festivals that drew Greeks from many parts of the Greek world, Homer could not only address diverse Greeks as regards their gods and a shared human past, but could reach them outside the diverse-yet-resembling local realizations of their religion. Stepping forward as a story-teller who, while different from the myth-maker, was yet inspired by a power that was of a kind—indeed was kin—with the powers of which Greek myth spoke, he could bring forward a vision of the divine powers and of human existence which, while able to resonate in his audience in virtue of their religious being (diverse as it may have been within the family resemblance of the various local realizations), was tied to no local realization in particular. As his audience would include aristocratic leaders who, however different they may have been in virtue of their local attachments and roots, were coming to find a kinship with each other, this vision could particularly impact this leadership elite of the emerging social order.

Third and finally, that impact could be—and was—complex and complexly grounded. But for the point at issue here, there is one factor that is of primary importance for understanding the ambivalent character of what issued from Homer's poetry. Even when singing on a religious occasion, Homer's voice sounded a distinctive note in its story-telling. When Zeus appeared in the symbolizing of myth-story, the ceremonial setting of the telling of the story offered a presence to which the presentational symbol related a listener. And to the extent that this carried over, with the help of ritual, into a being religious which was faithful to the disclosure, a Greek would have a living inward presence being maintained in life and affairs beyond ceremony. But when Homer sang of Zeus in the signifying representation of his poetry, Zeus remained a presence in the distance out there, unexperienced in the immediacy of the occasion and instead only known mediately under the anthropomorphic figure of the poet's devising. Now while the contrast in these modes of presence of Zeus in the different ceremonial occasions involves a difference that can potentially have quite divergent consequences, it is possible for these two different modes to reinforce each other, aided by the common anthropomorphic figure that is a symbol but also a figurative signifying image. Thus if under the sway of actual religious life the symbolizing were able to be sustained as prior, then the religious meaning of the signifying image could be successfully sustained as well, registered as a foreground. But even in that case, to the extent that the image, in its vividness and in its close interweaving with intensely vivid images of human figures, gained power as a 'clarifying' form and, in virtue of its association with a vivid and deeply resonating image of human life, came to fascinate as showing the god forth, Zeus could become a presence almost inseparable from his figurative image and be related to with it in mind. To the extent that this attachment became a fact in the times of and subsequent to Homer, his poetry had not only an impact with potential for supporting religious faith but also a potential working which could work against such faith.

In Part V, we will return to Homer and to what happened in the following several centuries to his poetry. But with the rise of philosophy in somewhat over a century in mind, this much is already clear: an individual voice, dealing reflectively with the problematic of existence in a comprehensive and direct way, and operating in a story-telling medium different from myth, has emerged and summoned others, in response to his poetizing, to practical and vocational reflection on the present and future in the light of its contrast with a strongly appealing and moving past. This is not yet philosophy, but neither is it still religion and myth-telling.

NOTES

1. Webster, MH, 210–5, argues (on the whole, plausibly) for a dating of the Homeric poems in the third quarter of the eighth century. My sense, that they belong to different phases of his life and reflect those phases, would fit with an interval of twenty years or so for the formative periods involved.

2. This is what seems most likely to me, for a variety of reasons. But if Homer composed only the *Iliad* and some successor composed the *Odyssey* as the only successful similar venture in monumental epic, that will make almost no difference in what I will be saying in connection with the two poems as important works setting the context for the beginnings of philosophy among the Greeks and providing an enduring problem for philosophical reflection among them.

3. Kirk would oppose the disbelief of A. B. Lord and others in the possibility of poetry as complicated as the two Homeric works being composed without the aid of writing. See SH, 72–3. In any case, such composition, for its possibility, presupposes a number of things. For one, there needs to be a rich tradition of shorter stories and of developed devices upon which to draw. (See Bowra, HP, 358.) For a second, it requires a bard with certain capacities enabling such a wholly memory-dependent composing: "such a process may well take years and implies an extraordinary gift not only of memory but of concentration and judgment" (Bowra, HP, 440–1). Further, there need to be certain current opportunities for performance which the bard can take advantage of. Even with the latter, there is required as well a change in the character of bardic performance, to introduce a relay of performers or to enable a solo performance which, with the needed breaks for the performer (to say nothing of the audience), will stretch over more than one day. That, in turn, requires an audience patience. As for the particular poems of Homer, there are further presuppositions expressed in the works themselves. For example, the allusion to numerous legends presumes an audience familiar with a wide range of stories which are not being told in the poems themselves. See Webster, MH, 267–75 for his account of the factors involved or presupposed in the performance of the Homeric poems.

4. See such a discussion as that of Webster, MH, 268–71, concerning festival performance. Webster also claims that, if the unity of such long poems was to be perceived by an audience, their performance must in each case have involved a relay of performers (as was the case at the Panathenaea from the 6th century on), and this, he claims, commits us to believing that the poems were reduced to writing before they were so recited. "It is credible that a poet could compose orally a poem of this length and perform it as he composed it (although such composition would lack all the subtle unity of the Homeric epics). It is not credible that, as he composed orally, he could teach his team a poem of such length and that they could remember it" (272). Yet assuming that writing in the new alphabetic script was known by the middle of the 8th century, even if it were involved in

the way Webster claims for the communication of the poems to other performers, what was written need not have been the whole poem but at most performance notes. For a questioning voice concerning the suitability of the festivals as opportunities for performing longer works like the Homeric, see Kirk, SH, 276–7.

5. See Kirk, SH, 255 and 274–81, for the statement of a similar thought.

6. It seems likely that Homer's poetry was preserved for awhile orally (with or without performance notes), with the consequence that it suffered some modification in the transmission, as oral poetry was wont to do at the hands of creative bards. But two things happen to maintain the poems, as Homer may have sung them, before the written text seems likely to have come into being. First, the power and appeal of the poems "as Homer sang them" seems to have been considerable, and the language in which they were composed—formulaic and metrical—is likely to have enabled the poems, once achieving a special status, to be resung by others with less variation than would otherwise be the case. (Kirk, "HPH", 826 argues such a point in contrasting the Homeric with oral poetry in the modern Slavic tradition. See also Kirk, SH, 319–320.) Second, the tradition of oral poetry lost its vitality soon after Homer, and a shift in the character of the performer took place, from a singer-poet to a rhapsode who recited the memorized work of others. Such a rhapsode was still a performer, and might take liberties; but they would be unlikely to change the coherence of the poem and the vision expressed in it.

7. Kirk ("HPH", 848–9: also SH, Ch. 14, 301–15 for a longer version) offers a brief summation of the history of the text. One should keep in mind that no written version of an oral poem will do more than record its performance on some one occasion, and thus fix it in a way that no oral poetry, alive as oral, is ever actually fixed. In fact, it may be that the written version does not record one single performance, but separate performances of parts of the whole. See the comments of Fränkel (EGPP, 23), for interpretations of certain passages in each poem with this, in mind.

8. In the *Iliad* the story of the Trojan War, which is central enough to give the poem its title, is nonetheless told only in the course of telling the story of the wrath of Achilleus. But more generally: in both poems there is an overall structure, an architecture, which subserves the telling of a single dramatic movement, but introduces a manifold of episodes that enlarge the scope of the presentation of the world in which the drama is taking place. Those episodes are connected together in numerous ways, ranging from the simple side-by-side (paratactic) to the larger balanced or reverse echo pattern, to the chronologically and thematically foreshadowing or advancing, and so on. But throughout there is a unifying dramatic movement under whose ultimate control the introduction of the variety of episodes and their development is held. For a very condensed discussion of such matters, slightly different from the preceding, see Hainsworth, "COH", 94–97. For discussions of the order of one or both poems, seen particularly in comparison with the order of contemporary Geometrical pottery, see C. Whitman, *Homer and the Heroic Tradition* (hereafter abbreviated HHT), and Webster, MH, 200–207 and 259–67, for example. The fact that the dramatic movement involves episodes which could be detached and developed in their own right, as (or as if) separate poems, does not necessarily mean the whole was simply put together of such parts. Indeed, the traces of such a treatment of a part of the *Odyssey* (see Bowra, HP, 325) may reflect simply one way in which the whole poem was performed over several days. Separate performance of its sections may have involved *ad hoc* introductions and recapitulations, to situate the audience each time in relation to the whole poem and its thread of continuity.

9. I mean here not simply the envisioning of the Olympian gods led by Zeus (apparently this vision is the work of Homer) but the sense of the deeper divine matrix

within which even Zeus operates, alluded to in the notion of Moira. On the former point, see the discussion of M. P. Nilsson, *The Mycenaean Origins of Greek Mythology* (hereafter abbreviated MOGM), Chapter IV. Apparently the religious horizon itself involved simply a multiplicity of divine powers and no uniform sense of order and hierarchy. Homer's vision simplifies and ranks, to give a definite sense of order, which probably had no close counterpart in religion itself, at least apart from Homeric influence. On the second point: there is a coherence in the whole, complicit with human life as active and with the achievement of meaning in such a life through active effort that realizes aspiration. The working of the divine, in the ordering of the whole and in the involvement of the gods in human effort and life, is orderly *in this reference*, in the achieving of an ordainment. It is not enough, then, to point to a 'natural order' and think to have grasped the orderliness of the whole as the Homeric poems are concerned with it. It is also not enough to look to the capriciousness, personal bias, and conflict with each other, reflected in the involvement of the Olympians, to successfully dispute the orderly character of the working of the divine.

10. Homer's is a vision of the heroic which, rather than glorifying the human at the expense of the divine, sees the humanity of human beings and the divinity of the gods as interlinked, and interlinked in focus around what really matters in the ongoing temporal existence of this whole of heaven and earth. For the achieving of what counts, both gods and human beings are essential; and the working of the gods does not deprive human beings of efficacy and a place in that achieving, or deny the heroic. See the discussion of such matters in the next Chapter.

11. Nilsson (MOGM, 23) seems right to suggest that Homer "infused new life and vigor into epic poetry, putting the psychology of his heroes into the foreground and planning a comprehensive composition under this aspect." Similarly, Webster (MH, 256–8) seems on the right track in pointing to "the consistent and rich characterisation of Homer's heroes" and the changes in language (such as the development of abstract nouns) to enable such characterization to be made. See J. Griffin, *Homer on Life and Death* (hereafter abbreviated HLD) for an extended elucidation of the subtlety and complexity of the Homeric use of the traditional and formal means, to provide a psychological characterization of figures and a connection and interplay of episodes fraught with reflective import.

12. On the matter of the central thematic of the two poems, Webster (MH, 297–8) seems right to the point in speaking of the emphasis in both poems upon "human responsibility and divine justice", and in characterizing the will of Zeus in the *Iliad* as directed "to government of the world in accordance with the principles of justice." Similarly with his concluding remarks: "Thus before Hesiod, who must be regarded as an independent development of the same traditional poetry, Homer in Ionia was also concerned with the problems of divine government, human responsibility, and justice in the polls. Homer not only inherits a tradition which descends from the singers of Mycenaean palaces but is also the forerunner of archaic and classical Greece" (298).

13. What does it tell us about the Greeks, that so many seem to have been able to respond to poems so monumental in size, in scope of vision, and in the greatness they bring into view? Does that signify not only an aspiration already toward a 'great' future, a desire to build loftily, but also a richness of resources that could attest the latent potentiality for such achievement and that would enable the Homeric poems to resonate in such persons excitingly and incitingly?

14. See Bowra, HP, 276–80 for a very brief discussion. Fränkel (EGPP, 40) notes how similes function for the poet and the audience, as complementing the subject—heroic, peculiar and unusual—with the everyday, the customary and familiar. In the similes the

speaker no longer simply reports but adds something of his own; placing himself in person-to-person relationship with the hearer, he takes from the domain of his own time and ordinary experience and provides a contrasting double that gives greater clarity and fulness to the ancient things being set forth and that stimulates the hearer to think the situation out thoroughly.

15. See Webster, MH, 296, for comments on Homer as the link between the old and the new, especially through his use of similes drawing on observations of everyday life.

16. See Webster, MH, 208–23 (esp. 220–23). One might see it, say, in a simple matter such as the bard speaking of a time when the gods were living presences showing themselves in person to heroic human beings, in (implicit) contrast with what obtains for human beings in his own time.

17. In neither case is the experience drawn upon likely to go back to Mycenaean times; both the language and the character of the experience point to later times. See Kirk, "HPH", 846–7, 848 for discussion and examples.

18. Whether that future might be as high as the past, is undetermined.

19. It is not enough to point, simply, to the reawakened concern with the Mycenaean past, to understand why the Homeric poems which recalled that past struck the responsive chord they did. Nor is it enough to say (as Hawkes does, in DG, 264) "it was because his poetry embodied the myths and other unconscious expressions of the Greek people from the beginning that it had such a tremendous grip of the Hellenic mind." There was other poetry which recalled that past and embodied such 'myths', without having the power which Homer's did. It is instead necessary to see how that power was granted these poems by the aptness with which they spoke to Greeks who were in flux about themselves, by the measure in which they could resound against those aborning energies and give a sense to the Greeks of themselves which they could find significant. Their specific envisioning of the past intimately linked with, and brought to speech for others, a condition and an experiencing of the world which was already in the process for being formed. In any case, so far as the Greeks were indeed coming to a new birth in a new world, their sense of themselves is not something which would be granted simply by the past (human or divine). In fact, the past was itself becoming, so to speak, changing in its character and mode of presence in and for these people involved in change; it was disclosing its power and definiteness for them differently as they changed. If Homer was able to have a power through his recall of the past, it was because he was able to recast it and to catch it in this changing manifestation of itself, one supportive of the venturing into the new which the 8th century Greeks were engaged in.

20. See, for example, Plato's *Republic*, and the allusion to this effect by Socrates (at 606e).

21. Kirk (in SH, 314) claims that by the close of the 7th century, at least, true oral composition was virtually dead.

22. The translations are those of Lattimore; I shall use his translations in my references, except where noted otherwise.

23. In the *Iliad* we find Achilleus himself involved in such singing, and that should remind that bardic poetry was not always a professional matter. It also need not be always a matter involving divine inspiration, whether expressly acknowledged (as in the invocations in question) or not.

24. See the earlier discussion of the innovative working of the singer-poet (in Chapter 7 above, 80–81, 83).

25. In this case, he might have heard from eye-witnesses first hand, but in other cases (that of Homer himself, for example) such witness could be maintained only in the stories

which are handed down through tradition, to others who neither themselves knew first-hand or knew others who were first-hand witnesses.

26. Perhaps only out of courtesy?

27. Apollo was also closely connected with the Muses, although it was Zeus who was their father, by Memory (Mnemosyne).

28. Note that this seems to be the sense of significant human action generally which the poems, in their development of drama and meaning, incarnate in their delineation of human beings and events.

29. Even if such confrontation were possible, whose witness would be worthy of crediting? Would just anyone be able to discern the truth of presence?

30. In the ensuing discussion, it is important to keep separate the question of truth as it may have been realized on the occasion of the bardic song and in the singing of the story, from the question of how Homer and his audience understood this matter of truth as it related to such poetry. The latter is an important matter, but it is not the same as the former. The difficulty in discerning the way Homer and his audience understood the truth claim of his poems does not lie solely in the dearth of explicit testimony. We are concerned in such a case with a sense of truth which has not yet begun to define itself to itself in contrast (say) with a notion of historical truth, or more broadly, a notion of scientific truth, however 'science' be understood. The attempt to understand this as yet relatively undifferentiated sense by categories and questions framed from later more differentiated perspectives can readily distort the phenomenon by introducing a more differentiated consciousness formed from a different standpoint as the frame of reference for the questions and requested answer. To avoid this, one needs at the very least to try to reenter into the poetry itself and form one's reflections from out of a sense of what happens in the experience of the drama there. There one may well find that truth as the poet brings it into speech is neither 'objective' or 'subjective': the categories are anachronistic and inadequate.

31. The initial presumption of most if not all students of Homer is that this is the mode of truth which it is appropriate to apply to the poems. And thus we turn to archaeology and any other sources, direct or indirect, which might give us a clue about whether the poems, in any way or ways, accurately represent anything in the actual Mycenaean world. See Kirk, SH, 109–25 for one assessment of the two poems in this vein; see also A. M. Snodgrass, "An Historical Homeric Society?".

32. In this sense of truthful disclosure, the distinctive insight of the divinely inspired poet is into a concrete meaning embodied in his tradition. It may well be that the depth of insight which the poet achieves under inspiration can vary from individual to individual, even in one individual from time to time. It may well also be that the poet's fathoming of what meaning is implicit in the past which is his focus can be more or less effective. It may also be that the variation in profundity of the poet's insight reflects the depth or shallowness of the past he would bring to speech. And as well, even if the poet, in the 'making' of the signifying 'world' which embodies such insight, does this 'making' under inspiration, it may be that the words that emerge to carry the story and enable others to share such insight are not adequate to the insight itself, or to its communication. But in any case, these are relevant dimensions in the sort of truthful disclosure in question here, which stems more from the divinely-intensified spiritual touch with the spirit of the past than from anything else. If we would find the poetry in its truthful disclosure in this sense, and that seems a precondition to our reflective understanding of such disclosure, it is not enough to sustain a fact-referent frame of mind while listening to the poem. That concern with fact may be relevant in the first mode of truthful disclosure, but it is alien to the

second. To find the poem working in this other mode, we have to enter into the poem and experience immersion in its 'world', and then reflect from out of that involvement upon what takes place within it. But would this demand for immersion mean: we would have to find that Muse at work in ourselves which inspired the poet in his making? If so, it might be that the most immediate response to such presence would be toward our own remaking of the poem, our working as poet rather than as thinker. To really feel that possibility is to discover how the competitive response of bard to bard might appropriately take place in the setting of religious festivals.

33. And which could again obtain in the present and future, of course.

34. To the extent that this side to the divine (the gods) is linked with the Homeric representation of another side, namely, Moira, an even fuller religious sense emerges. But again, as the focus of the story is upon the humans and not the gods, so such focus upon the divine as is involved is upon the gods rather than Moira. This power is left for the most part in the background, and in any case is not presented in anthropomorphic figure (the use of the name itself is not sufficient to constitute such a figure). Yet the very meaning of the drama itself, and the working of the foreground figures that brings the drama to pass, accomplishes destiny and attests to this distant and inscrutable presence.

35. Among their distant kin, the Aryans who invaded India, there was for long a comparable diversity, despite the early presence of a priestly class. It was only as the Aryan response to the indigenous people, together with the incursion of new Aryan tribes, brought into question what the true way of life was, and the priestly class succeeded in articulating a common vision which, at least by way of many priests, it would promulgate as an orthodoxy, that something like a formal and embracing religion for the increasingly integrated Aryan and non-Aryan in north India emerged. Greece never knew such a development, in any of its phases or aspects.

NANCY WORMAN

This Voice Which Is Not One:
Helen's Verbal Guises in Homeric Epic

The voices of many important female characters in Homeric epic differ from each other in vocabulary choice, tone, and formulaic expression. While occasion dictates these differences to some extent, the style of each female speaker is generally true to her character type. Just as Nestor's measured, honey-sweet tones and use of exempla suit his status as elder statesman, so do Andromache's mournful self-reference and admonishing use of the future tense serve to mark her further as the paradigmatic widow, even when her husband is still alive. If certain characters show a remarkable degree of consistency in their speech types, others speak in a manner that is more changeable, inclusive, and therefore difficult to categorize, the hybrid quality of which arises from their variegated roles in Homeric narrative. Of all the Homeric characters, Odysseus most thoroughly embodies this type of verbal mutability; in this study I focus on the speech patterns of the female figure in Homer who does so—Helen.

It has become standard practice among scholars of gender in Greek literature to emphasize the problem that female characters pose as producers of signs (since they are themselves signs of a sort traded among male agents), and to cite Lévi-Strauss' famous formulation of this conundrum.[1] Helen is in some sense the paradigmatic exchanged sign, in that her figure strikingly encapsulates both the process of objectification inherent in this symbolic

From *Making Silence Speak: Women's Voices in Greek Literature and Society* , edited by André Lardinois and Laura McClure. © 2001 by Princeton University Press.

exchange and its fundamental problems. Simultaneously the archetypal bride
and the most illustrious flouter of the marriage bond, Helen embodies the
dangerous potential of all women to be unfaithful to their men. She is also
the paradigmatic elusive object of male desire, whose semidivine status
underscores the impossibility of complete control over the female as a type,
and, on a more abstract level, of all that she might symbolize: the generative
forces of both plant life and poetry, the destructive powers of both sex and
dominion. Helen's cultic associations with the lover Aphrodite and the
parthenos Artemis indicate her failure to make the transition to a stable
marital status, as Claude Calame has argued.[2] She remains in circulation, the
glorious bride gone wrong. From the earliest discernible point in the
tradition of stories about Helen, she is this multiple, inclusive, and dangerous
figure, whose reputation fluctuates repeatedly between praise and blame.
Unlike her sister Clytemnestra, she is not only a figure of abuse; unlike
Penelope, her predominate story is not that of the faithful wife. Although
versions of Clytemnestra's and Penelope's tales suggest the possibility of
defending the one and accusing the other, only the figure of Helen comprises
both versions of the wife's story poised in tense competition.

    Plato relates an episode about the archaic poet Stesichorus that
revolves around Helen's praise and blame, in which the poet, struck blind by
the angry goddess, is said to have retracted his tale about her journey to
Troy.[3] A Hellenistic commentary explains that Stesichorus composed a poem
in which a phantasm of Helen went to Troy, while the real Helen was kept
safe in Egypt.[4] The episode highlights the dangerous power of Helen's anger
and her control of her own reputation, relating it specifically to poetic
production.[5] Euripides treats the story of the *eidolon* in his play *Helen*, where
her doubled figure makes manifest the epistemological problem at the heart
of theatrical representation. His *Trojan Women*, in some contrast, uses a
seductive Helen to suggest the moral threat of the misapplication of praise,
especially when couched in a decorative rhetorical style.[6] Archaic and
classical writers thus consistently treat Helen as signifying the dangerous
aspects not only of women but also of poetic and rhetorical effect. The
Homeric poet himself seems to respond to a preexisting tradition of
conflicting stories, apparent in the tensions between the more forgiving
depiction of Helen that he clearly favors and the darker implications that he
allows to intrude. Unlike more narrowly delimited characters in epic, Helen
represents a complex of forces in human life and a multitude of stories; her
biography constitutes a series of public events, each one a pivotal moment in
the lives of many.

    So what type of voice does such an inclusive figure have? A voice that
is not one, it seems; that is multiple and layered; that includes speech types

strongly associated with relatively consistent characters, but transposed into other contexts where standard meanings do not necessarily match particular intentions. Helen's special type of verbal mutability arises at least in part from a difference between the formal locutions she employs and the intended impact of her words, so that a gap repeatedly opens up between the usual meanings of familiar formulae and her singular implications. This gap between meaning and intention is not necessarily unique to Helen (again, cf. Odysseus), but it does take a unique form in her usage. Helen is a mimic, as her first husband is quick to point out (*Od.* 4.279); she takes on the voices of others (including both tone and typical phraseology), most often as a means of deflection. In practical terms, she thereby avoids direct blame, but this verbal mutability is also more profoundly related to her as the embodiment of multiple stories.

The Iliadic Helen is the only character in the Homeric poems to engage in self-abuse; no one else turns such barbs against themselves. Nor does any other Homeric character engage in abusing Helen, even though, as Linda Clader has discussed, she arouses in others the shudder that suggests the chilly gusts of Hades or the presence of Nemesis (Indignation, Retribution), whose child she sometimes is.[7] In both the *Iliad* and the *Odyssey* she refers to herself as "dog-faced", which, especially in the *Iliad*, serves as an important signal of her fateful connections. Dogs are linked to Hades; they attend Hecate, and feed voraciously on human carrion.[8] They are thus bound up with the fated end-point of all human life, which Helen brings about quickly for many Greek heroes. Gregory Nagy has noted the association of blame speech with carrion feeding (specifically the corpses of heroes),[9] while Margaret Graver has argued more recently that Helen's dog insult is evidence of a defaming tradition.[10] Graver's excellent discussion nevertheless overlooks the tension created by Helen's particular use of such insults, in part because she regards Homer's treatment of Helen as unproblematically gentle. But in Homer, the traces of this blame tradition confound any understanding of Helen as simply good or evil—as simply a goddess or a dog. In every scene in which she appears, her speech is edged threateningly with competing implications, with suggestions of precisely the blame that the Homeric poet's dominant images of her repeatedly counter.[11]

At least in part as a result of this narrative competition, attempts to find consistency of character in the figure of the Homeric Helen impede rather than promote an understanding of how she functions in the poems. In the *Iliad*, Helen's vocabulary and speech patterns seem to echo the mourner's voice[12] and that of some stricken or angry hero, combining the vocabulary of regret with self-abuse and/or abuse of others, in contexts that suggest a covert seduction of her interlocutors. In the *Odyssey*, she speaks in a manner that makes her look like an all-knowing and sympathetic poet-goddess, and she is treated by both the external narrator and her internal audience with such respect that her verbal interactions seem powerful and bewitching. Helen combines the coy perspicacity of the goddesses who host Odysseus in their beds with the commanding tones of both the Muses and the poet, representing her role in Odysseus' adventures as a singular mix of authoritative stances.

Many recent studies have exposed the doubling, fictionalizing aspects of Helen's figure in the *Odyssey*, in some general way supporting the notion that Helen's verbal type is multiple and changeable.[13] But these discussions analyze Helen from outside of her figure, as it were, tending to consider Helen's doubleness as symbolic of the poet's dilemma and not looking in any detail at how Helen's own speech patterns establish her as both a potentially dissembling speaker and one of consummate suitability, a central oratorical criterion for effective speaking.[14] For the purposes of this discussion, I am less interested in the epistemological problems that the figure of Helen poses than in what makes her speeches in the *Odyssey* seem so appropriate and therefore so persuasive. I argue against the grain of recent assumptions about the characterization of Helen in both poems, examining her speaking style in some detail to show how seductively fractious she is in the *Iliad* and how eerily calming she is in the *Odyssey*.

THE VOICE OF NEMESIS

Helen's character in the *Iliad* has usually been taken at face value by scholars: they describe her rueful responses to Priam and Hector and her angry rejection of Paris and Aphrodite as sympathetic depictions, often without analyzing in any detail the ambiguous quality of these verbal exchanges.[15] I suggest, in contrast, that in these exchanges 1) Helen's apparent tone often does not match her ultimate intention, and 2) the speech types she uses—which range from the mournful widow's to the flyting warrior's—are transposed from their usual contexts to form locutions unique to her. Helen is also significantly aware of her centrality to the narratives of others, manifesting a concern for reputation (*kleos*) that connects her to the Muses, the Sirens, and ultimately the poet, as a number of scholars have recognized.[16] In the Teichoscopia (*Il.* 3.141–244), for example, when she is asked by Priam to name a warrior, Helen uses her identification of Agamemnon to frame an elegiac look at her own past, thus substituting her story for his. Her reply is not particularly suited to the context. In fact, it somewhat resembles in content Andromache's mournful speech in book 6, when the latter bewails her widow's fate to her living husband. Andromache's voice, however, is consistently grief-stricken, and her use of the mourner's topoi (e.g., lamenting family ties, dilation on the effect the death will have on one's life) coheres with her role as loyal wife.[17] Helen's rueful self-reference instead mingles regret with an emphatic awareness of her own singular status. When Priam asks Helen to name Ajax, her identification moves quickly from his epithets (e.g., 3.229) to the Cretan leader Idomeneus, who as a guest-friend of Menelaus reminds her again of her own story, and she remarks on the absence of her brothers from the battlefield (3.234–42). She then conjectures that their absence can be explained by their fears of shame and reproach that are rightfully hers (3.242).

Since she views the actions of others as dependent on her error and rues bitterly this damage to her reputation, Helen assigns herself the crucial role in others' stories, thereby giving voice to the blame tradition that the narrator avoids. Her sense of her public reputation is anomalous among the female figures in Homeric epic; *kleos* is rightfully the concern of the warrior, not of the warrior's prize. Like any good warrior (and unlike her paramour), she fears the insults of others (3.242, 3.412, 24.767–68) and recognizes the vulnerability of her public position. Helen, in contrast to the chaste Andromache, treats her story—in part the battles waged essentially for her that she weaves in her second husband's halls (*Il.* 3.125–28)—as if it were the story most central to every warrior's life. And this in some sense is the case: whereas the mourning wife's story would only be properly told in keening over her husband, Helen's story is on the lips of everyone, since it is relevant to all the warriors. As the catalyzing, fateful figure for these heroes, her story is their story; her own *kleos* is inevitably bound up with the *kleos* of each.[18]

But the complexity of Helen's figure and voice in this scene does not end there. Before she lapses into self-reflection in response to Priam's first inquiry, she says that he is worthy of veneration and fearsome in her eyes (3.172), using a show of extreme respect that implies an apologetic attitude consistent with her penchant for self-abuse, the primary stylistic tendency unique to her. Helen then declares, in reference to her coming to Troy, "Would that evil death had pleased me" (3.173–74), invoking in a sensuous manner the end point with which she is associated.[19] She makes a similar (though blander) declaration in her mourning speech over the body of Hector in book 24: "Would that I had been destroyed before" (764). Andromache uses a related construction when, as Hector is dragged around the city walls, she regrets that Eetion bore her (22.481).[20] In book 21, fearing an unheroic end to his life, Achilles cries out to Zeus in prayer: "Would that Hector had killed me" (279). In the *Odyssey*, the shade of Achilles wishes something similar for Agamemnon: "Would that you had met your death and fate in Troy" (24.30–31). Most famously, in *Odyssey* 5 Odysseus exclaims as he faces the storm near Scheria, "How I wish I had died and met my fate in Troy" (5.308); he repeats the exclamation in the fictional account of his travails that he gives to Eumaeus (14.274).[21]

The *ophelon* phrase thus seems to be a locution used both by those in mourning and by Homeric heroes caught in threatening or painful situations—or, in the case of Odysseus, when telling about them in guest-friendship situations. The phrase does not, however, only communicate bitter despair (which may be either a *cri du coeur* or a persuasive tactic). When turned on another, it may also be used as an insult in verbal contests, reproaches, and taunts, an important aspect of its usage for analyzing Helen's speeches.[22] In the *Odyssey*, Odysseus most frequently utters the phrase, deploying it twice (of four times in the *Odyssey* and once in the *Iliad*) when he is trying to use a painful situation to gain sympathy, a complex deployment similar to Helen's. In the *Iliad*, it is Helen's favorite locution for expressing both despair and scorn, which she usually does with some other end in mind (of all characters she uses the phrase most often, five times in the *Iliad*). As a stranger in Troy, her usage in the *Iliad* resembles that of Odysseus in the *Odyssey*, who must make clever use of guest-friendship situations to win his way home. Just as Odysseus, when seeking empathy from the Phaeacians (*Od.* 11.547), regrets that he won Achilles' arms instead of Ajax, Helen, when seeking empathy from Priam and Hector (*Il.* 3 and 6), regrets that she followed Paris. Though each time she employs the phrase Helen's aim is slightly different, never is it simply the direct outpouring of emotion that it sounds. Although its repetition links her tone both to mourning diction and to the hero's emotions and concern for *kleos*, her application of this type of phrase is unique. Rather than actually being a widow or a hero in challenging circumstances, Helen echoes their outbursts by employing an emotional appeal that sounds like self-address, a layered locution whose related aims are deflecting blame and cementing allegiances. In her use of the phrase to cast scorn on Paris, for example, once she seems to be teasing him and once to be flattering his brother.

The earlier scene in book 3 involving Paris alone is plotted by Aphrodite, whose machinations irk her protegée and who inspires in her a passion that seems suspended between desire (for the beautiful Paris whom Aphrodite describes, 3.391–94) and anger at the very goddess with whom she is so closely associated.[23] Note that Helen herself calls her painful feelings ἄκριτα (3.412), the most common meaning of which is "confused, indeterminate," a word that thus underscores both the complexity of Helen's passion and (what comes to the same thing) the merging of roles in this scene, so that Helen's abuse of Aphrodite comes close to self-abuse.[24] Helen has been referred to as a "faded Aphrodite";[25] their conversation resembles an internal dialogue—a debate not only between Helen and her *daimon* but also between two of the facets that make up her many-sided figure, with its multiple motivations and opposing traditions. Moreover, her scornful responses to her intimates resemble each other: she exhorts both Aphrodite and Paris with dismissive imperatives (3.406, 432) and pictures each in a compromised position (3.407–9, 434–36); correlatively, she uses the *ophelon* phrases of both herself and Paris. Her reproach of Aphrodite for using seductive talk (3.399) also recalls Hector's insulting of his brother for being a seducer (3.49). Helen engages in this derogatory language only with those closest to her;[26] a significant variation on the normal context of such blame speech, her usage parallels as well Hector's treatment of Paris.

The scornful abuse of one so intimate can sound similar to the dueling speech of warriors (e.g., the use of negative epithets and goading imperatives). Coupled with Helen's self-abusive epithets, this speech and that in which she reproaches Paris mimic the aggressive challenge of the hero on the battlefield.[27] When Helen returns to the bedroom as ordered by Aphrodite, her expression and tone suggest pique,[28] while her taunting phrases recall the flyting warrior: "Would that you had died there," she says, "subdued by the better man, who was once my husband" (3.428–29). At the beginning of book 3 Hector similarly chastises his brother on the battlefield, declaring that he wishes Paris had never been born or had died unmarried (3.40). In the bedroom Helen changes her tack with brusque abruptness, first telling Paris to go and challenge Menelaus for a second time, then remarking that he had better not, since Menelaus would probably kill him (3.432–36).[29] Compare first Achilles, who goads Aeneas with a parallel insult in a famous flyting scene, when he urges him to retreat into the mass of soldiers lest he be harmed (20.197). And compare again Hector, who challenges his brother in similar terms ("Couldn't you stand up to Ares-loving Menelaus?" 3.51), and then predicts that if he did he would end up "mingling with the dust" (3.55). Both Helen and Hector contrast Paris unfavorably with Menelaus, and point up the superiority of the Greek by giving Paris' defeat sexual overtones (e.g., "mingling" 3.48, 55], "subduing" [3.429, 436]). For Paris the lover, even encounters on the battlefield have a tincture of the bedroom.[30] These two scornful acknowledgments of his unwarlike attitude serve to frame book 3, so that it begins and ends with Paris' sensual presence and the bellicose types who reproach him: Hector and Helen. Helen's use of this stance is not nearly so straightforward as her brother-in-law's, of course. She imports a verbal style that belongs on the battlefield, and that here in the intimate context of the bedroom takes on an additional layer of meaning—offering a sexual as well as a military challenge.

Indeed, Paris (lover that he is) responds to this goading by treating it as a kind of bitter foreplay. And it appears that Helen's amorous husband has interpreted her taunts in some sense rightly, for Helen follows him to bed. By invoking her war-loving first husband in order to prick her bed-loving second, she employs the militaristic attitude of the one in order to denigrate qualities that she herself shares with the other, and her physical acquiescence reiterates her reluctant bond with him. That is, when she turns the emotional phrasing of the angry wish against her too-tender husband, she links herself to him and both of them to Aphrodite (since she and the goddess are the other recipients of such reproach). The hero's despair as well as his scorn thus take on a singular usage in Helen's mouth: in challenging those who share her affinities, she implicates herself in the abuse that she levels at them, while also preempting the criticism of others. In this way she stands poised against the gentle judgments of those who would forgive her, her character operating as a window on this defamatory tradition.

Something similar occurs in book 6, although Helen's tone has changed somewhat since her interaction with Paris in book 3, and now she speaks with a post-coital combination of enticement and gentle abuse. When Hector comes to rouse Paris from his sensuous reverie in the bedroom, Helen tries to get her manly brother-in-law to sit down by scorning her soft and lovely husband.[31] She engages in a delicate seduction of Hector, addressing him with "honey-sweet words" (6.343). Both Nestor and the Sirens also speak in a honeyed manner, so that the term delimits a range of speech types from the authoritatively but gently persuasive to the dangerously seductive,[32] a mesmerizing quality that marks Helen's speaking style in this passage. When Hector first enters and reproaches his brother, the mild Paris responds that Helen had just been urging him to return to battle with "soft words" (6.337)—unusual content for such beguiling tones. The enticing associations that attend *malakos* ("soft") thus contrast strangely with the stringency of her message, while those that attend *meilichios* ("honey-sweet") lend her words a potentially threatening quality. Thus Hector's refusal to sit with her becomes a refusal to play the victim role to her Siren, a role that his brother willingly takes on. While the Homeric poet may counter this ominous seductive quality at the surface level of the scene, it nonetheless resonates there as a disturbing subtext.

From this perspective, it should not be surprising that Helen begins her conversation with Hector by invoking her threatening qualities, but in the self-debasing mode that she employed with his father. She calls herself an "evil-devising, shudder-inspiring dog" (6.344; cf. 6.356; 3.180). The wish construction that follows is an elaborate expansion of her earlier use of it. Rather than simply desiring to die, she declares that she wishes that on her day of birth a gust of wind had carried her off to the mountains, or into a wave of the many-voiced sea (6.345–48). Helen purports to desire a type of end that Jean-Pierre Vernant relates to being seized by a god, invoking a connection between erotic love and death that he considers especially relevant to Helen's type.[33] An echo of her wish in book 3 that death had "pleased" her (3.173), Helen's lyrical desire for rapture here in *Iliad* 6 lends sensuous overtones to her speech. While her words explicitly depict regret, her flowery turns of phrase and sweetened tones suggest an attempt to soften Hector's attitude toward herself if not her husband: she sides with Hector in his chastising of his brother, yearns aloud for divine seizure, and notes ruefully her and Paris' future fame. Recall the similarity of Hector's and Helen's reproaches in book 3; here again she mimics his attitude, this time to his face with the goal of cementing her connection to him. Her maneuver is a delicate one. She must acknowledge her alliance with Paris in order to show her awareness of their shame; but she thereby also isolates herself from him, since he assumes no responsibility for his actions. As in book 3, Helen brackets herself with Paris as objects of abuse, highlighting their status here by using the *ophelon* phrase twice in expressions of heroic bitterness to apply to herself and her husband (6.345, 350). Homer thus has Helen transform the typical intentions of the phrase by using it for this anomalous speech act, layering self-abuse, scorn for an intimate, and a seductive allegiance of perspective, all of which ultimately aim at softening the heart of her interlocutor. While Hector does not in the end sit down with Helen, neither does he speak roughly to her, instead responding with a respect that resembles his father's treatment of her. By introducing a defamatory tradition that threatens to reveal her infamous side and yet ultimately serves an apotropaic function, Helen succeeds in deflecting blame: again, no one else abuses her as she abuses herself.

At the end of the *Iliad* (24.760–75), Helen has the final mourning speech over Hector's dead body—a surprising status that supports Graver's argument that the Homeric poet is forcefully asserting an alternate tradition that elevates Helen and questions her blame. But if we look more closely at precisely how she mourns Hector, beyond her use of the mourner's topos of bewailing her fate as vulnerable survivor, we can see that her lament in this case focuses entirely on the threat of blame—the threat, that is, of the other story, the tale of bad-dog Helen. This is not to say that other mourners do not fear ill repute: Andromache certainly does, but mostly for her son Astyanax (e.g., *Il.* 22.494–501).[34] Helen's lament, in some contrast, is only about repute; in detailing her fears for the future, she makes no mention of other horrors such as slavery and remarriage, which are often voiced by newly bereft female mourners in both epic and tragedy.[35] After expressing her usual sentiment of regret (24.764), Helen notes that she had never heard a debasing or disrespectful word from her brother-in-law. She adds that if anyone else in his family ever reproached her, Hector would fend them off verbally with his gentle mind and words (24.768–72). She concludes by declaring that everyone else shudders in her presence (24.775).

Helen's final word in the *Iliad* resonates with the dread that she might inspire, as the dog-faced daughter of Nemesis whose self-blame in Homer repeatedly suggests this other story. Hector, like the poet, may be gentle-minded toward Helen, but her description of his protection reveals how tenuous this praise tradition is; here as elsewhere in the poem her words declare one thing but point to another—this time her dangerous qualities, which cause a sensation in those around her like the chilly hand of Hades. At these moments Helen's figure suggests the deadly side of the female, to which Greek poets often attribute the downfall of men in some profound and sweeping manner. These figures are the embodiment of Fate, the Medusa who freezes the bones, the Nemesis who is the end of the hubristic man, even the Aphrodite who (dog-faced) devours the husband's energy and wealth alike.[36] The word *nemesis* ("retribution") in fact surfaces repeatedly in Helen's speech and that of those who speak in her presence (e.g., 3.156, 3.410, 6.3 35–36,6.351). That is, in the scenes where Helen appears, her presence seems to call forth the *nemesis* that is an essential aspect of her story. And her speeches, in their insistence on her infamous associations, serve as constant reminders of the just indignation and deserved retribution that acts of hubris bring down on the heads of those who commit them.

THE PAINLESS STORY

While Helen is a weaving narrator of her own story in the *Iliad* (3.125–28),[37] in the *Odyssey* the objects that associate her with weaving signal the context of formal ritual conducted by people of high status. In book 4, she descends from her bedroom accompanied by handmaidens and weaving implements that were gifts from Egyptian royalty—her own gifts, as the narrator points out, not those obtained by her husband (4.130). Moreover, she is accompanied by the handmaiden Adraste, a name that Clader notes recalls Adrasteia, a cult title of the goddess Nemesis;[38] the scene of her descent into the *megaron* in its entirety strongly suggests the entrance of a goddess—if a dangerous one. In book 15 she gives to Telemachus a gown of her own fine weaving as a token of guest-friendship, requesting that he accept it as a memory token of herself and that he give it to his future wife (15.124–29). The gesture should possess a disturbing ritual power, since a wedding gown from Helen would symbolize both the marriage bond and its transgression.

And yet in both scenes Helen plies, without recoil from others, implements of guest-friendship (the condolence drug and the marriage dress) that not only are profoundly associated with her figure, but also suggest and then eerily suppress the problems that she embodies for story-telling on the one hand and gift-giving on the other.

Helen's speeches, which accompany her handling of these objects, invoke various models of authoritative speech—the Muses, the poet or choral performer, the speaker of prophecy—and demonstrate her sensitivity to the appropriate locution. Helen's first words to her audience draw purposeful attention to her perceptive abilities and narrative control. When she recognizes Telemachus as the son of Odysseus, she asks, "Should I lie or should I speak the truth?" (4.140), recalling the power that the Muses possess.[39] In this scene Helen gives shape and purpose to the conversation and saves the dinner party (albeit in questionable fashion) by doling out to her hearers a condolence drug. The narrator terms this substance "no-pain" (4.221), while emphasizing the grotesque effects of such emotional benumbing. But the ambiguous and powerful drug, in combination with Helen's words, staunches the flow of tears among the diners, which her husband had tended to augment. The *nepenthe* thus serves as an essential complement to her control of verbal interaction and storytelling. And although the juxtaposition of Helen's and Menelaus' stories also encourages the audience to question her true inclinations, it similarly promotes her narrative authority. She implicitly associates herself with Zeus, the Muses, and the epic poet, while Menelaus approves her story openly and imitates the structure of her narrative frame.

Most readers have focused on the ominous qualities of both Helen and her drug, and seemed to accept that Menelaus' is the true version of events. But Helen's command of verbal interaction is such that the *Odyssey*, unlike the *Iliad*, almost succeeds in suppressing completely the disturbing implications of her hosting strategies. These surface only briefly and cause little reaction in Helen's interlocutors, leaving behind in the external audience an eerie sense that they have been seduced by a rhetorically agile speaker and that all may not be well in Sparta.[40] As a measure of this near-success, Helen only refers to herself once with the dog epithet (4.145). That is, her defamatory tradition is not nearly so dominant as it is in the *Iliad*, and even her husband's story avoids blaming her directly for her actions. Although, as a metapoetic figure, Helen does seem in this scene to represent the doubling nature of storytelling,[41] as an adept speaker she calms indecision and effectively overshadows her husband's potentially upsetting tale.

Helen first explains that she will not recount all the feats that Odysseus undertook during the war; rather, she says, she will only describe his achievements within the walls of Troy. The phrase she uses in introducing her narrative resembles her husband's to Peisistratus (4.242, cf. 204–5); later he repeats her phrase almost exactly (4.271).[42] Her usage calls attention to her sensitivity to conversational context: she signals the suitability of her story by sounding like her husband, who has been speaking with great warmth and familiarity about both Odysseus and Nestor. Helen also establishes her status as a narrator by suggesting that, like Telemachus' father, she possesses one of the primary attributes of the authoritative speaker: great perspicuity. Describing Odysseus' appearance in Troy disguised as a slave, she claims that she alone recognized him and taxed him with her knowledge. She emphasizes the extent of his disguise by repeating phrases that mark his likeness to a man of low status, a rhetorical strategy that underscores both his cleverness at deception and hers at detection (4.244–51). Odysseus, having beaten himself with blows that are unbefitting (4.244) of the hero, is so unlike himself—so like a household slave or a beggar (4.245, 247–49)—that he slips into Troy (4.246, 249) unnoticed, except by Helen herself. Odysseus counters her probing eye by refusing to confirm her identification until she has bathed and anointed him, dressed him well, and sworn a great oath of secrecy to him—that is, until she has treated him as do those other dread goddesses Calypso and Circe, from the care of the hero's body to the swearing of an oath not to harm him.[43]

Helen then explicitly claims that, after she played the role of ministering goddess, Odysseus told her the "whole plot" (4.256) of the Greeks. Once again she emphasizes her omniscience, or at least the vast extent of her knowledge, leaving open the possibility that she may have even been told then about the Trojan horse (the device that would end the war)—as her probing response to it in Menelaus' story suggests. Helen also describes her heart's rejoicing amid the wail of the Trojan women at Odysseus' subsequent killing of Trojans (4.259–60), which (as she implies) she made possible by being loyal to those with whom she now dines.[44] Sitting once again with her first husband, she ends her story by implicitly comparing Menelaus favorably to Paris, calling the former "my husband" (4.263), who, she declares, is not inferior to "anyone" (4.264). Helen's self-portrait is carefully calibrated both to support her claims to narrative authority and to gratify her audience; it could not be more delicately balanced or more suitably told.

This elegant story is thrown into some question by Menelaus' depiction of Helen's loyalties in the war (4.265–89), although how well he succeeds in doing so or even how much he desires to has, I think, been exaggerated by recent readers of the scene. He initially responds to his wife's tale by remarking that she has told everything "in a fitting fashion" (4.266), an interesting characterization for a speech whose pivotal sympathies he seems himself to refute. In rhetorical terms, phrases such as *kata moiran* do not assess the truth of the speech, but rather whether the speaker is behaving appropriately with her words. Gregory Nagy has argued convincingly that in Homer the phrases *kata moiran* and *kata aisan* indicate conformity to epic diction in particular.[45] Helen's speech would then meet the criteria not only of dinner-table etiquette but also of the poet's genre, further supporting her status both as an authoritative speaker and as a metarhetorical figure whose implications for speech-making help delineate the boundaries of the genre itself.

Menelaus thus implicitly approves Helen's ability to tell a story that highlights Odysseus' ingenuity and his military prowess and that thereby flatters and gratifies his son. He then reaffirms the aptness of her speech by using a similar frame for his own tale. Helen's first words had paid homage to Zeus, father of the Muses and of Helen herself, so that she established her unparalleled authority as a knower and a speaker by implied association with both (a connection aided by the repetition of "all" [*apantia ... panta*, 4.237, 240])—in effect collapsing the roles of the Muses and the poet.[46] And perhaps most important, by underscoring her role as a knowing story-teller, she allied herself with Odysseus. In his introduction Menelaus echoes one phrase of Helen's exactly (4.242 and 4.271); he also employs a similar introductory strategy, pointing up his own status and exclaiming over the endurance of Odysseus in the service of the Achaeans (4.267–73).[47] Most pointedly, he declares that, although he has encountered the strategies and mental types of many men and traveled far (like Odysseus), he has never seen such a one as Odysseus. Both introductory strategies seek to control the reception of the tale by pointing (either implicitly or explicitly) to the wisdom and experience of the tellers, thereby grounding the authority of both as narrators in their known characters and their fortuitous resemblance to the authoritative type whose story they tell (i.e., Menelaus is a hero-traveler, Helen is an associate of the Muses). In affirming the appropriateness of his wife's speech and echoing her verbal strategy, Menelaus effectively weakens the negative impact of his own story.

This potential conflict is further mitigated by the fact that Menelaus blames his wife's actions on Aphrodite, who intended that Helen be driven to bring ruin to the Trojans (4.274–75). In the end, Odysseus' protector Athena leads Helen away from the horse, so that in Menelaus' story, goddesses compel both her arrival on the scene and her leave-taking. The only event not motivated by the goddesses—and for which Helen may thus be held responsible—is her imitation of the voices of the warriors' wives. In this she is met and matched by Odysseus. As in her own story, here in her husband's

Helen and Odysseus are paired as singularly clever, especially in relation to verbal manipulation. If Helen can don multiple verbal disguises (something the hero does elsewhere in the *Odyssey*), Odysseus can effectively see through her disguise (as she alone saw through his).

Thus while Odysseus sits inside the Trojan horse, alone in his recognition of Helen, she—still a sharp-eyed detector—literally probes its significance, fondling its sides as if touching all the Greek husbands and mouthing the voices of their wives (4.277–79). This mimetic ability matches that which the female chorus is said to have (to its great glory) in the *Hymn to Delian Apollo* (162–64).[48] Like the Muses, Helen can tell the truth or not; like the rhapsode or choral performer, she can imitate the voices of others to the delight and/or danger of her audience. And although as an object of narrative she does signal the doubling, dissimulating nature of mimesis, as a speaking subject she exhibits a formidable facility to detect the identities of others, to assume the roles of various authoritative types, and to suit her tale to the context of its utterance. Helen herself merely claims before she tells her story that she will speak "suitable things" (4.239)—things that, if they are not true, ought to be, by virtue of the extent to which they fit the context in which they are told. *Eoikota* are ethically "true"; they suit character and situation and are thus the mainstay of the rhetorically adept speaker.

Compare the scene in book 15, where Helen's extraordinary control of signifying objects (e.g., the gown, but also the eagle and the goose in the omen that she deciphers) effects a near-complete suppression of the troubling aspects of her figure, to the extent that she is able to hand over an item that she explicitly labels as a marriage gift without any negative reaction on the part of its recipient. When Helen gives Telemachus the robe, she calls it "a memory token from the hands of Helen for the much-desired wedding time" (15.126), precisely the ritual whose luxurious trappings and illicit transgression she symbolizes. This scene echoes one in *Iliad* 6 where Hecuba chooses a gown to dedicate to Athena, but with emphatically different effect. There the poet states explicitly that Paris took these gowns from Sidon on his way home with Helen (6.289–92), so that Hecuba's offering—which she makes when the Greeks are effectively at the door—is a precisely matched payment for Helen's having been brought to Troy with these same items. In this scene Helen's figure surfaces as a reminder of Paris' transgression, as another ruinous object, whose return may not bring about the gods' protection (as the dedication of the gown does not, 6.311). When Helen gives the marriage dress to Telemachus in *Odyssey* 15, it is of her own making (i.e., she is associated with it as a craftsman, rather than as a fellow object). She is its author, in effect, and she assigns to it the label and type of narrative that she desires for it.[49] While the object, in its connection to marriage and gift-giving, may still resonate with negative connotations for the external audience, Helen exercises impressive control over its signification for the internal audience, transforming it from a would-be ruinous object into one with happy associations.

This scene also adds another model of authoritative speech to Helen's repertoire. Her agile reading of the omen that marks the departure of Telemachus and Peisistratus from Sparta (15.160–78) precisely forecasts Odysseus' interpretation of Penelope's dream (*Od.* 19.555–58), thereby linking Helen both to the seer's role and, once again, to Odysseus himself. Helen's prophecy foreshadows Odysseus', and like a good seer she foretells what does come to pass. Most interestingly, she relates with striking brevity the plot and conclusion of the *Odyssey* ("Thus Odysseus having suffered many evils and wandered much, will return home and exact retribution"),[50] again collapsing the roles that mark a special authority: the omniscience of the Muses and the narrative compass of the poet. Compare especially the opening of the *Odyssey* (1.1–5), with its similar repetition of "many/much", its juxtaposition of wandering and suffering, and its reference to *nostos*, Odysseus' primary goal.[51] Where the Homeric poet holds off the end of the story, Helen includes it, spanning the entire narrative in a single sentence.[52]

In *Odyssey* 15, then, Helen seems in possession of an inhuman knowledge, and as usual Menelaus is greatly overshadowed by his more mentally and rhetorically agile wife. Here he "ponders how he might express his thoughts judiciously" (15.169–70), while his wife prophesies with startling alacrity. Note that Menelaus is unsure how to speak in a context that requires a suitable response, precisely the kind of response that Helen is capable of, as her husband himself had acknowledged earlier (4.266). Helen's mantic capabilities elicit an avowal from Telemachus that he will worship her as a goddess in his own land, pledging the establishment of a cult in Ithaca like that which did exist in the archaic period in Sparta and perhaps elsewhere.[53] Thus the scene's final words on Helen acknowledge her status not merely as prophet or poet but also as herself divine—as one, that is, who might know more than the average human, not just about the details of the story but also about how to tell it in a deeply appropriate manner. In the *Odyssey*, Helen is persuasive enough that she nearly manages to circumvent entirely the obvious problem with her voice in the first place: that it is changeable and multiple, just as her figure is symbolic of the multiplicity of stories to be told.

Both the *Iliad* and the *Odyssey* depict Helen as a subtly appropriate and appropriative speaker. She echoes the typical phrases of the mournful wife and the challenged hero in a unique form of self-abuse, often deploying this emotional tone to draw her audience into sympathy with her. Or she speaks like a divinely persuasive narrator, while the self-image she projects invokes the inevitable suitability of her words. The changeable quality of Helen's voice reflects her indeterminate and yet authoritative status in Homeric epic: she is half god, half mortal, a forbidding presence even among aristocratic men; she is the wife of too many men, and so the contested possession of everyone and no one; her speaking style is similarly that of everyone and no one. In the *Iliad* Helen's voice is not openly authoritative, but she succeeds in using her despairing, self-abusive tone to maintain a covert control of verbal exchanges. The *Odyssey* represents Helen as being in easy command of the conversation; her voice is authoritative and deeply suitable in manner, if often ambiguous or possibly deceptive in content. In her verbal guises of the mournful wife, the despairing or scornful warrior, the perspicacious poet-goddess, or the gracious host, she shows herself capable of the mimesis with which Menelaus charges her—with all the subtle enticement and potential danger that implies. Helen's variegated speaking style and striking narrative control signal her encompassing role in the Homeric poems as the embodiment of Nemesis. She is the beginning and end of the Trojan War story for both the Greeks and the Trojans, and the figure whose conflicting characterizations and multiple voices repeatedly raise the specter of fateful competition, be it military or poetic.

NOTES

1. Lévi-Strauss [1958] 1963: 61: "For words do not speak, while women do; as producers of signs, women can never be reduced to the status of symbols or tokens." See, e.g., Bergren 1983; du Bois [1978] 1996; Suzuki 1989; Joplin 1991; Katz 1991; Wohl 1998.

2. Calame [1977] 1997: 191–93.

3. Pl. *Phdr.* 243a3–b2.

4. *P. Oxy.* 2506, fr. 26, col. 1.

5. On Stesichorus and Helen's relationship to the construction of an authoritative tradition, see Bassi 1993; and cf. Nagy 1990: 419–23.

6. I argue elsewhere (Worman 1997) that this play shares with Gorgias' *Helen* the use of her body to demonstrate the erotic effects of persuasive style.

7. *Cypria* fr. 7; see Clader 1976: 18–23, esp. nn. 30 and 31. Her detailed discussion— which predates by fifteen years the more recent flurry of attention around Helen—has served as the basis for many studies, often without sufficient recognition of her work. Vernant ([1985] 1991b: 102–3) similarly associates Helen with Kêr, Fate, and the Erinyes. Cf. Vermeule 1979: 159.

8. See Redfield [1975] 1991: 193–203; also Clader 1976: 18; Graver 1995: 58.

9. Nagy 1979: 224–31.

10. Graver 1995: esp. 55–59.

11. Clader (1976) is not explicit about this alternate tradition, but she does note a number of times the threatening character of Helen's presence in the *Iliad*.

12. Martin (1995) has suggested this similarity, and pointed to the use of *ophelon* phrases in Helen's Iliadic speeches. See below.

13. Zeitlin [1981] 1996; also Bergren 1983; Suzuki 1989; Doherty 1995a.

14. Arist. *Rh.* 1405a.

15. See, e.g., Redfield [1975] 1991: 122; Edwards 1987: 195–96; Suzuki 1989; Austin 1994; Graver 1995.

16. See esp. Pucci ([1979] 1998), who associates the Muses' ability with the Sirens, Circe, and Helen; also Crane 1988: 42; Suzuki 1989: 69; Wohl 1993: 33–34; Doherty 1995b, 1995a: 135–38. For broader discussions, see Clader 1976; Bergren 1983; Austin 1975, 1994.

17. See Alexiou 1974; Holst-Warhaft 1992; and Murnaghan 1999. Andromache repeats nearly the same set of fears and regrets three out of the four times she speaks (6.407–39, 22.450–59, 24.725–45).

18. See esp. Clader 1976: 10–12.

19. Again, see Vernant ([1985] 1991b: 102–3), who argues that *eras* ("love") and *thanatos* ("death") are strongly linked in the Greek social imagination and calls Helen a "fatal beauty"; cf. Vermeule 1979: 159.

20. Cf. Priam of Hector in the same scene (*Il.* 22.426); also Thetis when she wishes that Achilles had just stayed by the ships (1.415–16), Achilles when he wishes that his mother had stayed among the sea nymphs (18.86–87).

21. Cf. Andromache (*Il.* 6.412) to Hector; and Aeneas in Vergil (*Aen.* 1.94–96). Odysseus also wishes he had remained among the Phaeacians when he lands on his own disguised island (13.204–5).

22. Cf. *Il.* 11.380–81 (Paris taunts Diomedes); *Il.* 14.84–85 (Odysseus curses Agamemnon); *Il.* 24.253–54 (Priam curses his living children); *Od.* 2.183–84 (Eurymachos taunts the old seer Halitherses); *Od.* 18.401 (the suitors taunt the beggar Odysseus).

23. On the extreme proximity of type between Aphrodite and Helen, see Boedeker 1974:48, 54–55, 61; Clader 1976: 74; also Suter 1987.

24. See Martin 1989: 111–13 on the interpretation of the epithet ἀκριτόμυθε, which Odysseus uses of Thersites (*Il.* 2.246; cf. Iris regarding the μῦτθοι ... ἄκριτοι of Priam, *Il.* 2.796).

25. See Friedrich 1978: 46–47. Lyons (1997: 72) notes that the "faded god" theory of such figures is no longer popular among scholars, but cites Clader's 1976 treatment of Helen as a convincing exploration of her close connections to Aphrodite and Artemis. See also Calame [1977] 1997: 191–92.

26. Among female characters, only the confrontational and devious Hera uses such a vitriolic response to an intimate, although she fears Zeus when he responds angrily to her (1.568), just as Helen fears Aphrodite (but not Paris; 3.418).

27. Dog epithets are common flyting tools (Graver 1995: 49); Helen's self-abuse is thus a technique common in verbal dueling that uniquely boomerangs on the speaker. On the typical contexts of flyting in epic, see Parks 1990. Although he is not sanguine about the transference of flyting patterns to suit amorous or familial conflict, Parks does admit the similarity between these and warrior conflicts (12–13). I am most interested in shared speech patterns, which Parks does analyze, but not in any great detail and not in relation to what he considers non-dueling verbal exchanges. In contrast, Murnaghan (1999) points out that lament is also an agonistic genre. On the abuse of Paris in particular, see Suter 1993.

28. "Averting her eyes, she reproached her husband" (3.427).

29. Attempts have been made to explain Helen's seeming shift of direction and her ultimate acquiescence to Paris' suggestion as due to her weakness and attraction to him

(e.g., Hooker 1979; Edwards 1987:195–96). Kirk (1985: 327), in some contrast, regards the entire speech as "bitterly sarcastic and hostile."

30. Cf. Hector's disparaging reference to Paris' "gifts of Aphrodite" (3.54) and Paris' own affirmation of the same (3.64).

31. Mackie (1995: 118–19) remarks that Helen's phrases seem carefully chosen to suit Hector's outlook.

32. See Dickson 1995: 38.

33. Vernant [1985] 1991b: 102–3; cf. above, note 19. Penelope makes a similar despairing wish to be borne away by a gust of wind (*Od.* 20.61–65); see Johnston 1994 for comparable connections to the Erinyes, etc.

34. When alive, Hector seeks to cheer his weeping wife with grim praise for himself (*Il.* 460–61); see above regarding Helen's fear of ill repute, which is a hero's fear rather than a hero's wife's fear.

35. Holst-Warhaft 1992: 112–13.

36. See Graver 1995: 51.

37. Clader 1976: 6–11; Austin 1975: 127–28; 1994: 37–42; Bergren 1980; Zeitlin [1981] 1996: 409–11; Kennedy 1986; Suzuki 1989: 40–43.

38. Clader 1976: 62.

39. Hes. *Theog.* 27; Homer's Muses "know all things" (*Il.* 2.485), which implies both truth and lies.

40. See Austin 1975: 187–89; he "corrects" his reading in his later analysis of the same scene (1994: 81–82).

41. Zeitlin ([1981] 1996) has suggested that the scene depicts Helen as the embodiment of the double story and thus of the dissimulating potential of mimesis itself, see also Bergren 1983. Bergren (1981) argues that Helen's use of the drug, in combination with her tale, effects a seduction of her audience that recoils on the epic poet, hinting at his own narrative seduction. (Homer's epithets associate the drug with epic, as a number of scholars have noted.) Cf. Olson 1989; Doherty 1995a: 130–35.

42. See further discussion below and in note 47.

43. Cf. *Od.* 5.177–79, 5.263–64, 10.342–44, 358–65.

44. Zeitlin [1981] 1996; Bergren 1983; Suzuki 1989: 42–43.

45. Nagy 1979: 40 and n. 2, 82n., 134; cf. the related phrase "beyond measure", which denotes the opposite—that is, a hubristic inattention to fitting measure, an excess that is anathema to epic.

46. Cf. *Il.* 2.484–93 (Catalogue of Ships), and see Ford 1992: 72–74 (*Il.* 2.488 = *Od.* 4.240); on this collapse of roles by Hesiod, see Lardinois 1995: 201. Helen's use of the phrase makes it sound as if she might be able to tell all, while the poet emphasizes his incapability (*Il.* 2.489–90). See note 47 below for details.

47. Helen:

ἀτὰρ θεὸς ἄλλοτε ἄλλῳ

Ζεὺς ἀγαθόν τε κακόν τε διδοῖ δύναται γὰρ ἅπαντα·	} narrator's status
ἤ τοι νῦν δαίνυθε καθήμενοι ἐν μεγάροισι	↓
καὶ μύθοις τέρπεσθε· ἐοικότα γὰρ καταλέξω.	↓
πάντα μὲν οὐκ ἂν ἐγὼ μυθήσομαι οὐδ᾿ ὀνομήνω	} narrator's status (cf. *Il.* 2.488)
ὅσσοι ᾿Οδυσσῆος ταλασίφρονος εἰσιν ἄεθλοι.	} subject + epithet
ἀλλ᾿ οἷον τόδ᾿ ἔρεξε καὶ ἔτλη καρτερὸς ἀνὴρ	} deed + subject
δήμῳ ἔνι Τρώων, ὅθι πάσχετε πήματ᾿ ᾿Αχαιοί.	} site of deed; reference to pain (Trojan → Greek) (4.242–43)

Menelaus:

ἤδη μὲν πολέων ἐδάην βουλήν τε νόον τε	} narrator's status
ἀνδρῶν ἡρώων, πολλὴν δ' ἐπελήλυθα γαῖαν·	}(cf. *Od.* 1.3)
ἀλλ οὔ πω τοιοῦτον ἐγὼν ἴδον ὀφθαλμοῖσιν	
οιον Ὀδυσσῆος ταλασίφρονος ἔσκε φίλον κῆρ.	} subject + epithet
οἷον καὶ τόδ' ἔρεξε καὶ ἔτλη καρτερὸς ἀνὴρ	} deed + subject
ἵππῳ ἔνι ξεστῷ ἵν· ενήμεθα πάστες ἄριστοι	} site of deed;
Ἀργείων Τρώεσσι φόνον καὶ κῆρα φέροντες.	} reference to pain
	(Trojan → Greek)
	(4.242–73)

48. In the *Hymn. Hom. Ap.*, the poet calls this feat a "wondrous thing" (156), and his praise of the Delian maidens is covert praise for himself, just as Helen's narrative seduction suggests the poet's own. See further on this passage in the *Hymn. Hom. Ap.* in Richard Martin's contribution to this volume.

49. Note that Helen uses the word μνῆυα, a word that designates some sort of ritual marker—like a monument, or tombstone—something often *inscribed*, which is analogous to what Helen effects with her speech.

50. 15.176–77.

51.

Ἄνδρα μοι ἔννεπε Μοῦσα, πολύτροπον, ὃς μάλα πολλὰ
πλάγχθη, ἐπεὶ Τροίης ιερὸν προλίεθρον ἔπερσε
πολλῶν ἀνθροώπων ἴδεν ἄστεα καὶ νόον ἔγνω
πολλὰ δ' γ' ἐν πόντῳ πάθεν ἄλγεα ὃν κατὰ θύμον,
ἀρνύμενος ἥε τε ψυχὴν καὶ νόστον ἑταιρῶν.

52. Contrast Helen's imperfect knowledge of events in the Teichoscopia (Lynn-George 1988: 33).

53. See Clader 1976: 63–64, 69, 72–78; Skutsch 1987: 189, 190–91.

MARGALIT FINKELBERG

Homer as a Foundation Text

The Greek heroic tradition once embraced a much wider range of epic poems than merely the *Iliad* and the *Odyssey* with which it eventually became associated. Side by side with the Trojan cycle, to which the Homeric poems belong, additional heroic subjects were treated in epic cycles such as the Argonautic saga, the Theban cycle, and others, some of them also attributed to Homer. At an early stage, all the traditional poems dealing with the events of the Trojan War were assumed to be authored by Homer; later, only the *Iliad* and the *Odyssey* came to be seen as genuinely "Homeric", whereas the other Trojan epics were attributed to other poets and subsumed under the so-called Epic Cycle. A handful of fragments and a brief summary of the contents excerpted from the *Chrestomathy* of Proclus is all that has remained of the Cyclic poems, and even less than that of other epics.[1] Only the *Iliad* and the *Odyssey* survived transmission, eventually to form part of the so-called "Western Canon". While it is pretty obvious that this outcome has much to do with the privileged status that the Homeric poems enjoyed in ancient Greece,[2] it is much less obvious how they acquired this status. In what follows, I will argue that the *Iliad* and the *Odyssey* were intended to supersede the other traditional epics from the very beginning and that they achieved this goal by means of a thorough revision of the heroic tradition and

From *Homer, the Bible, and Beyond: Literary and Religious Canons in the Ancient World*, edited by Margalit Finkelberg and Guy G.Stroumsa. © 2003 by Koninklijke Brill NV.

169

its deliberate adaptation to the new self-image of Greek civilization that emerged in the early Archaic period.

1. HOMER AND THE EPIC TRADITION

It is generally recognized today that both the *Iliad* and the *Odyssey* lean heavily upon the nomenclature of Trojan subjects dealt with in the poems of the Cycle.[3] Take for example Books 2–7 of the *Iliad*, which form a digression from the narrative succession of the story of the Wrath of Achilles. Quite a few episodes in these books are connected with the beginning of the Trojan War, which was the subject of the Cyclic *Cypria*. Odysseus' account of the mustering of the troops at Aulis and the Catalogue of Ships in *Iliad* 2; the Teichoscopia, the duel of Paris and Menelaus and the Helen–Paris encounter in *Iliad* 3; Agamemnon's inspection of the troops in *Iliad* 4; the Trojan scenes in *Iliad* 6; the negotiations about the return of Helen and the building of the Achaean wall in *Iliad* 7—each of these offers a retrospective of an initial stage of the war. The beginning of the war may be evoked in a direct reminiscence, as in Odysseus' reminiscence of the Aulis episode in *Iliad* 2 or Anterior's reminiscence of the embassy of Odysseus and Menelaus to Troy in *Iliad* 3, both told in the *Cypria*.[4] But more often than not the *Iliad* adopts a subtler strategy, in that the episodes properly belonging to the beginning of the war are incorporated into the chronological and narrative setting of its last year. Thus, the seduction of Helen by Paris and Aphrodite in *Iliad* 3, rather than being simply a reminiscence, provides, as was aptly put by Mark Edwards, "a reenactment of the original seduction", the proper context of which is again the *Cypria*.[5] In a similar way, the mustering of the troops described in *Iliad* 2 or the negotiations about Helen and the building of the Achaean wall described in *Iliad* 7, properly belonging to the beginning of the war but introduced so as to suit the context of the last year, can hardly be anything else than such "reenactments" of the war's initial stages, again closely parallel to the *Cypria* account.[6]

In fact, what we have here is a narrative technique characteristic of the *Iliad* as a whole, because in the second half of the poem the same strategy of "reenactment" or, to borrow the expression used by Wolfgang Kullmann, "an imitation of a narrative known to us from one of the Cyclic epics", is employed.[7] There, this strategy is used to evoke the last stages of the war which, again, are not described directly in the *Iliad*. It was noticed long ago that the duel between Patroclus and Sarpedon in *Iliad* 16 directly evokes the Achilles–Memnon duel as recounted in the Cyclic *Aethiopis*; again, although the lamentations of Thetis and the Nereids over Achilles in *Iliad* 18.22–72 are prompted by the death of Patroclus, they evoke Thetis' bewailing of

Achilles, also presented in the *Aethiopis*.[8] Likewise, although the Fall of Troy properly belongs with the events described in the Cyclic *Iliu persis*, the death of Hector is represented in *Iliad* 22 as if the city of Troy were already in flames.[9]

What the *Iliad* does for the Trojan War as a whole, the *Odyssey* does for the Fall of Troy and the Returns: the former was the subject of the *Cyclic Aethiopis, Ilias parva* and *Iliu persis* whereas the latter was treated in the Cyclic *Nosti*. The *Aethiopis* is evoked in the story about Achilles' funeral told by Agamemnon in the Underworld; *Ilias parva* in Odysseus' meeting with Ajax in the Underworld described by Odysseus in *Odyssey* 11 and in the story of Odysseus' entering Troy as a spy told by Helen in *Odyssey* 4; *Iliu persis* in the story of the Wooden Horse told by Menelaus in *Odyssey* 4 and by Odysseus in *Odyssey* 11; this same story is also the subject of Demodocus' third song in *Odyssey* 8.[10] The Returns are evoked in Nestor's reminiscences and his story of Agamemnon's death in *Odyssey* 3, in Menelaus' reminiscences in *Odyssey* 4, in Agamemnon's account of his own death in *Odyssey* 11 and, of course, in Odysseus' reminiscences embracing Books 9–12 of the poem; this is also the subject of a song performed by Phemius in *Odyssey* 1.[11] As a result, the *Odyssey*, besides being a poem of the return of the last of the heroes, also acts as a large-scale compendium of the part of the Epic Cycle dealing with the final stages of the Trojan War and the fate of the survivors.

The above seems to indicate that, although they begin *in medias res* and describe two single episodes of the Trojan saga, the *Iliad* and the *Odyssey* also function as symbolic compendia of the entire history of the Trojan War and the Returns. While the literary merits of this compositional technique were commended as early as Aristotle,[12] it has rarely been taken into account that what is being dealt with is far from purely a matter of composition. As Laura Slatkin and Irad Malkin have shown for the *Iliad* and the *Odyssey* respectively, Homer not only evokes other traditions but also neutralizes them by adapting them to his own agenda: thus, the traditional theme of the immortality conferred on Achilles by Thetis is turned in the *Iliad* into one of "heroic experience as a metaphor for the condition of mortality, with all its contradictions", whereas the *Odyssey* transforms the tradition of Odysseus' leaving home for foreign lands into a story of homecoming.[13] This strongly suggests that Homer and the Cyclic epics cannot be placed on one plane as if they were variations on the same theme. By the very fact of reinterpreting the other versions of the Trojan saga, Homer signalizes their subordinate status as regards his own poems and privileges the version that he offers.

At some point in the Archaic Age, Homer's narrative of the Trojan War acquired the extraordinary status of the only narrative worthy of being told at all. In the *Odyssey*, where the Trojan War is already viewed as belonging to the heroic past, "The Doom of the Achaeans and Troy" engages everybody's attention, including that of the gods themselves. The inhabitants of Ithaca, of Phaeacia, of the Island of Aeolia, and even Odysseus himself, are eager to listen to songs and stories about the Trojan War (which, in fact, are the only songs and stories they listen to), and this is the very subject that is included in the Sirens' promise of bestowing a knowledge greater than human—a promise nobody can resist. That only a savage like the Cyclops can remain ignorant of the Trojan War, as well as of any other mark of human civilization, shows clearly enough that acquaintance with the Trojan saga— and, by implication, with the poems of Homer—was envisaged as a cultural code that united the civilized world.[14]

To sum up, the relationship between Homer and the Trojan tradition is anything but symmetrical. Homer both reshapes the tradition he inherited and adapts it to his own agenda, which as a rule do not concur with those of his sources. This would mean that, rather than offering just another variant of the common tradition, Homer turns earlier traditions about the Trojan war and the Returns into raw material for his poems. That he is nevertheless anxious to show his awareness of his sources indicates that he meant the *Iliad* and the *Odyssey* not simply to absorb the other traditions but to supersede them, thus claiming for them the unique status of metaepics.[15] Our next task is to see why this claim became universally accepted.

2. THE SHAPING OF COLLECTIVE MEMORY

The political and dialectal maps of historic Greece are both the direct outcome of two events that took place at the end of the second—the beginning of the first millennium B.C.E.: the emergence of the Dorians and other northwestern tribes in central Greece and the Peloponnese, and the mass migration of the Mycenaean population to the Aegean shore of Asia Minor and other parts of the Mediterranean. Neither of these events makes an appearance worthy of mention in the Homeric poems.[16] This is not to say that they were not dealt with in the Greek epic tradition as a whole. Thus, it is almost certain that the lost traditional epics *Aegimius* (often ascribed to Hesiod) and *Naupactia* dealt with the coming of the Dorians, whereas the migration to Asia Minor was certainly treated in the lost epic poem *Melampodia*, also ascribed to Hesiod. And, judging by the evidence of literary sources, the Dorian saga of the "Return of the Children of Hercules" gave the Dorians' own distinctive version of the population movements that shook Greece at the end of the Bronze Age.[17] None of these became part of the mainstream epic tradition, which sees the Trojan War as the main if not the only factor that brought about the end of the Heroic Age. Yet, the very fact that such alternative versions of the end of the Heroic Age did exist strongly suggests that Homer's silence regarding the coming of the Dorians and the subsequent migrations to the East was a matter of deliberate choice. This is not to say that Homer simply ignored the Dorians. Consider for example the map of Argos as drawn in the Homeric Catalogue of Ships:

> And those who lived in Argos and walled Tiryns, in Hermione and Asine which lie on a deep bay, in Troezen and Eiones and Epidaurus rich in vineyards, and in Aegina and Mases, sons of the Achaeans: these were led by Diomedes, master of the war-cry, and Sthenelus, dear son of the famous Kapaneus.... but the commander of all was Diomedes, master of the war-cry.[18]

The Argos of Diomedes is presented in the Homeric Catalogue as spreading over the entire territory of northeastern Peloponnese and the island of Aegina. This picture is boldly anachronistic, in that it corresponds to what were thought to have been the original domains of Dorian Argos (the so-called "lot of Temenus"), presumably restored under king Pheidon in the seventh century B.C.E.[19] As a result, Heroic Age Argos emerges in Homer as if it had already possessed the political and tribal structure that was associated with it in the Archaic period.

Not only does the Argos of Diomedes reflect the Dorian Argos but the Sparta of Menelaus fairly well corresponds to the Dorian Sparta. However, such geographical entities as Argos or Sparta do not properly belong to the Heroic Age. The centres of the relevant territories were Mycenae, Tiryns, and Amyclae, all of them abundantly represented in Greek legend. Characteristically, Mycenae is the only one of the three whose treatment is historically consistent, in that it was made the capital of the antiquarian kingdom of Agamemnon. Tiryns and Amyclae, whose functions as the administrative and cult centers of pre-Dorian Greece were well known to the Greeks of the Archaic period, were replaced by the more up-to-date Argos and Sparta and, accordingly, marginalized. That is to say, although it was a matter of common knowledge that the Dorians were post-Mycenaean newcomers into the Peloponnese, their descendants could nevertheless easily locate themselves on the map of Heroic Greece that Homer supplied. This suggests that in drawing his picture of Heroic Greece Homer systematically updated the past in such a way that it might fit the present. The most likely motive underlying this practice seems to have been the need to represent the Greece of the Heroic Age as a harmonious Panhellenic whole, already containing the political and ethnic elements present in the Archaic period. Evidently, this could only be done by ignoring the historical facts of the coming of the Dorians and the mass emigration to Asia Minor that it triggered, and by marginalizing the alternative traditions that accounted for those events.

It is difficult to tell what kind of authority, if any, could have lain behind the strategy of updating the past in accordance with the contemporary agenda that Homer adopted. The only thing that can be said with a considerable degree of certainty is that this strategy cannot be separated from large-scale developments that took place at the same period and that are sometimes given the collective name "the eighth-century Renaissance". The Panhellenic cult of Zeus and other Olympians; the Olympian games and other Panhellenic festivals in which these cults found their fullest expression; the free-standing temple with the cult statue of an Olympian deity within it; the canonic epics of Homer and Hesiod celebrating these very deities;[20] the emergence of the hero-cult, and above all the rise of the city-state itself—all these seem inextricably connected with each other. The emergence of the hero-cult is especially pertinent to the present discussion. This characteristically Greek cult, closely connected with the cult of the dead, consisted in the worship of personages of Greek legend—many of them the same heroes who were celebrated in the poems of Homer and Hesiod— performed at ancient tombs which were supposed to be their burial places. This remarkable coincidence between the traditional poetry on the one hand and the new religious practice on the other has even given rise to the suggestion that the hero-cult developed under the direct influence of the epic tradition, above all of Homer. But it is perhaps more likely that both expressed the same tendency towards establishing a continuity between prehistoric and historic Greece that became dominant at that period.[21]

Since at least 700 B.C.E. the Dorians of Sparta celebrated a cult of Menelaus, who was generally believed to have been king of Sparta at the time of the Trojan War. Some hundred years later, the Spartans made a considerable effort to locate and to bring to their city the bones of Menelaus' son-in-law Orestes, whom they also made the recipient of a hero-cult. For the Spartans, Orestes was first and foremost king of Amyclae, which had by then become part of their territory. But it was the same Orestes who was universally believed to have been the last pre-Dorian ruler of what was to become the territory of Sparta and whose descendants led the Achaeans, whom the Dorians expelled from their lands, to what was to become the district of Achaea in the northern Peloponnese and eventually to Asia Minor.[22] The Spartans' identification with Menelaus and Orestes, the leaders of the population that they replaced, is consistent with the treatment of Sparta in the Homeric epics. Both clearly indicate the direction in which the updating of the past proceeded at this period.[23]

We have seen that Homer marginalized the epic traditions that offered alternative versions of the end of Mycenaean Greece. "There is reason to suppose that at some later stage a similar thing happened both to the tradition represented in the Cyclic epics, which had also once been credited with Homeric authorship,[24] and to the traditional poetry associated with the name of Hesiod. Take for example the theme of the destruction of the Race of Heroes, prominent in the Hesiodic tradition as well as in the poems of the Cycle. According to these sources, the Heroic Age came to an end in two great wars, the Theban and the Trojan, which were especially designed by Zeus to put an end to the Race of Heroes.[25] Although Homer was also engaged in perpetuating the glorious memory of the Trojan War, the theme of the End of Heroes is conspicuously absent in his poems. As Ruth Scodel put it in an important article, "In Homer, the continuity of history from the heroes to the poet's contemporaries is complete."[26] It is clear that Homer's suppressing of the traditional myth of the destruction of the Race of Heroes was again part of a larger strategy purporting to transform the heroic past into one of the main factors in establishing the self-image of the new Greek civilization that replaced Mycenaean Greece at the beginning of the first millennium B.C.E. As a result, it became possible to mention Achilles and Brasidas, Nestor and Pericles in the same breath, as for example in Plato's *Symposium*, simply because they were seen as belonging to the same historical space.[27] Clearly, this could not have been done had the Race of Heroes continued to be envisaged, as in Hesiod and the Cycle, as an extinct race having nothing in common with the degenerate Iron Race of the present.[28]

Let me emphasize again that we have no reason to doubt that Homer and his contemporaries were well aware that the Dorians were not part of the Heroic Age milieu or that the population of historic Greece was distinctly heterogeneous.[29] Yet this awareness did not prevent them from ignoring such facts or moulding them in accordance with their own agenda. As far as I can see, this agenda consisted in answering the need of creating, beyond the differences dividing the heterogeneous tribes that settled in Greece at the beginning of the first millennium B.C.E., the overarching identity of "Hellenes". By modifying the inherited picture of the heroic past, the new Greek civilization not only acquired the unity it initially lacked but also established a continuity between the Greece of the Heroic Age and historical Greece, in that the former was envisaged as already possessed of the ethnic and political structure characteristic of the latter. It is reasonable to suppose that this attitude to the past issued from a cultural strategy which, to borrow the expression used by the biblical scholar Nadav Na'aman, may be defined as "the shaping of collective memory".[30] The Homeric poems were both a by-product of this strategy and its most effective vehicle. The picture of prehistoric Greece that they promulgated became the standard if not the only account of their past that the later Greeks could imagine. So much so that, in his discussion of the Homeric Catalogue of Ships, even so critically minded an historian as Thucydides took it for granted that the Trojan War was the first genuinely Panhellenic enterprise in Greek history.[31]

3. THE ILIAD AND THE POLIS

The change of attitude towards the heroic past could of course not be achieved simply by updating the traditional geography or avoiding reference to the destruction of the Race of Heroes. As far as Homer is concerned, the speeches were the main vehicle in carrying his message. Since the traditional subjects dealing with the Heroic Age were not only universally known but also accepted as historical truth, no poet could permit himself to mould them in a free and independent way: the Trojan War will end with the Trojan rather than the Achaean defeat, Hector will be killed by Achilles and not vice versa, and so on. This is why dissonances between the plot of the poems and what is expressed in the speeches are so important: while the plot is fixed in tradition, the content of the speeches is not; accordingly, the speeches are amenable to expressing the poet's reaction to what he had received from his tradition.[32]

The result may be that the same episode is treated from two perspectives, the traditional and the poet's own. Thus, at *Iliad* 14.364–9 the disguised Poseidon says in his exhortation to the heavily pressed Greeks: "Argives, are we once more to yield the victory to Hector, son of Priam, so he can take our ships and win glory for himself? That is what he thinks and prays, because Achilles is staying back by the hollow ships in his heart's anger. But we will not feel his loss too strongly, if the rest of us stir ourselves to support each other." The entire concept of the *Iliad* is based on the premise that without Achilles' individual contribution Achaean victory is impossible, and the weight the poem places on the single combats of other Achaean leaders shows that this is indeed the prevailing attitude. Poseidon's words, in that they give equal weight to the value of the ordinary soldiers' mutual effort, contradict this attitude, and this is why they leave no trace on the development of the action. But the same idea of the importance of mutual effort occasionally emerges again, as for example in a description of the Greek army on the march at the beginning of *Iliad* 3: "But the Achaeans came on in silence, breathing boldness, their hearts intent on supporting each other." This passage, one of the few Homeric passages commended by Plato in the *Republic*, is closer to the spirit of the hoplite phalanx as celebrated in the poems of Tyrtaeus (characteristically, this is how it was taken by the scholiast) than to the standard behaviour of the Homeric warrior.[33]

The poems of Hesiod contain very little direct speech, and we can actually be sure that the same was true of the poems of the Epic Cycle. In his discussion of epic poetry in *Poetics* 24, Aristotle writes:

> Homer, admirable in all respects, has the special merit of being the only poet who rightly appreciates the part he should take himself. The poet should speak as little as possible in his own person, for it is not this that makes him an imitator (*mimêtês*). Other poets appear themselves upon the scene throughout, and imitate but little and rarely. Homer, after a few prefatory words, at once brings in a man, or woman, or other personage; none of them wanting in characteristic qualities, but each with a character of his own.

Aristotle's remark that poets other than Homer are very rarely engaged in mimesis can only refer to the composers of other epics, which indicates that the narratives of the latter contained practically no direct speech.[34] This would mean, as simply as possible, that the Cyclic poets had very little to add to the traditional material they inherited. Nothing could provide a sharper contrast to Homer, in whose poems speeches constitute about two thirds of the entire text, serving the main means of characterization and providing, so to speak, a running commentary on the plot. I shall use the *Iliad* as an example.[35]

There is little doubt that the *Iliad* originated in the cultural and political milieu of aristocratic chiefdoms which preceded the formation of the city-state. Contrary to the system of values established with the rise of the polis, according to which the distribution of honour should follow personal achievement, the distribution of honour in pre-city-state society corresponded to a person's social status, which was determined by superiority in birth and wealth. Nowhere is this shown more clearly than in the description of the athletic contests held by Achilles at Patroclus' tomb in *Iliad* 23. In the chariot race, Eumelus who lost the competition is offered the second prize because he is "the best", *aristos*, and Menelaus who came third is again offered the second prize on exactly the same grounds, while in the throwing of the spear Agamemnon receives the first prize without even participating in the contest, only because he is *aristos* and superior to all others.[36] "After all," Moses Finley wrote of Homeric society, "the basic values of the society were given, predetermined, and so were a man's place in the society and the privileges and duties that followed from his status".[37] No wonder, therefore, that the chief motivation behind the Homeric warriors' behaviour was the drive to meet the expectations that ensued from their status. Together with risking one's life in war, these expectations also embraced assistance to and the protection of those to whom the person was tied by the mutual obligations of military alliance, guest-friendship, or vassal relations.[38]

It is however highly symptomatic that the lack of social equality and insufficient recognition of personal merit which directly result from the aristocratic ethos prevailing in the *Iliad* are questioned in the body of the *Iliad* itself. This can be seen first of all in Homer's treatment of the central issue of the poem, the conflict between Achilles and Agamemnon. "I have sacked twelve of men's cities from my ships", Achilles says bitterly in *Iliad* 9, "and I claim eleven more by land across the fertile Troad. From all of these I took many fine treasures, and every time I brought them all and gave to Agamemnon son of Atreus: and every time, back there by the fast ships he had never left, he would take them in, share out a few, and keep the most for himself."[39] Homer makes Achilles question the view of honour as bestowed automatically, according to status and birth, and pose the claim of merit as against the claim of rank. "Stay at home or fight your hardest—your share will be the same. Coward and hero are given equal honour", Achilles says elsewhere in the same speech. It is not surprising, therefore, that in his *Politics* Aristotle adduces these Homeric lines in support of the argument that the distribution of honour must be proportionate to one's contribution to the well-being of the community.[40]

But Homer's criticism of aristocratic values goes even further. The main conflict of the *Iliad* is the conflict of honour. It was because of considerations of honour which went against the common interest that Agamemnon took Briseis from Achilles and it was, again, considerations of honour that caused Achilles to withdraw from participation in the Trojan campaign from the moment that his prize of honour, *geras*, was taken from him. The issue of honour is thus woven into the core of the *Iliad* plot. At the same time, it would be wrong to say that the poet of the *Iliad* sides unambiguously with the considerations of personal honour and prestige which move his heroes and the plot of his poem. As I have argued elsewhere, in his treatment of the theme of Achilles' wrath in *Iliad* 11, 16, and 18 Homer criticizes aristocratic individualism and its self-serving value of personal honour, *timê*, and reinterprets the inherited plot of the *Iliad* in the spirit of the city-state value of *aretê*, personal excellence which benefits the entire community.[41] When in *Iliad* 11 Nestor says that Achilles' abstention from participating in the war will result in that he "will be the only one to profit from his excellence", or when in *Iliad* 16 Patroclus asks Achilles "what will any other man, even yet to be born, profit from you, if you do not save the Argives from shameful destruction?", and, finally, when in *Iliad* 18 Achilles himself comes to the conclusion that his chosen line of behaviour has resulted in that, instead of being "a saving light to Patroclus or many other companions", he has become "a useless burden on the earth", the concept underlying all these utterances is that by keeping his excellence, *aretê*, to himself Achilles has actually invalidated it and thus almost annihilated his own worth as "the best of the Achaeans".[42]

There can be no doubt that this was not the message which originally informed the poem. Consider again Achilles' words of self-reproach in *Iliad* 18: "I have not been a saving light to Patroclus or my many other companions who have been brought down by godlike Hector, but sit here by the ships, a useless burden on the earth." Whereas Achilles' obligations to Patroclus, Achilles' "own" man, are among those values which are seen in terms of the aristocratic code of honour, the very design of the *Iliad* shows that no such terms could originally have been applied to Achilles' attitude to the rest of the Greeks: an aristocratic chieftain is only responsible for his own men and owes nothing to the soldiers led by other chieftains. The clash between the individualistic values of the nobility and the communal values of the city—state produced by this and similar Homeric usages shows that the social perspective adopted in the *Iliad* is a double one.

In his *Reciprocity and Ritual* Richard Seaford defined the *Iliad* situation as Homer's "ideological contradiction", namely, that "aristocratic individualism is on the one hand vital to the community and on the other hand a danger to be controlled by the community". Seaford tends to see this contradiction as reflecting a transitional stage within a single society and thus allows for a degree of historicity in the Homeric poems as we have them; Kurt A. Raaflaub has recently expressed a similar opinion.[43] This, however, is by far not the only contradiction that can be found in the Homeric poems. As A. M. Snodgrass famously argued, the contradictions in Homer's depiction of social institutions cannot be resolved and should be interpreted to the effect that, rather than reflecting a concrete historical society, the Homeric poems offer an amalgam created as a result of centuries-long circulation in oral tradition.[44] Indeed, if we take into account that the language of Homer is a "Kunstsprache" never spoken by any living person; that his formulae for weapons exhibit an impossible combination of military technologies used at different historical periods, and that the same is true of his view of death and the afterlife,[45] we shall see that there is no reason why the situation of Homeric values should be any different.

In so far as the pursuit of the communal values of the polis emerging in *Iliad* 11, 16, and 18 and the pursuit of the individualistic values of the aristocracy as found in the rest of the poem are mutually irreconcilable, they could not have been held as supreme values at one and the same time. In view of this, it seems wiser to admit that, more than reflecting the state of a concrete historical society, contradictions in Homer's account of values reflect the state of the Homeric text itself. We can suggest, therefore, that at some stage in their history the Homeric poems underwent a thorough reinterpretation which made them relevant to the city-state society. Owing to Homer's extensive use of direct speech, it became possible to incorporate this reinterpretation into the text of the poems without changing their plots. As a result, like the Bible and some other ancient corpora, Homer's became a manifold text, which carried within itself both the original message and its reinterpretation in the vein of later values.

We have seen that the need to consolidate the heterogeneous populations of historic Greece was the most likely reason why the myth of the Heroic Age as delivered by Homer became the foundation myth of the new Greek civilization that replaced Mycenaean Greece at the beginning of the first millennium B.C.E. This however was far from the only function that this myth fulfilled. Greek civilization, perhaps for the first time in history, created a civic society whose ideal of man was not identical to that proposed by religion or philosophy. The Greek concept of human excellence, *aretê*, which embodied this ideal, played a central role in the poems of Homer.[46] No wonder, therefore, that for generations of Greeks the world of Homer became a timeless model against which their own lives were enacted. This is why Plato's Socrates, for example, found it appropriate to account for his position at his trial by comparing his situation with that of Achilles in *Iliad* 18.[47] There was no need for Socrates to embark on a lengthy argument in order to explain why he preferred death to exile. The example of Achilles brought his message home with an efficacy that no argument could ever equal.

4. THE BIBLE OF THE GREEKS

The codification of the *Iliad* and the *Odyssey* in Athens of the sixth century B.C.E. granted the Athenian state a monopoly over the standard text of Homer. The Homeric poems began to be recited at the prestigious Panathenaic festival, which was among the central events of the public life of the city and of the whole of Greece.[48] They also became the basis of elementary education, to be memorized at schools all over the Greek world. This is why the history of the Homeric poems after their fixation in writing is not simply a history of a written text but that of a written text highly privileged in the civilization to which it belonged. In that, its status is closer to the status of the Bible than to that of other works of literature created in ancient Greece.[49]

Needless to say, the Greek world continued to change also after the codification of Homer. The beliefs and values that informed the Homeric poems altered considerably in the course of time. The Homeric religion especially, with its all too human-like and human behaving gods, soon enough began to be felt inadequate by many. Already in the sixth century B.C.E. Xenophanes accused Homer and Hesiod of having attributed to the gods "everything that is a shame and reproach among men",[50] and Plato's attack on Homer in the *Republic* was very much in the same vein. Nevertheless, in the entire history of Homeric reception, Plato seems to have been the only one who actually recommended systematic censoring of the *Iliad* and the *Odyssey* and even replacing them with hymns to the gods and the praises of good men, which alone would suit the educational reforms he proposed in the *Republic*.[51] It was by interpreting the standard text of the poems rather than by interfering with it that Homer's adaptation to changing circumstances normally proceeded.[52] To borrow the terms introduced by Moshe Halbertal, "textual closure" of the Homeric corpus was accompanied by "hermeneutical openness" towards it—a sure sign of the canonical status that the text of Homer had acquired.[53]

As early as the end of the sixth century B.C.E., Theagenes of Rhegium for the first time applied the method of allegorical interpretation to the Homeric religion. As far as we can judge, Theagenes approached the battle of gods, the Theomachy of *Iliad* 20 and 21, in terms of the conflict of physical and cosmic elements. In the fifth century, Metrodorus of Lampsacus interpreted the whole of the *Iliad* in the vein of the cosmological doctrine of the philosopher Anaxagoras.[54] The allegorical approach was also favoured by the early Stoics: their chief purpose seems to have been the identification of the gods of Homer and Hesiod with cosmic elements and forces. The Neoplatonist and Neopythagorean allegorization of Homer, which explicitly aimed at defending the poet against Plato's criticisms, began to appear in the first centuries C.E. and reached a climax in the fifth century, in the work of Proclus.[55]

Another widespread method of interpretation, closely connected with allegory but not identical with it, was to update Homer by reading into his text the scientific and practical knowledge that accumulated in later epochs, first and foremost after the conquests of Alexander. The Stoics especially were notorious for their attempts to make Homer into an advanced astronomer and geographer. In his readings of Homer, a contemporary of Aristarchus and founder of the Pergamene school, Crates of Mallos, ascribed to the Poet the knowledge of a spherical earth and universe, of the arctic circle and regions of the Far North, of the Atlantic ocean and the western lands in general, and so on, whereas Strabo tried to adjust the geographical horizons of Augustan Rome to Homer's picture of the world. Strabo's polemics with Eratosthenes and his followers in Book 7 of the *Geography* is a good example of the Stoic exegesis of Homer. Eratosthenes claimed, sensibly enough, that although Homer knew Greece fairly well, he was not acquainted with lands and peoples far away from it. Homer's failure to mention the Scythians served as a conspicuous example of his geographical incompetence. In his defense of Homer, Strabo seeks to rehabilitate the Poet by arguing that the fabulous tribes of Hippemolgi, "mare-milkers", and Galactophagi, "curd-eaters", could be none other than the Scythians in poetic disguise.[56]

Moral and values were perhaps even more difficult to adjust than religion and science. We have seen that before being codified the Homeric poems were brought into correspondence with the values of the city-state, above all the communal value of *aretê*. This guaranteed their relevance to city-state society at least till the time of Aristotle, whose treatment of arete still does not differ essentially from what we find in Homer.[57] Yet the ethical theories of the Hellenistic Age no longer addressed the traditional city-state society. As Joseph M. Bryant puts it, "The retreat from Polis-citizen ideals ... occurred along all philosophical fronts during the Hellenistic period, as the Cynics, Cyrenaics, Skeptics, Epicureans, and Stoics each sought to distance the well-being of the individual from the collapsing Polis framework and to detach arete, or "virtue", from its former dependence on communal service through performance in the roles of warrior and self-governing citizen."[58] This is why Homer's words "Zeus increases and diminishes man's arete"[59] were found inappropriate by Plutarch, who approached them from the standpoint of the second century C.E. In his treatise *How the Young Man Should Study Poetry* Plutarch wrote:

> Particular attention must be paid to the other words also, when their signification is shifted about and changed by the poets according to various circumstances. An example is the word *aretê*. For inasmuch as *aretê* not only renders men sensible, honest, and upright in actions and words, but also often enough secures for them repute and influence, the poets, following this notion, make good repute and influence to be *aretê*.... But when ... in his reading, he finds this line, "Zeus increases and diminishes man's *aretê*," ... let him consider that the poet has employed *aretê* instead of repute, or influence, or good fortune, or the like.[60]

Plutarch's treatise deserves our special attention also because it reveals some of the actual methods of guiding students towards what was envisaged by their tutors as the appropriate reading of a given Homeric passage. Thus, he suggests that where Homer's moral judgment is not made clear enough, "a distinction is to be drawn by directing the young man's attention in some such manner as the following":

> If, on the one hand, Nausicaa, after merely looking at a strange man, Odysseus, and experiencing Calypso's emotions toward him, being, as she was, a wanton [child] and at the age for marriage, utters such foolish words to her maid-servants, "If only such a man as this might come to be called my husband" [*Od.* 6. 244], then are her boldness and lack of restraint to be blamed. But if, on the other hand, she sees into the character of the man from his words, and marvels at his conversation, so full of good sense ... then it is quite right to admire her.[61]

According to the thorough treatment of the Homeric poems as the ultimate source of all knowledge in the anonymous *Essay on the Life and Poetry of Homer*, which was once believed to be written by Plutarch, the fact that Homer often presents "wicked deeds" should not prevent us from attributing to him every virtue, for owing to the mixture of good and evil that the Homeric poems offer, "the recognition and choice of the better becomes easier."[62]

Contrary to what one might have expected, the transition to Christianity did not bring about a radical change in the Greek attitude to Homer. The Homeric poems and especially the *Iliad* retained their status of school texts till the very end of the Byzantine empire. What is perhaps even more surprising, no serious attempts were made to Christianize them.[63] Offered instead were, again, various methods of interpretation. This for example is how St Basil instructed Christian youths to read pagan texts so as to "accept from them only that which is useful":

> Whenever they [the poets] recount for you the deeds or words of good men, you ought to cherish and emulate these and try to be as far as possible like them; but when they treat of wicked men, you ought to avoid such imitation, stopping your ears no less than Odysseus did, according to what those same poets say, when he avoided the songs of the Sirens.

This meant don't admire the poets "when they depict men engaged in amours or drunken, or when they define happiness in terms of an over-abundant table of dissolute songs", and above all don't pay attention to them "when they narrate anything about the gods, and especially when they speak of them as being many, and these too not even in accord with one another". These reservations aside, Basil, just as generations of pagan interpreters before and Christian interpreters after him, simply took it for granted that "all Homer's poetry is an encomium of virtue" and therefore cannot be easily dispensed with.[64]

The capture of Constantinople in 1453 put an end to two and a half millennia of continuous development of Greek civilization. The epic tradition of the Trojan War, which gradually crystallized into the Homeric poems as we know them, accompanied this civilization through all the stages of its existence, thus fulfilling the function of what the sociology of culture calls "the dominant cultural arbitrary".[65] These poems became the universally accepted frame of reference, in fact, the only frame of reference upon which the cultural language common to all those who belonged to the ancient Greek civilization was formed, and therefore an inseparable part of the identity of those who saw this civilization as their own.[66] This would not only explain why the *Iliad* and the *Odyssey* outlived other epics that once circulated in the Greek tradition but also justify treating them on a par with other foundation texts known to us from the history of civilization.

NOTES

1. For general collections see G. Kinkel, *Epicorum Graecorum Fragmenta*. Vol. 1 (Leipzig, 1877); M. Davies, *Epicorum Graecorum Fragmenta* (Göttingen, 1988); A. Bernabé, *Poetarum Epicorum Graecorum Testimonia et Fragmenta*. Vol. 1 (Stuttgart and Leipzig, 1996) (henceforth, Bernabé). For the Epic Cycle see T.W. Allen, *Homeri Opera*. Vol. 5 (Oxford, 1912) (henceforth Allen); H. Evelyn-White, *Hesiod, the Homeric Hymns and Homerica* (Cambridge, Mass., 1914); E. Bethe, *Homer, Dichtung und Sage* (2nd ed.). Vol. 2 (Leipzig and Berlin, 1929) (reprinted as E. Bethe, *Der Troische Epenkreis* (Stuttgart, 1966)).

2. See M. Finkelberg, "The *Cypria*, the *Iliad*, and the Problem of Multiformity in Oral and Written Tradition", *Classical Philology* 95 (2000), 1–11.

3. The growing recognition of this fact has been one of the major achievements of the Neoanalytic trend in Homeric scholarship. The works most representative of the methods of Neoanalysis are J.T. Kakridis, *Homeric Researches* (Lund, 1949) and W. Kullmann, *Die Quellen der Ilias* (Wiesbaden, 1960); for comprehensive discussions in English see W. Kullmann, "Oral Poetry Theory and Neoanalysis in Homeric Research", *Greek, Roman and Byzantine Studies* 25 (1984), 307–23; M.W. Edward, "Neoanalysis and Beyond", *Classical Antiquity* 9 (1990), 311–25; L. Slatkin, *The Power of Thetis: Allusion and Interpretation in the Iliad* (Berkeley, 1991), 9–12. I treat the subject in some detail in M. Finkelberg, *The Birth of Literary Fiction in Ancient Greece* (Oxford, 1998), 141–50. See now also J.S. Burgess, *The Tradition of the Trojan War in Homer and the Epic Cycle* (Baltimore and London, 2001).

4. *Il.* 2. 284–332; 3. 204–24; cf. Allen, 104.1–3; 105. 3–5.

5. M.W. Edwards, *Homer: Poet of the Iliad* (Baltimore and London, 1987), 196. Cf. W. Kullmann, "Ergebnisse der motivgeschichtlichen Forschung zu Homer", in J. Latacz, ed., *Zweihundert Jahre Homer-Forschung* (Stuttgart and Leipzig, 1991), 434. For the *Cypria* episode see Allen 103, 2–10.

6. Allen 105.3–5, 17–18.

7. Kullmann, "Oral Poetry Theory and Neoanalysis", 310.

8. Allen 106. 11–13; the episode is also evoked in *Od.* 24. 36–97.

9. *Il.* 22. 405–411, cf. Allen 108.6–7.

10. Achilles' funeral *Od.* 24. 35–92, cf. Allen, 106. 9–16; Odysseus and Ajax *Il.* 541–64, cf. Allen 106. 20–23; Odysseus the spy 4. 235–64, cf. Allen 107.4–7; the Wooden Horse 4. 265–89; *Il.* 504–37; 8. 499–520, cf. Allen 107. 16–21; 107. 27–108.2.

11. Nestor *Od.* 3. 103–200; 253–312; Menelaus 4. 351–585; Agamemnon 11. 404–34; Phemius' song 1. 325–27; cf. Allen 108–109.

12. *Poet.* 1451a 23–30; 1459a 30–b7.

13. Slatkin, *The Power of Thetis*, 39; I. Malkin, *The Returns of Odysseus. Colonization and Ethnicity* (Berkeley, 1998), 120–55. Cf. M. Finkelberg, "Homer and the Bottomless Well of the Past", *Scripta Classica Israelica* 21 (2002), 243–50 (a review article of Malkin, *The Returns of Odysseus*).

14. *Od.* 12.183–93 (the Sirens); 9. 258–80 (the Cyclops). Cf. Finkelberg, *The Birth of Literary Fiction*, 73–74, 95–98; D. Clay, "The Archaeology of the Temple of Juno in Carthage", *Classical Philology* 83 (1988), 195–205.

15. Cf. R. Martin, "Telemachus and the Last Hero Song", in H.M. Roisman and J. Roisman, eds., "Essays on Homeric Epic", *Colby Quarterly* 29 (1993), 222–40; K. Dowden, "Homer's Sense of Text", *Journal of Hellenic Studies* 116 (1996), 47–61; Finkelberg, *The Birth of Literary Fiction*, 154–55. I discuss this issue in greater detail in M. Finkelberg, "The Sources of *Iliad* 7", in H.M. Roisman and J. Roisman, eds., "Essays on Homeric Epic", *Colby Quarterly* 38 (2002), 151–61.

16. The only explicit reference to the Dorians is *Od.* 19.177.

17. On the Dorian charter myth see esp. 1. Malkin, *Myth and Territory in the Spartan Mediterranean* (Cambridge, 1994), 33–45.

18. *Il.* 2.559–567. Tr. M. Hammond.

19. Str. 8.3.33, p. 358; cf. N.G. Hammond in *Cambridge Ancient History* (3rd ed.) 2.2 (1975), 694–5. and *Cambridge Ancient History* (2nd ed.) 3.1 (1982), 715. The pseudo-Hesiodic *Catalogue of Women* gives a different and apparently a more consistent picture of the domains of Heroic Age Argos; see M. Finkelberg, "Ajax's Entry in the Hesiodic *Catalogue of Women*". *Classical Quarterly* 38 (1988). 38–41.

20. It is noteworthy that, according to some sources, Homer and Hesiod were directly responsible for the introduction of the mythological stories relating to the Olympian gods, their domains of authority, and their very names. See Xenoph. 21 B 11 DK, Hdt. 2.53.

21. See J.N. Coldstream, "Hero-Cults in the Age of Homer", *Journal of Hellenic Studies* 96 (1976), 8–17; F. De Polignac, *Cults, Territory, and the Origins of the Greek City-State*, Tr. J. Lloyd (Chicago 1995; French edition 1984) 128–49; J. Whitley, "Early States and Hero Cults: A Reappraisal", *Journal of Hellenic Studies* 108 (1988), 173–82; I. Morris, "Tomb Cult and the 'Greek renaissance': the past in the present in the 8th century B.C.E.", *Antiquity* 62 (1988), 750–61.

22. Polybius, himself an Achaean, adduces what was in all probability the standard Achaean version of the events: 'The state of the Achaean nation ... may be summarized as follows. Their first king was Tisamenos, the son of Orestes, who had been expelled from

Sparta on the return of the Heraclidae, and who then proceeded to occupy Achaea.' Polyb. 2.41; cf. Str. 8.7.1 p. 383; Paus. 7.1.2. In addition, the founders of the Aeolian colonies in Asia Minor claimed to be descendants of Orestes' son Penthilos, see Str. 9.2.3, p. 401, 9.2.5, p. 403; 13.1.3, p. 582; Paus. 2.18.6; 3.2.1; cf. 7.6.1–2.

23. Malkin, *Myth and Territory*, 30, interprets, the reburial of the bones of Orestes and other cases of the Spartans' appropriation of the pre-Dorian past as indicative of their 'political use of cult and myth vis-à-vis other Greeks'. Yet, the fact that the same practices are paralleled in the Homeric poems strongly suggests that there was a broad Panhellenic consensus in favour of crediting the Spartans with a Heroic Age past for the sake of their fuller integration into the body of the 'Hellenes'.

24. Cf. G. Nagy, *Pindar's Homer: The Lyric Possession of an Epic Past* (Baltimore and London, 1990), 72–3.

25. *Cypria* fr. 1 Bernabé; Hes. *Erga* 159–73; Hes. Fr. 204. 95–105 Merkelbach-West.

26. R. Scodel, "The Achaean Wall and the Myth of Destruction", *Harvard Studies in Classical Philology* 86 (1982), 35. Cf. B. Hainsworth, ed., *The Iliad: A Commentary*. Vol. 3 (Cambridge, 1993), 320; Slatkin, *The Power of Thetis*, 121.

27. Pl. *Symp.* 221.

28. See esp. Hes. *Erga* 174–78: 'Thereafter, would that I were not among the men of the fifth generation, but either had died before or, been born afterwards. For now truly is a race of iron, and men never rest from labour and sorrow by day, and from perishing by night; and the gods shall lay sore trouble upon them.' Tr. H.G. Evelyn-White.

29. Some regions, such as Attica, Arcadia, or Achaea, have never become Dorian, whereas in others the Dorians settled side by side with the former inhabitants to form a symbiosis which often lasted till the end of antiquity. The non-Dorian tribe of Argos, the Hyrnathioi, immediately comes to mind in this connection, but a considerable 'Achaean' population was also present in Triphylia, formally part of Dorian Messenia, and in Laconia itself, where several cities, most notably Amyclae, were captured from 'Achaeans' as late as the beginning of the Archaic Age.

30. N. Na'aman, "Historiography, the Shaping of Collective Memory, and the Creation of Historical Consciousness in the People of Israel at the End of the First Temple Period", *Ziyon*, 1996, 449–72 [Hebrew]. See also N. Na'aman, *The Past that Shapes the Present: The Creation of Biblical Historiography in the Late First Temple Period Jerusalem*, 2002) [Hebrew].

31. Thuc. 1.3.

32. Cf. W. Nicolai, "Rezeptionssteurung in der Ilias", *Philologus* 127, 1983, 1–12, on the distinction between the 'affirmative' and the 'kritische Wirkungsabsicht' in the *Iliad*.

33. *Il.* 14. 364–69; 3. 8–9. Cf. Pl. *Rep.* 389e.

34. *Poet.* 1460a 5–11. Cf. S. Halliwell, *Aristotle's Poetics* (London, 1986), 126; Finkelberg, *The Birth of Literary Fiction*, 155–56.

35. I treat the topic discussed in this and the following section also in M. Finkelberg, "Canon-Replacement Versus Canon-Appropriation: The Case of Homer", forthcoming in H. Vastinphout and G. Dorleijn, eds., *Structure, Function and Dynamics of Cultural Repertories* (Leuven).

36. *Il.* 23. 536–8, 586–96, 884–97.

37. M.I. Finley, *The World of Odysseus* (2nd ed.), (Harmondsworth, 1978), 115.

38. See A.A. Long, "Morals and Values in Homer", *Journal of Hellenic Studies* 90 (1970), 123–26. On the values of Greek aristocracy see esp. W. Donlan, *The Aristocratic Ideal in Ancient Greece*, (Wauconda, Illinois [repr. of Coronado Press, 1980], 1999).

39. *Il.* 9. 328–33.

40. *Il.* 9. 318–19; Ar. *Pol.* 1267a1–2.

41. M. Finkelberg, "*Timê* and *Aretê* in Homer", *Classical Quarterly* 48 (1998), 15–28.

42. *Il.* 11. 762–4, 16. 29–32, 18. 98–106.

43. R. Seaford, *Reciprocity and Ritual: Homer and Tragedy in the Developing City-State* (Oxford, 1994), 5–6; K.A. Raaflaub, "Homeric Society", in I. Morris and B. Powell, *A New Companion to Homer* (Leiden,1997), 646–48.

44. A. Snodgrass, "An Historical Homeric Society?", *Journal of Hellenic Studies* 94 (1974), 114–25.

45. Weapons: D. Gray, "Homeric Epithets for Thing", *Classical Quarterly* 41 (1947), 109–21, reprinted in G.S. Kirk, ed., *The Language and Background of Homer* (Cambridge, 1964), 55–67; death- and afterlife: C. Souivinou-Inwood, '*Reading*' *Greek Death to the End of the Classical Period* (Oxford, 1995), 12–3, 73–6, 89–92.

46. For the *Odyssey* version of the same ideal see M. Finkelberg, "Odysseus and the Genus 'Hero'," *Greece and Rome* 42 (1995), 1–14.

47. Pl. *Ap.* 28cd: 'He [Achilles], if you remember, made light of danger in comparison with incurring disgrace when his goddess mother warned him, eager as he was to kill Hector, you will die yourself—"Next after Hector is thy fate prepared." When he heard this warning, he made light of his death and danger, being much more afraid of living as an unworthy man and of failing to avenge his friends. "Let me die forthwith," said he, "when I have requited the villain, rather than remain here by the beaked ships to be mocked, a burden on the ground." Do you suppose that he gave a thought to death and danger?' Tr. H. Tredennick, with slight changes.

48. While some scholars connect the standardization of the Homeric text with the tradition of the so-called Pisistratean recension, that is, the codification of the Homeric poems in sixth-century Athens, others place it much earlier, in eighth-century Ionia. At the same time, all these scholars share the contention that Athens of the sixth century B.C.E. played a central role in the transmission of the text of Homer.

49. Cf. Finkelberg, "The *Cypria*, the *Iliad*, and the Problem of Multiformity", 11.

50. Xenoph. 21 B I 1 DK (cf. also 21 B 1. 19–23).

51. *Rep.* 607a, 398d–400d. Note, however, that, according to Richard Janko, it is not out of the question that Zenodotus (3rd century B.C.E.), tried to apply Plato's principles in his editorial work; see R. Janko (ed.), *The Iliad: A Commentary*. Vol. IV (Cambridge), 23.

52. According to Plutarch, the great Alexandrian scholar Aristarchus (2nd century B.C.E.) deleted 'out of fear' four lines from Phoenix's speech in *Iliad* 9 (458–61), which described how Phoenix considered killing his father in revenge for the curse put on him. Yet, as far as we know, Aristarchus was mainly preoccupied with the *numerus versuum*, working hard on purging the text of Homer from meaningless repetitions that had accumulated in the course of time, and was not in the habit of deleting Homeric lines on account of their content. When he wanted to cast doubt on a line or a passage he simply athetized them (cf. R. Lamberton, "Homer in Antiquity", in Morris and Powell, *A New Companion to Homer*, 44). This is why I find it more plausible that, as Stephanie West argued in a recent article, the lines in question, known to us only from Plutarch's quotations, should rather be taken as belonging to one of the Cyclic poems. See S. West, "Phoenix's Antecedents: A Note on *Iliad* 9", *Scripta Classica Israelica* 20 (2001), 1–15.

53. M. Halbertal, *People of the Book: Canon, Meaning, and Authority* (Cambridge, Mass., 1997), 32–40, esp. 32–33: 'Canonizing a text results in increased flexibility in its interpretation, such as the use of complex hermeneutical devices of accommodation to yield the best possible reading.'

54. D-K 8.2; 59 A 1 par. 11. Cf. N. Richardson, "Homer and His Ancient Critics", in N. Richardson. ed., *The Iliad: A Commentary*, Vol. VI (Cambridge, 1993), 27–29.

55. See further R. Lamberton, "The Neoplatonists and the Spiritualization of Homer", in R. Lamberton and J.J. Keaney, *Homer's Ancient Readers: The Hermeneutic of Greek Epic's Earliest Exegetes* (Princeton, 1992), 115–33.

56. Str. 7.3.6–10, pp. 298–303. On Strabo and Homer see now D. Dueck, *Strabo of Amasia: A Greek Man of Letters in Augustan Rome* (London, 2000), 31–40.

57. See Finkelberg, "*Timê* and *Aretê* in Homer", 23–24.

58. J.M. Bryant, *Moral Codes and Social Structure in Ancient Greece: A Sociology of Greek Ethics from Homer to the Epicureans and Stoics* (Albany, 1996), 461. Cf. also M. Finkelberg, "Virtue and Circumstances: on the City-State Concept of Arete," *American Journal of Philology* 123 (2002), 35–49.

59. *Il.* 20. 242.

60. *Mor.* 24 C.E.: tr. F.C. Babbitt.

61. *Mor.* 27 AB.

62. *De Homero* 218, tr. J.J. Keaney and R. Lamberton.

63. See R. Browning, "The Byzantines and Homer", in Lamberton and Keaney, *Homer's Ancient Readers*, 146–47.

64. *Ad adulescentes* 1.5; 5.6; 4.1–2; 4.4. Tr. R.J. Deferrari and M.R.P. McGuire.

65. Cf. P. Bourdieu and J.-C. Passeron. *Reproduction in Education, Society and Culture* (2nd ed.), tr. R. Nice (London 1990), 5–11.

66. Cf. Browning, "The Byzantines and Homer", 147: 'The Byzantines were well aware that their own culture and their own peculiar identity had two roots—pagan and Christian.... History and tradition had made Homer the very symbol of a complex and tenacious culture that distinguished the Greek from the barbarian and also from the non-Greek Christian, Orthodox though it might be.'

D. N. MARONITIS

The Space of Homilia and Its Signs in the Iliad and the Odyssey

I

This essay is based on a more general working hypothesis, the basic propositions of which, very briefly formulated, are as follows:

1. The *Iliad* is constructed around the interplay of two main themes that might, on account of their scope and depth, be termed megathemes of heroic poetry. The first and most obvious one is that of "war," divided into individual and named clashes or into collective and anonymous ones, the result of which is death or injury. The second theme is that of *"homilia,"* as this was identified and specified by the Alexandrian scribes in order to characterize corresponding scenes from the *Iliad* and the *Odyssey*: the *homilia* between Hector and Andromache, Odysseus' *homilia* with Eumaeus, the *homilia* between Odysseus and Penelope.

2. The theme of *homilia* in the *Iliad* exhibits three complementary aspects: the "conjugal," the "extra-conjugal," and the "companionate." All three aspects of the theme of *homilia* are interwoven in an exemplary way into Book VI of the *Iliad*, either set out one after the other or subordinated one to the other. The book begins with the companionate *homilia* between Glaucus and Diomedes, which serves as a preparation for the subsequent

---

From *Homeric Megathemes: War–Homilia–Homecoming.* © 2004 by Lexington Books.

conjugal *homilia* between Hector and Andromache, which, in its turn, highlights the extra-conjugal relationship between Paris and Helen.

3. However, Book VI of the *Iliad* does not provide the only example of the theme of *homilia*. We only have to recall that the epic has as its starting point the double extra-conjugal involvement (first between Agamemnon and Chryseis and then between Agamemnon and Briseis) and ends with the companionate *homilia* (between Achilles and Priam). Between these two limits, other signs of the theme of *homilia*[1] corresponding to its three formal aspects can also be seen.

4. The relationship between war and *homilia* in the *Iliad* can be defined, using a chemical term, as "antipathetic": in other words, the weakening of the one theme involves the strengthening of the other and vice versa. Because, however, this is a heroic epic, the theme of war not only proves to be stronger than that of *homilia*, but also has a relationship of container to contained: that is, all aspects of the Iliadic *homilia* are either strained or disrupted under pressure of the Iliadic war.

5. The disruptive influence of the war comes to bear on the conjugal *homilia* between Hector and Andromache and on the companionate relationship between Achilles and Patroclus. The end of the latter *homilia*, with the slaying of Patroclus by Hector, also leads to the end of the former. In other cases, the outcome of the companionate *homilia* could be characterized as ironic. This appears more clearly in the nature of the companionate *homilia* between Glaucus and Diomedes with the exchange of gold and bronze weapons.

6. The extra-conjugal relationship contributes either to the start of the war or to its escalation: the Trojan war is provoked by the extra-conjugal relationship between Paris and Helen and the Iliadic war is started[2] by the extra-conjugal relationship between Agamemnon and Chryseis, which develops into the extra-conjugal relationship between Agamemnon and Briseis. Behind the Iliadic war, the extra-conjugal relationships end or tend toward their end: Chryseis returns to her father even as early as Book I; Briseis returns, albeit it with some delay, to Achilles during the course of Book XIX; and, finally, the return of Helen is proposed in Book III with the duel between Menelaus and Alexander, but is postponed for the post-Iliadic development of the Trojan myth.

7. Among other things, the *Odyssey* inherits from the *Iliad* its two major constituent themes: "war" in its postwar, internecine version, and "*homilia*." Since, however, this is an epic belonging to the wider, postwar cycle of "*Nostoi*," the two themes vary[3] and, above all, their importance is reversed. Here the theme of *homilia* takes precedence over the theme of war. This is evident in the course and the outcome of the conjugal *homilia* between Odysseus and

Penelope. This relationship which, because of the Trojan war and primarily because of the hero's many wanderings following the war, was in danger of coming to an end is reestablished for good following the *Mnêstêrophonia*.

8. Yet the extra-conjugal relations in the *Odyssey* also function positively, as a rule. Circe, Calypso, and Nausicaa, albeit latently, are all eventually transformed from being obstacles into aids to Odysseus' homecoming.[4] As for the extra-conjugal designs of the suitors, the constant postponement is due to Penelope's cunning resistance, while the final foiling of these designs is due effectively to the slaughter of the suitors.

9. The aspect of the companionate *homilia* in the *Odyssey* is similarly divided. Odysseus' companions from Troy are wiped out by their own fault, though showing their leader to be a good companion.[5] Moreover, Odysseus' companions on Ithaca (Eumaeus and Eurykleia, for example, and the goddess Athena on another level) collaborate in bringing about the slaughter of the suitors and in consolidating Odysseus' homecoming.

10. More generally, in the *Odyssey*, the theme of *homilia* is presented, both quantitatively and qualitatively, much more strongly than in the *Iliad*, though without turning the epic into a sentimental romance. Apart from anything else, this is due to the way that *homilia* is constantly interwoven with the Odyssean war: whether the external war of the *Apologoi* or the internal war on Ithaca. *Homilia* and war in the *Odyssey* are linked primarily by Odysseus' excellence of mind, by his cunning genius.[6]

II

If the above hypothesis holds true, then the next question in this study could be posed as follows: Is the threefold Iliadic *homilia* located in its own familial space? And if so, what space is this and what are its signs? And further, to the extent that the space of war and *homilia* can be discerned in the *Iliad*, is the same true of the *Odyssey*? Or is there a difference and divergence between the two epics on this important issue?

The list of questions already points to a wide field of investigation, which is outside the scope of the present study. Here, I will confine myself to the absolutely essential, leaving side issues undiscussed and unresolved.

This field of investigation, however, is further enlarged when my own group of questions is included in its wider context. By this I mean the more general problem concerning the presentation and function of space in the two Homeric epics. In the first part of his work, W. Kullmann attempts his own investigation in this direction.[7] Moreover, this controversial issue has been covered by what is, in my opinion, an exhaustive and incisive study published by Brigitte Hellwig in 1964.[8]

Although Hellwig does not refer to the distinction between the space of war and that of *homilia*, except indirectly and in only one sentence in her long study,[9] her general descriptions and conclusions, at least, concerning the presentation and function of space in the *Iliad* and *Odyssey* may be seen as a presupposition for my own study and, indeed, a necessary introduction to it.

Let me begin with the three main specifications of space in the *Iliad*, as these were set out by Hellwig:

1. Space in the *Iliad* is not described per se and consequently it is not autonomous in narrative terms; it is simply outlined as a generally broad background for the narrative action, which it serves.

2. Two basic circles of space can be discerned in the *Iliad*: the divine and the heroic or human. The latter is inscribed as an inner ring within the former, which forms the outer ring. The outer circle defines and delimits the largest radius of narrative action from the point of view of space. Divine and heroic space communicate with each other in other ways too, primarily through the incursions of the gods from the outer into the inner ring.

3. The seat of the divine space is Mount Olympus. However, from time to time, the gods are also located elsewhere: among the Aethiopians, on Mount Ida, on the mountain in Samothrace, on the wall of Heracles, and on Mount Kallikolone. Moreover, the outline of the heroic space appears more clearly defined and almost symmetrical. Presented as its outer limits and as the poles of its narrative action are the walled city of Troy on the one hand and, on the other, the camp of the Achaeans, which is also protected by a ditch and a makeshift wall. In between lies the plain of Troy as the major field of battle in the Iliadic war, which, nevertheless, moves alternately from the one pole to the other: from the walled city of Troy to the ships of the Danaans.[10]

With this general outline of the Iliadic spatial arrangement in mind, we can again pose the question whether *homilia* in the *Iliad* commands its own specific space. A concise answer to this question would be affirmative, if the spatial circumstances of the *homilia* between Hector and Andromache are taken into account together with the underlying extra-conjugal *homilia* between Alexander and Helen. Both these examples of *homilia* presuppose a shift from the field of battle to the inner safety of the walls of Troy, which functions as a closed and secure space. Through its walls and its towers, Troy constitutes the limit of the conflict and threat of war.

Similarly, the space of the instances of companionate *homilia* is also delineated outside the field of battle, with one sole exception as we shall see. The companionate exchange between Priam and Achilles in Book XXIV is located in Achilles' tent and in the camp of the Myrmidons.[11] Roughly the same scene surrounds the companionate relationship between Achilles and Patroclus, while the two renowned friends both remain out of the war. In these terms, the typical space of companionate *homilia* in the *Iliad* may be seen as closed, distinct, and secure, corresponding symmetrically to the walls of Troy.

An exception to this rule appears to be the companionate *homilia* between Diomedes and Glaucus in the first part of Book VI. Here, at least in the first instance, the space of war and that of *homilia* are merged to the extent that they outwardly coincide. This exception calls for a more careful examination, which, however, requires discussion first concerning the clear-cut cases of the distinct space of *homilia*, as this is seen above all in the *homilia* between Hector and Andromache in Book VI.

III

The scene is well-known. I shall present, then, its main features, stressing the signs of *homilia*, both primary and secondary, which relate to the space and act of *homilia*.[12]

Helenos' command to his brother (6.86–101) initiates Hector's move from the warring to the non-warring space. However, the reason for this unexpected change of place is still the war, while in Helenos' advice there is no allusion to a meeting between Hector and Andromache.

Following the end of the intervening companionate *homilia* between Diomedes and Glaucus, Hector arrives at the Scaean Gates, which are presented here, and will be presented again at the end of the scene, as the clear boundary between the warring and non-warring space. It is precisely at this boundary that the first act of *homilia* takes place, between Hector and the anonymous throng of mothers, daughters, and wives, who ask about the fate of their husbands, sons, and brothers.[13]

Hector then goes toward Priam's palace and, exceptionally here,[14] there is a description of the fifty and twelve facing chambers of the sons and daughters of the ruler of Troy. In my view, this long description of the chambers and the albeit discreet reference to the cohabitation of the spouses may be seen as planned indications of the heart of the theme of *homilia*, at least when this concerns conjugal or extra-conjugal relationships.

In any case, it is before this setting of the chambers, and in particular that of Laodice (the fairest of Priam's daughters), that the meeting takes place between Hector and Hecuba (I note that Hecuba, Helen, and Andromache also participate, in part or in full, in the dramatic continuation of the conjugal *homilia*: in the final phase of Book XXII and in the funeral rites in Book XXIV).[15] Opposed to his mother's arguments, the son rejects the offering of wine in the next exchange, considering it a sign of unwarlike relaxation. Consequently, this constitutes an indirect and complementary indication of the respite necessary for *homilia*.

Next, there follows the delivery of Helenos' command and its execution. Meanwhile, the meeting between Hector and Alexander is foreshadowed[16] and, in this way, the extra-conjugal union of Paris and Helen is introduced as a contrast[17] to the subsequent conjugal *homilia* between Hector and Andromache.

The infamous illicit couple in the *Iliad* and the Trojan myth are in their chamber when visited by Hector, in a state that could be characterized as "between *homilia* and war." In this instance, the erotic union,[18] instigated by Aphrodite, has just preceded. Nevertheless, Helen's words to Hector also constitute a form of indirect challenge to him, still standing and armed as he is, to enter into the space of *homilia*. Helen invites him to enter the chamber and sit on a chair. For a second time, Hector rejects this conduct concerning *homilia* (the respite on the part of the warrior, which entails at least partial disarming, indicates it once again), appears to be in a hurry to return to the space of war, though expresses his desire to see his wife and son as he foresees that he will never return to Troy alive. The way has opened for the conjugal *homilia* at exactly the point where the distinction between the space of war and *homilia*, between the conduct of war and *homilia*, has become most clear: when, that is, the two adjacent and complementary areas have been sufficiently marked.

To the extent that the chamber has, until now, proved to be the main sign of the space of *homilia*, we would expect the conjugal *homilia* between Hector and Andromache to find its natural setting in the couple's chamber. However, this expectation, shared by Hector, is proved wrong. The husband arrives at the threshold of his house, only to be informed by the maids that his wife (together with their son and his nurse) are already roaming the city, hoping to meet him. Her desire for *homilia*[19] drives her to the hasty action of going in search of him, which almost proves fatal. The meeting between the couple eventually takes place at the exit from the space of *homilia*, at the very moment when Hector is preparing to lave it and return to the war. In this way, the Scaean Gates are presented as the ultimate and crowning setting for *homilia*, since they have already served as the introductory opening for Hector's act of *homilia*.

There follows the presentation of Andromache and the young Astyanax, which, among other things, has as its purpose to complete the triangle of *homilia*: the spouses are shown as constituting the base, the child as the unifying apex.[20]

In order for the conjugal *homilia* to begin, its constituent parties have to pass from their hasty motion to an expressive halt: Hector smiles at his son, who is still in the arms of his nurse. In tears, Andromache stands beside him and holds his hand. Her first words mainly highlight her anxiety concerning her husband's fortune in the war. She endeavors to drag him into the periphery at least of the space of *homilia*, using the argument of her own impending widowhood and the consequent orphaning of the child. At the same time, she admits her exceptional dependence on her husband, who, for her, has become father, mother, brother and, of course, θαλερός παρακοίτης—a discreet allusion to the warmth of the conjugal bed.

Hector rejects his wife's invitation to *homilia* in the name of heroic glory; he nevertheless confirms his superlative bond with Andromache, setting out his own corresponding scale, in which his father, mother, and brothers are all downgraded in favor of his wife. Moreover, the possibility of Andromache being made into a slave is a nightmarish thought, to which he prefers death.

What follows adds two more formal and highly significant characteristics to the already multiple characteristics of the conduct surrounding *homilia*: the albeit partial disarming and the indirect embracing. This is achieved with the help of Astyanax: the infant goes from his nurse's arms into his father's embrace and then gives himself up to his mother's bosom, managing in the meantime, through his crying, to get Hector to remove his helmet. Moreover, the infant's crying causes the parents to laugh, a fact which, in its turn, points to the *homilia* of their carefree prewar life.[21]

It is precisely at this point that the homiletic scene reaches its climax. As the woman takes the boy from his father's arms, she smiles tearfully, and this tearful smile provokes the husband's compassion and tenderness so that, for the first and last time, he caresses her.

This is followed by the almost violent[22] end to the *homilia*: Hector sends Andromache home. He himself again dons his armor and leaves. She watches him with a still restrained sobbing that worsens and becomes a mournful γόον when she returns to her chamber.

As he leaves, he meets with his brother, who is satiated[23] by the extra-conjugal *homilia*. Together, Hector and Alexander proceed "from *homilia* to war," leaving behind the walls of Troy.

We arrive at the following conclusions:

1. *Homilia* in the *Iliad* (in this case conjugal *homilia* and, as an insert, extra-conjugal *homilia*) is, in a manner of speaking, begotten by the Iliadic war. After its asphyxiating development, it is again absorbed by this. In other words, while the *homilia* is progressing and flourishing, the signs of war decrease, but do not vanish; when the *homilia* begins to wane, the signs of war again grow strong. Consequently, this circular movement acquires a

crosswise form: from war to *homilia* and from *homilia* to war. In this way, the suppression of the theme of *homilia* becomes evident.

2. This *homilêtic* scene demands that we distinguish the act and conduct of *homilia* from its space. The latter serves the former, though it adds to it its own complementary signs.

3. The conjugal (or extra-conjugal) bed and the chamber are correspondingly highlighted as the focus of the space of *homilia*, with Priam's palace and Troy in general as its inner ring, the walls of Troy and the towers as its outer ring, and, finally, the Scaean Gates as the symbolic entrance and exit from the space of war to that of *homilia* and vice versa.

4. Moreover, the act and conduct of *homilia* are presented here as a progressive focussing and then as an almost violent departure.[24] This is clearly seen during the course of Hector's *homilia*. If his previous warring activity re quires movement on the field of battle, his mission concerning *homilia* demands his moving from the warring to the non-warring space; then his successive visits to the chambers of Laodice, of Helen and Paris, and of Andromache; his halting at the Scaean Gates so that the conjugal *homilia* might take place; and, finally, his exit with Alexandros in order to submit himself once again to the motion of the warring clash.

5. A corresponding spiraling is also formed in the area of language: if a violent exchange often accompanies the warring contest between two opponents, here we can speak of a mild exchange during the *homilia*, which develops into the tender words of *homilia*, only to revert once again into a rebuffing exchange.

6. Obviously, lying together in the conjugal or extra-conjugal bed marks the essence of the act of *homilia*. The entrance and remaining of the warrior in the chamber indicate the approach of *homilia*, which is why this is rejected by Hector. The conjugal *homilia* between Hector and Andromache takes place at the farthest limit of the space of *homilia*, and this demands the, so to speak, metonymic[25] stating of the act of *homilia*. The most obvious signs of this conduct of metonymic *homilia* are: the approach and first formal contact of the parties concerned in the *homilia*; the albeit partial disarming of the hero; the indirect embrace between the couple, by means of Astyanax; the husband's compassionate caressing of his wife. As secondary signs, we have: the father's smiling at his son; the momentary laughter of the parents and the tearful smile of Andromache.

I am not going to dwell on the companionate *homilia* between Glaucus and Diomedes,[26] so as to examine, as necessary, the apparent coincidence of the spaces of *homilia* and of war. I will confine myself simply to a number of general observations and explanations:

The recognition scene between Glaucus and Diomedes, included as it is in the context of the Argive hero's valiant deeds, bears all the formal characteristics in its prologue of the dual warring clash (6.119–122): the isolation of two warriors amidst the warring throng, who at some moment come face to face as they stalk the battlefield; the exchange of names; the lone or reciprocal defiant address before the onset.

Here, the defiant address is assigned to Diomedes, who seeks to learn whether his brash adversary is a mortal or a god, so that he may act accordingly. Though this double question is unexpectedly prolonged, it ends with the repetition of the murderous threat, which usually precedes the murderous blow. The suspension of the murderous clash is further prolonged by the insertion of Glaucus' long genealogical account (divided into the prologue, main part, and epilogue), both through its tone[27] and through its content, in which it is easy to detect the motifs of, first, extra-conjugal and then conjugal *homilia*. The eventual postponement of the warring clash is achieved with Diomedes' second recognition speech, which results in a companionate agreement: the two companions will not henceforth engage in combat with each other, even though they belong to opposing camps, since they are bound together through the act of hospitality in their genealogical roots. This is followed by what I have already called an ironic exchange of gold and bronze gifts, since, in the meantime, the two heroes dismount, embrace, and swear an oath of friendship to each other.

Despite its warlike typology, on the level of the conduct of *homilia*, this companionate *homilia* exhibits the basic signs of the conjugal *homilia* between Hector and Andromache: the warring and hasty motion is here turned into a static *homilia*, the warlike retorts into a dialogue; moreover, the exchange of weapons presupposes the albeit momentary disarming, while the dismounting of the heroes, their going over to each other and, finally, their embracing constitutes their physical contact. There is still the question, however, of the autonomy of the space of *homilia*.

The careful reading of the scene leads us to say that the war space is only clearly defined in the introductory lines (ll. 119–122) and in a latent way in the epilogue (ll. 2.32–236). This space disappears, however, in the inner part of the *homilia*.[28] In its place, through Glaucus' genealogical account and Diomedes' recognition speech, the common companionate space is shown to be Argos.[29] As a conclusion, we can say that the primary space of war is transformed along the way into the secondary space of *homilia*, created by the companionate *homilia*, given that it is impossible for it to be found elsewhere.

IV

I will now turn to the *Odyssey*. It is not possible, of course, for me to deal with the more general problem of the presentation and function of space in the *Odyssey*, other than to stress that in this matter it shows a characteristic deviation from the *Iliad*.

Kullmann,[30] too, shows that both inhabited and open space is presented in the *Odyssey* with much greater detail and regularity than in the *Iliad*, and, above all, is functionally interwoven with the narrative action and sometimes specified in the extreme. In the case of Odysseus' palace, Kullmann rightly observes that the functional role of this space in the preparation and carrying out of the Mnêstêrophonia recalls a crime novel.

Hellwig's general observations concerning space in the *Odyssey* are similar. Of these, I will refer to just four for reasons of brevity:[31]

1. In the *Odyssey*, the dominance of the heroic or human space is almost total with regard to the narrative composition and structure. From the beginning, the divine space (with its seat on Mount Olympus) programs the end of the narrative and henceforth imbues the human space with gods, usually as messengers or helpers for the heroes.

2. Moreover, although the human space retains Ithaca and Odysseus' palace as its focus, nevertheless it constantly shifts throughout two-thirds of the epic. This is the result, on the one hand, of Telemachus' journey of quest and, on the other, of Odysseus' ten-year wandering journey of return.

3. If, however, the human space in the *Odyssey* has to be divided into two complementary areas, then the one could be termed "homeland" and the other "foreign land." Their difference lies in the fact that the former is a familiar and recognizable space in its every detail; whereas the latter is presented as an unfamiliar and indistinct place, inhospitable or only in exceptional cases hospitable. Both areas form, in each instance, a minor, medium, or major radius, though particularly the space of the *Apologoi* (that is, Odysseus' inner narrative) could be characterized not only as exotic, precivilized, and utopian, but also as multicentric.

4. The presentation of space in the *Odyssey* takes place (in accordance with the model of the *Iliad*) either in an indirect way (contributing its spatial support to the narrative action) or (and for the first time and in blatant contrast to the *Iliad*) in a direct way (in the form of a virtually autonomous and static description). Characteristic examples of the direct presentation of space are: the land and cave of Calypso in Book V (ll. 63 ff.), the garden and Palace of Alkinous in Book VII (ll. 86 ff.), and the harbor of Phorkys and the cave of the Nymphs in Book XIII (ll. 96 ff.). How the indirect presentation of space proceeds in the *Odyssey* with astounding specificity can already be

seen in Book I, when Athena, in the guise of Mentes, visits Odysseus' palace. There, located and named in turn are: the threshold and the αὔλειος οὐδός, the doors, the hall and its furnishings, a tall column, the upper room, where Penelope dwells, and, finally, the room in the courtyard where Telemachus sleeps. The differences, then, from the *Iliad* are seen to be significant in this more traditional presentation of space.[32]

I shall now go back to my own line of questioning: more specifically, to the presentation and functioning of the space of war and *homilia* in the *Odyssey*. The most important and also the most characteristic application of armed conflict in the *Odyssey* is, of course, the *Mnêstêrophonia*, which from a formulaic point of view is usually characterized as Odysseus' valiant deeds. If this is indeed so, then we have to accept it on the understanding that in this particular case the external conditions of the valiant deeds have to a large extent been modified.

The suitors, who through their conduct attempt to transform the conjugal relationship between Odysseus and Penelope into an extra-conjugal one, are finally destroyed before the recognition of the spouses and the consolidation of their *homilia* on both the level of conversation and that of sexual union, which acquires the ritual form of a second marriage.[33]

Nevertheless, the *Mnêstêrophonia* and the conjugal *homilia*, if taken as a whole (that is, as both preparation and execution), not only happen at the same time in the *Odyssey*, but also in the same space: in Odysseus' palace. This is an exceptionally daring coincidence, particularly when compared to the corresponding data in the *Iliad*. Whatever the model was for this temporal and spatial coincidence between two narrative acts which are clearly distinguished in the *Iliad* (Kullmann suggests the epic Nostos of Agamemnon as a model in this context),[34] the way that the poet of the *Odyssey* handles this odd combination reveals, in my view, the magnitude of his narrative skill. I will attempt to explain exactly what I mean.

In the following study, I suggest that the theme of conjugal *homilia* in the *Odyssey* reaches its climax in three stages, corresponding to the stages of the conjugal *homilia* between Hector and Andromache in the *Iliad*, though with a reverse outcome: the first stage can already be recognized in Book XVI (ll. 505–588); the second in Book XIX (ll. 96–604); the third and final stage in Book XXIII (ll. 1–345). The problem is to place these three stages in their individual time and space in order to ascertain their total or partial isolation from the time and space of the *Mnêstêrophonia*.

The first instance of *homilia* between Penelope and Odysseus is indirect and tentative: it takes place during the course of the day, with the stranger again withdrawn inside the μέλινον οὐδὸν of the chamber, following Antinous' insulting remark and with the rest of the suitors having finished their sumptuous meat. Penelope, who, obviously from an adjacent room, hears the unpleasant exchange between Odysseus and the suitors, calls Eumaeus and through him summons the stranger to her chamber, specifying beforehand the topic of the conversation she desires with him. Odysseus, however, refuses the invitation for the time being and asks that the *homilia* be postponed for later that evening, when the suitors have left the palace, specifying also the place: παραὶ πυρί (XVII, 572). In this way, the space and time of the *homilia* are secured for the present and the immediate future.

At the end of Book XVIII, the suitors retire and Odysseus (with Athena's perceptible presence and Telemachus' physical help) renews his plan for *Mnêstêrophonia*, giving orders to this effect to his son, who immediately afterwards also retires to his bed. The time of the already planned second *homilia* has arrived and Penelope undertakes to provide its setting.

She emerges from her chamber and takes her place on her own ornate throne beside the fire. The maids clean away the traces of the suitors' meal from the tables and replace the torches in the sconces. A chair covered in soft hides is offered to the stranger for him to sit facing his wife. And the *homilia* begins, continues deep into the night, reaches the verge of recognition, and there remains in midair. However, the profit from this second, direct communicative exchange between Odysseus and Penelope proves decisive in the impending slaughter of the suitors. Penelope proposes the next day as the final trial for her passage from a conjugal to an extra-conjugal state. Everything will be decided by a contest: the passing of the arrow through the twelve axes. Whichever of the suitors performs this feat, which was child's play for Odysseus, will win her. Odysseus agrees and urges Penelope not to postpone the carrying out of this final test. So the *Mnêstêrophonia*, extra-conjugal, and conjugal *homilia* are interwoven in the specific time and place of this stage of the *homilia*.

The *Mnêstêrophonia* takes place the next day, the penultimate day in the *Odyssey*, in Penelope's absence. Still covered in blood, Odysseus orders that the bodies of the suitors be carried out into the courtyard so that the hall and the courtyard may be cleansed with fire and brimstone, so that the space of the palace may be decorated anew; so that, at last, Eurykleia might fetch the queen.

There are three scenes and three particular spaces in the third and final stage of conjugal *homilia*: the upper room, Penelope's permanent living quarters; the hall and its center, the hearth; and, finally, the chamber with the unmovable conjugal bed. The upper room is the setting for the preliminary discussion between Penelope and Eurykleia; the hall for Penelope's testing and the recognition; the bed in the conjugal chamber is the setting for the sexual union and the ensuing brief accounts given by the couple. Meanwhile, the bodies of the suitors remain piled in the courtyard, the hall has been fumigated, a wild celebration, with music and dance, has been arranged in the palace, so that passersby will think that Penelope has succumbed and taken one of the suitors. In reality, the whole palace space is now given up to the conjugal *homilia*, though without the traces of the *Mnêstêrophonia* and the illusion of the extra-conjugal relationship being altogether eradicated.

I consider that any further commentary would be superfluous. No matter how the acts of the *Mnêstêrophonia* and of the conjugal *homilia* as a whole are presented together in time and space, the poet of the *Odyssey* allots that com mon time and space in such a way (through the method of abstraction, division, and addition) that each theme has its own temporal and spatial setting. It is a model of poetic economy.

NOTES

1. The most prominent companionate relationship in the *Iliad* is that between Achilles and Patroclus. However, there is no corresponding scene of *homilia*, in the strictest sense of the word, between the two companions in the *Iliad*, with the exception of their "musical" *homilia* in Book IX (ll. 191–192). Also worthy of note is the dispersion of the extra-conjugal aspect of the theme of *homilia*. This can be found, for example, in Glaucus' recognition account to Diomedes (6.160–170), and also in Phoenix's admonitory account to Achilles (9.447–457).

2. The linking of the themes of extra-conjugality and war should, in my opinion, be regarded as formulaic: it is present both at the beginning of the *Cypria* as the cause of the Trojan War (see K. Reinhardt, "Das Parisurteil," 16–36; W. Kullmann, *Die Quellen der Ilias*, 248 ff.) and in the *Iliad* as the cause of the Iliadic War (see W. Schadewaldt, *Iliasstudien*, 148; R. Rabel, "Chryses and the Opening of the *Iliad*," 473). One could also refer to the macroscopic and microscopic use of this dual theme in the *Cypria* and the *Iliad*, respectively.

3. The war in the *Odyssey* may be termed a "postwar" to the extent that it is interwoven with Odysseus' homecoming following the end of the Trojan War. The peculiarities of the Odyssean war appear in the warring clashes in the *Apologoi* (e.g., in the episode with the Cicones) and, above all, in the preparations for and the carrying out of the *Mnêstêrophonia*. Moreover, the theme of *homilia* is projected in the *Odyssey* much more than in the *Iliad* and in its three basic aspects: conjugal, extra-conjugal, and companionate. One only has to recall Odysseus' extra-conjugal relationships with Circe, Calypso and, latently, with Nausicaa, or his long companionate *homilia* with Eumaeus.

4. Whereas at first (each in her own way) Circe, Calypso, and Nausicaa set up obstacles before Odysseus' homecoming, they eventually facilitate his return. See, for example, K. Reinhardt, "Die Abenteuer des Odysseus," 77–87; S. L. Schein, "Female Representations and Interpreting the *Odyssey*," 17–27.

5. I have discussed the "companionable" Odysseus at length in my work Ἀναζήτηση καὶ νόστος τοῦ 'Οδυσσέα, 92–102. See also Ἡ ποίηση τοῦ Γιώργου Σεφέρη, 44–62.

6. Odysseus' well-known cunning is utilized not only in his warring activities, but also in his conduct with regard to *homilia*: with Athena, Eumaeus, Penelope, and also with

the suitors. Moreover, in the context of the *Mnêstêrophonia*, the hero's dual sharpness of wit becomes more than evident; see R. Schröter, *Die Aristie als Crundform homerischer Dichtung und der Friermord in der Odyssee*, 121 ff.

7. "Die poetische Funktion der Palastes des Odysseus in der *Odyssee*," 41–56, and in particular the "Introduction," 41–48, which deals with the more general problem of the presentation and function of space in the Homeric epics and which contains all the recent bibliography.

8. *Raum und Zeit im homerischen Epos*, v–viii and 1–153, with the relevant detailed bibliography.

9. B. Hellwig, *Raum und Zeit im homerischen Epos*, 25.

10. The alternative symmetry proves to be complete. See B. Hellwig, *Raum und Zeit*, 24–28.

11. See F. I. Kakridis, "Ὁ ὁμηρικός οἶκος σὲ σχέση μὲ τὴν εἰρήνη καὶ τὸν πόλεμο," 153–157.

12. This scene has previously been studied and discussed many times and the relevant bibliography is long. See, for example, W. Schadewaldt, *Von Homers Welt und Werk*, 207–233; D. Lohmann, *Die Andromache-Szenen der Ilias*; T. Krischer, "Zur Z der *Ilias*," 16–22. I simply note here that, at least from my reading of this bibliography, it is not based on the hypothesis that the famous scene in the *Iliad* constitutes a formal theme; what I call here the theme of "conjugal *homilia*" is both complementary and in opposition to the theme of "war."

13. This first instance of *homilia* between Hector and the Trojan women is presented by the poet in an indirect narrative form and extremely concisely. Nevertheless, in the list of women, who besiege Hector with their questions, the two basic subjects of conjugal *homilia* are prominent: the words ἄλοχοι and πόσιας are prominent at the beginning and end of the list. Following Hector's despondent yet ambiguous reply, we find in line 241 the comment: πολλῆοι δὲ κῆδε᾽ ἐψῆπτο. It is not easy to decide whether this comment belongs to the poet or is a continuation of Hector's indirect reply to the women. It seems to me, most probably, the former.

14. The description of the royal chambers, which form the inner ring of *homilia*, in which Hector will henceforth move, is again provided by the poet; in such a way, however, that the impression is created in the listener that the poet is recording, or better, conveying, everything that Hector knows as he goes from the Scaean Gates toward Priam's palace. See F. Müller, *Darstellung und poetische Funktion der Gegenstände in der Odyssee*, 89–90.

15. Hecuba: 22.405–428 and 24.746–759, Andromache: 22.460–514 and 24.72–745, Helen: 22.760–775.

16. It is clear that Hector exceeds Helenos' commands. This means that he arbitrarily undertakes responsibility for the *homilêtic* scenes that will follow: with Alexander and Helen on the one hand, and Andromache on the other. In other words, he moves toward the center of the space of *homilia* and temporarily moves away from the space of war. Nevertheless, the theme of war continues to weigh upon him and to be the ultimate goal of his visit to Troy. In order to strengthen this projection of the theme of war as we approach the peak of the conjugal *homilia*, the hero, in the form of a pretext for his visit to the chamber of Helen and Paris, puts forward his intention of returning to the war with his brother, who, meanwhile, with Aphrodite's help, has given himself up to extra-conjugal love.

17. Alexander and Helen are about to come out of their extra-conjugal respite when Hector comes to see them: Paris is handling his weapons, while Helen uses her erotic wiles

to persuade her paramour to return to the field pareipous alokhos malakois epeessin, says the text (l. 337).

18. The erotic union between Paris and Helen, for which Aphrodite is responsible, is described in Book III (ll. 421–426) with particular emphasis. Nowhere else in the epic do we have a corresponding description of an erotic scene referring to heroes. The poignancy of the erotic description is also strengthened by the fact that it is "boxed" within the narrative context of the duel between Menelaus and Alexander. In this instance, the contrast between the themes of war and *homilia* becomes most acute: the erotic *homilia* not only violently interrupts the warring contest, but it virtually ridicules it.

19. Andromache's rash haste is evidently due to her growing desire for *homilia*, which draws her out of her home in the hope of catching up with her husband at exactly the same time that he is hastening to the conjugal chamber to see her. Andromache exhibits a similar rashness in Book XXII (ll. 437–446): at the moment when the whole of Troy is up on the walls lamenting (Hector's maltreatment after being killed by Achilles, she remains inactive in the conjugal chamber. She attends to her weaving, while at the same time she has ordered the maids to prepare a hot bath for her husband, still expecting his homecoming from the battle. The two scenes, which correspond to the two stages of the descending conjugal *homilia* between Hector and Andromache (the third is in Book XXIV), are obviously similar and comparable: the excessive desire for *homilia* leads for a while to the postponement of the *homilia* scene, a delay which increases its dramatization in the extreme.

20. The presence of Astyanax in this *homiletic* scene (in Books XXII and XXIII, in the respective laments of Andromache, Astyanax is indirectly evoked through the references made to him by his mother) shows that, apart from the couple themselves, the child too belongs to the formula of conjugal *homilia*. If the two spouses constitute the angles at the base of the triangle of *homilia*, then the child constitutes its unifying apex. A corresponding role is played by Telemachus in the conjugal triangle of the *Odyssey*, in the recognition scene in Book XXIII. The formulaic necessity of the child for forming the triangle of conjugal *homilia* is also shown by the variation that we encounter in Sophocles' *Ajar*. See the following essays in this volume: "The Theme of Conjugal *Homilia* in the *Odyssey*" and "Conjugal *Homilia*: From the *Iliad* to Sophocles' *Ajax*."

21. That the theme of conjugal *homilia* is considered as being in opposition to the theme of war is also apparent from the fact that, elsewhere, it is directly linked with the prewar time of peace, as shown by lines 153–156 in Book XXII. It could be said that the two themes of *homilia* and war reciprocally annul themselves: the development of the one eliminates the other. Nevertheless, in the *Iliad*, without this archetypal opposition being discarded, the two themes sometimes concur, with the result that their opposing nature and function becomes even more evident.

22. Hector's final speech (ll. 486–492) is divided into two: the first part is comforting and inclines more toward the side of conjugal *homilia*, which just previously has reached its peak; the second part transforms the admonition into a command, almost into a rebuttal of Andromache. Hector prepares to return alone to the space of war. Andromache is sent back to the conjugal chamber, now isolated from her husband, as if the entire theme of war is henceforth to be undertaken by Hector and that of *homilia* by Andromache. This forcible separation of the two themes is final and is expressed by Andromache's premature mourning.

23. The sense of erotic satiety is conveyed by the simile in lines 506–514.

24. This double motion (to and from the space of *homilia*) is repeated and amplified in the *Odyssey*. Odysseus goes from Eumaeus' hut to his own palace; lingers in his courtyard;

remains, as long as is necessary, in the surrounds; enters the hall, first as a beggar, later to become its lord through the slaughter of the suitors; goes up to the conjugal chamber and the conjugal bed. And this centripetal motion is supplemented in Book XXIV by the hero's corresponding centrifugal motion: first into the open-air space to meet with his father and bring about their overdue recognition. Afterwards, together with Laertes, he deals in the center of the town with the uprising of the people, who for the present want to avenge the murder of the suitors. See also my work ᾿Αναζήτηση καὶ νόστος τοῦ ᾿Οδυσσέα, 65–66.

25. Hector and Andromache never see each other alive again in the *Iliad*. This is their only encounter in the whole epic which develops into conjugal *homilia* and, latently, into conjugal union. In my opinion, the whole gamut of their reciprocal gestures may be seen as metonymic signs of erotic union.

26. See O. Andersen, *Die Diomedesgestalt in der Ilias*, 95–110.

27. A melancholic yet antiwar note has already been announced through the simile in lines 145–205 in Glaucus' narration, where there is talk of the "misanthropic" isolation of Bellerophon and his wanderings in the ᾿Αλήιον πεδίον.

28. The space of the Trojan war is completely engulfed in lines 145–205 in Glaucus' narration, as also in lines 215–225 in Diomedes' final recognition and reconciliatory speech.

29. Argos is named in particular in lines 152 and 224 by both companions. Consequently, it functions as the setting for the ancestral companionate *homilia* between Oineus and Bellerophon, which is now being "imitated" by their grandchildren.

30. W. Kullmann, *Die Quellen der Ilias*, 48.

31. B. Hellwig, *Raum und Zeit*, 28–35. Hellwig's observations are not only summarized at certain points, but are also supplemented and made more specific.

32. In comparison with the *Iliad* (see H. Willenbrock, *Die poetische Bedeutung der Gegenstände in Homers Ilias*), the world of objects, which now plays a functional role in the narrative action, is noticeably enlarged in the *Odyssey*.

33. Eurynome and Eurykleia prepare the nuptial bed; immediately afterwards, Eurynome leads the couple to the conjugal bed (23.288–296). The ritual, nuptial manner is obvious. See J. Scott, "Eurynome and Eurykleia in the Odyssey," 78, and U. Hölscher, "Die Erkennungsszene im 23. *Buch der Odyssee*," 403.

34. W. Kullmann, *Die Quellen der Ilias*, 49 ff.

Chronology

1400–200 BC	What is today known as Greece exists as Balkan Peninsula, composed of many small kingdoms.
1250–1200 BC	Troy destroyed. Some historians believe Trojan War did occur; yet Homer's writings are not to be construed as an accounting of that occurrence.
8th century BC	Homer born and lived in Eastern Greece or Asia Minor.
8th or 7th century BC	Homer composes *Iliad* and *Odyssey*.
776 BC	Panathenaic games, models for modern-day Olympics, first occur. Homer's works recited at such Greek festivals .
6th or 7th century BC	Written manuscripts of Homer's work available.
1488	First printed works of Homer appear in Florence. Prepared by Chalcondyles of Athens, who taught Greek in Italy.

Contributors

HAROLD BLOOM is Sterling Professor of the Humanities at Yale University. He is the author of 30 books, including *Shelley's Mythmaking* (1959), *The Visionary Company* (1961), *Blake's Apocalypse* (1963), *Yeats* (1970), *A Map of Misreading* (1975), *Kabbalah and Criticism* (1975), *Agon: Toward a Theory of Revisionism* (1982), *The American Religion* (1992), *The Western Canon* (1994), and *Omens of Millennium: The Gnosis of Angels, Dreams, and Resurrection* (1996). *The Anxiety of Influence* (1973) sets forth Professor Bloom's provocative theory of the literary relationships between the great writers and their predecessors. His most recent books include *Shakespeare: The Invention of the Human* (1998), a 1998 National Book Award finalist, *How to Read and Why* (2000), *Genius: A Mosaic of One Hundred Exemplary Creative Minds* (2002), *Hamlet: Poem Unlimited* (2003), *Where Shall Wisdom Be Found?* (2004), and *Jesus and Yahweh: The Names Divine* (2005). In 1999, Professor Bloom received the prestigious American Academy of Arts and Letters Gold Medal for Criticism. He has also received the International Prize of Catalonia, the Alfonso Reyes Prize of Mexico, and the Hans Christian Andersen Bicentennial Prize of Denmark.

SCOTT RICHARDSON teaches at St. John's University. He is the author of *The Homeric Narrator*.

LOUISE H. PRATT teaches classics at Emory University. She is the author of *Lying and Poetry from Homer to Pindar: Falsehood and Deception in Archaic Greek Poetics*.

AHUVIA KAHANE teaches classics at Northwestern University and has worked on several books, including *Diachronic Dialogues: Authority and Continuity in Homer and the Homeric Tradition*. He has edited *The Oxford English-Hebrew Dictionary* and has also been a co-author and co-editor.

ANDREW FORD is professor of classics at Princeton University. His published work includes *The Origins of Criticism: Literary Culture and Poetic Theory in Classical Greece* as well as *Homer: The Poetry of the Past*.

RICHARD GOTSHALK teaches at the University of Montana. He is the author of several works, including *Beginnings of Philosophy in Greece* and *Temporality of Human Excellence: A Reading of Five Dialogues of Plato*. He also has edited books.

NANCY WORMAN teaches classics at Barnard College, Columbia University. She has authored *Cast of Character: Style in Greek Literature* and also has published essays on Greek poetry and rhetorical theory.

MARGALIT FINKELBERG is professor and chair of classics at Tel Aviv University. She has authored *The Birth of Literary Fiction in Ancient Greece* and *Greeks and Pre-Greeks: Aegean Prehistory and Greek Heroic Tradition*; she also has published numerous articles on Greek language, literature, and civilization.

D. N. MARONITIS is professor emeritus of pkhilosophy at the Aristotle University of Thessaloniki, Greece. He has written books, monographs, and essays on Homer, Herodotus, Hesiod, the ancient lyric poets, and modern Greek poetry and prose.

Bibliography

Albracht, Franz. *Battle and Battle Description in Homer: A Contribution to the History of War*, translated and edited by Peter Jones, Malcolm Willcock, and Gabriele Wright. London: Duckworth, 2005.

Alvis, John. *Divine Purpose and Heroic Response in Homer and Virgil: The Political Plan of Zeus*. Lanham, Md.: Rowman & Littlefield Publishers, 1995.

Bakker, Egbert J. *Poetry in Speech: Orality and Homeric Discourse*. Ithaca, N.Y.; London: Cornell University Press, 1997.

Baldick, Julian. *Homer and the Indo-Europeans: Comparing Mythologies*. London; New York: I.B. Tauris, 1994.

Bebbington, D. W. *The Mind of Gladstone: Religion, Homer, and Politics*. Oxford; New York: Oxford University Press, 2004.

Benardete, Seth. *The Argument of the Action: Essays on Greek Poetry and Philosophy*, edited by Ronna Burger and Michael Davis. Chicago: University of Chicago Press, 2000.

Bennett, Michael J. *Belted Heroes and Bound Women: The Myth of the Homeric Warrior-King*. Lanham, Md.: Rowman & Littlefield Publishers, 1997.

Beye, Charles Rowan. *Ancient Epic Poetry: Homer, Apollonius, Virgil*. Ithaca: Cornell University Press, 1993.

Braund, Susanna, and Glenn W. Most, eds. *Ancient Anger: Perspectives from Homer to Galen*. Cambridge, U.K.; New York: Cambridge University Press, 2003.

Burgess, Jonathan S. *The Tradition of the Trojan War in Homer and the Epic Cycle*. Baltimore, Md.: Johns Hopkins University Press, 2001.

Carlisle, Miriam, and Olga Levaniouk, eds. *Nine Essays on Homer*. Lanham, Md.: Rowman & Littlefield Publishers, 1999.

Carter, Jane B., and Sarah P. Morris, eds. *The Ages of Homer: A Tribute to Emily Townsend Vermeule*. Austin: University of Texas Press, 1995.

Clark, Matthew. *Out of Line: Homeric Composition beyond the Hexameter*. Lanham, Md.: Rowman & Littlefield Publishers, 1997.

Clarke, Michael. *Flesh and Spirit in the Songs of Homer: A Study of Words and Myths*. Oxford: Clarendon Press; New York: Oxford University Press, 1999.

Crotty, Kevin. *The Poetics of Supplication: Homer's* Iliad *and* Odyssey. Ithaca, N.Y.: Cornell University Press, 1994.

de Jong, Irene J. F., ed. *Homer: Critical Assessments*. London; New York: Routledge, 1999.

Dihle, Albrecht. *A History of Greek Literature: From Homer to the Hellenistic Period*, translated by Clare Krojzl. London; New York: Routledge, 1994.

Emlyn-Jones, C., L. Hardwick, and J. Purkis, eds. *Homer: Readings and Images*. London: Duckworth in association with the Open University, 1992.

Finkelberg, Margalit. *The Birth of Literary Fiction in Ancient Greece*. Oxford; New York: Clarendon Press, 1998.

Foley, John Miles. *Homer's Traditional Art*. University Park: Pennsylvania State University Press, 1999.

Garner, Richard. *From Homer to Tragedy: The Art of Allusion in Greek Poetry*. London; New York: Routledge, 1990.

Griffin, Jasper. *Homer*. London: Bristol Classical, 2001.

Hershkowitz, Debra. *The Madness of Epic: Reading Insanity from Homer to Statius*. Oxford: Clarendon Press; New York: Oxford University Press, 1998.

Higbie, Carolyn. *Heroes' Names, Homeric Identities*. New York: Garland, 1995.

Kahane, Ahuvia. *The Interpretation of Order: A Study in the Poetics of Homeric Repetition*. Oxford: Clarendon Press; New York: Oxford University Press, 1994.

King, Katherine Callen. *Homer*. New York: Garland, 1994.

Knox, Bernard MacGregor Walker. *Backing into the Future: The Classical Tradition and Its Renewal*. New York: W.W. Norton, 1994.

Latacz, Joachim. *Homer, His Art and His World*, translated by James P. Holoka. Ann Arbor, Mich.: University of Michigan Press, 1996.

————. *Troy and Homer: Towards a Solution of an Old Mystery*, translated by Kevin Windle and Rosh Ireland. Oxford; New York: Oxford University Press, 2004.

Lowenstam, Steven. *The Scepter and the Spear: Studies on Forms of Repetition in the Homeric Poems*. Lanham, Md.: Rowman & Littlefield, 1993.

McAuslan, Ian, and Peter Walcot, eds. *Homer*. Oxford; New York: Oxford University Press on behalf of the Classical Association, 1998.

O'Donnell, Mark. *Getting over Homer*. New York: Knopf, 1996.

Pavlock, Barbara. *Eros, Imitation, and the Epic Tradition*. Ithaca, N.Y.: Cornell University Press, 1990.

Powell, Barry B. *Homer and the Origin of the Greek Alphabet*. Cambridge, U.K.; New York, N.Y.: Cambridge University Press, 1991.

Pucci, Pietro. *The Song of the Sirens: Essays on Homer*. Lanham, Md.: Rowman & Littlefield, 1998.

Raaflaub, Kurt. "A Historian's Headache: How to Read 'Homeric Society'?" In *Archaic Greece: New Approaches and New Evidence*, edited by Nick Fisher and Hans van Wees. London: Duckworth, 169–193, 1998.

Reece, Steve. *The Stranger's Welcome: Oral Theory and the Aesthetics of the Homeric Hospitality Scene*. Ann Arbor: University of Michigan Press, 1993.

Romilly, Jacqueline de. *Hector*. Paris: Editions de Fallois, 1997.

Rutherford, Richard. *Homer*. Oxford; New York: Oxford University Press, 1996.

Scully, Stephen. *Homer and the Sacred City*. Ithaca, N.Y.: Cornell University Press, 1990.

Seaford, Richard. *Money and the Early Greek Mind: Homer, Philosophy, Tragedy*. Cambridge, U.K.; New York: Cambridge University Press, 2004.

Shankman, Steven. *In Search of the Classic: Reconsidering the Greco-Roman Tradition, Homer to Valéry and beyond*. University Park, Pa.: Pennsylvania State University Press, 1994.

Sissa, Giulia, and Marcel Detienne. *The Daily Life of the Greek Gods*, translated by Janet Lloyd. Stanford, Calif.: Stanford University Press, 2000.

Spariosu, Mihai. *God of Many Names: Play, Poetry, and Power in Hellenic Thought from Homer to Aristotle*. Durham: Duke University Press, 1991.

Van Duzer, Chet A. *Duality and Structure in the* Iliad *and* Odyssey. New York: P. Lang, 1996.

Acknowledgments

"Special Abilities" by Scott Richardson. From *The Homeric Narrator*: pp. 109–139. © 1990 by Scott Richardson. Reprinted by permission.

"*Aletheia* and Poetry: *Iliad* 2.484–87 and *Odyssey* 8.48–91 as Models of Archaic Narrative" by Louise H. Pratt. From *Lying and Poetry from Homer to Pindar: Falsehood and Deception in Archaic Greek Poetics*: pp. 11–53. © 1993 by the University of Michigan. Reprinted with permission of The University of Michigan Press.

"Hexameter Progression and the Homeric Hero's Solitary State" by Ahuvia Kahane. From *Written Voices, Spoken Signs: Tradition, Performance, and the Epic Text*, edited by Egbert Bakker and Ahuvia Kahane: pp. 110–137. © 1991 by the president and fellows of Harvard College. Reprinted by permission.

"Epic as Genre" by Andrew Ford. From *A New Companion to Homer*, edited by Ian Morris and Barry Powell: pp. 396–414. © 1997 by Koninklijke Brill. Reprinted by permission of Brill Academic Publishers.

"The Homeric Transformation of Bardic Poetry" by Richard Gotshalk. From *Homer and Hesiod, Myth and Philosophy*: pp. 89–110. © 2000 by University Press of America. Reprinted by permission.

"This Voice Which Is Not One" by Nancy Worman. From *Making Silence Speak: Women's Voices in Greek Literature and Society*, edited by André

Lardinois and Laura McClure: pp. 19–37. © 2001 by Princeton University Press. Reprinted by permission of Princeton University Press.

"Homer as a Foundation Text" by Margalit Finkelberg. From *Homer, the Bible, and Beyond: Literary and Religious Canons in the Ancient World*, edited by Margalit Finkelberg and Guy G.Stroumsa: pp. 75–96. © 2003 by Koninklijke Brill NV. Reprinted by permission of Brill Academic Publishers.

"The Space of *Homilia* and Its Signs in the *Iliad* and the *Odyssey*" by D. N. Maronitis. From *Homeric Megathemes: War–Homilia–Homecoming*: pp. 29–45. © 2004 by Lexington Books. Reprinted by permission.

Index

DATE DUE
